TONY ASPLER'S
Vintage
CANADA
SECOND EDITION

*The Complete Reference
To Canadian Wines*

TONY ASPLER'S

Vintage
CANADA
SECOND EDITION

The Complete Reference
To Canadian Wines

McGraw-Hill Ryerson Limited
Toronto, New York, Auckland, Bogota, Caracas, Lisbon, London, Madrid,
Mexico, Milan, New Delhi, San Juan, Singapore, Sydney, Tokyo

Vintage Canada, 2nd edition

First published in 1995 by
McGraw-Hill Ryerson Ltd.
300 Water Street
Whitby, Ontario
L1N 9B6

1 2 3 4 5 6 7 8 9 0 BG 4 3 2 1 0 9 8 7 6 5

Canadian Cataloguing in Publication Data

Aspler, Tony 1939-
 Tony Aspler's Vintage Canada : the complete reference to Canadian wines

2nd ed., rev. & updated.
Includes index.
ISBN 0-07-552604-2

1. Wine industry - Canada - History. 2. Wineries - Canada. 3. Wine and wine making - Canada. I. Title. II. Title: Vintage Canada.

TP559.C3A85 1995   338.4'76632'00971
                                     C95-931691-4

Publisher: Joan Homewood
Production Coordinator: Sharon Hudson
Cover Design and Photography: Dave Hader / Studio Conceptions
Page Makeup: Dave Hader / Studio Conceptions
Copy Editor: Don Loney / Word Guild
Printed in Canada

*F*or my late father
who drank wine for
sacramental purposes only,
but shared his life as if he
were a winemaker.

ABOUT THE AUTHOR

Tony Aspler is the most widely read wine writer in Canada. He has been active on the international wine scene since 1964. As a consultant and wine judge, he makes frequent trips to the vineyards and wine fairs of Europe and the new world and is recognized as the leading authority on Canadian wines.

His previous books include *Aligoté to Zinfandel, Tony Aspler's Wine Lover's Companion, Tony Aspler's Dinner Companion* (with Jacques Marie), *Cellar and Silver* (with Rose Murray) and *Tony Aspler's International Guide to Wine.* He contributed to Jancis Robinson's *Oxford Companion to Wine* and the *Larousse Encyclopedia of Wine.*

He is the editor of *Winetidings Magazine* and has been *The Toronto Star's* wine columnist since 1980. He writes for a variety of wine magazines around the world including *Wine Spectator, The Wine News* (U.S.), *Wine & Spirits* (England), *Liquor News (Australia)* and *FoodService & Hospitality.*

Tony Aspler is a member of the North American Advisory Board of the Institute of Masters of Wine.

He has also created a wine writer detective, Ezra Brant, who has appeared in *Blood Is Thicker than Beaujolais* and the soon-to-be-published *The Beast of Barbaresco.*

CONTENTS

BRITISH COLUMBIA   103

British Columbia Wines   273

ACKNOWLEDGEMENTS

Sharing is second nature to wine lovers. Show interest and a winemaker will lead you into the cellar and introduce you to all his "children".

Over the past twenty years, I have been privileged to meet virtually all of Canada's winemakers and through their generosity I have tasted an unprecedented number of Canadian wines. I thank them for the opportunity and for their continuing dedication. And I would like to pay a special tribute here to all those people who are not winemakers but whose efforts behind the scenes to turn Canada into a globally recognized wine-producing country have made this book and its previous two editions possible. I refer specifically to such institutions are The Wine Council of Ontario, The British Columbia Wine Institute, The Vintners Quality Alliance, The Ontario Grape Growers Marketing Board, The Association of British Columbia Grape Growers, The Grape Growers Association of Nova Scotia and the Association of Winemakers of Quebec.

I would also like to thank some special individuals who have made my research much easier and more pleasurable: Peter Gamble, director of Ontario's VQA; Dave Gamble (no relation), editor of *B.C. Wine Trails* and *Ontario Wine Trails* (who did many of the tasting notes for the B.C. section); Chris Coletta, executive director of B.C.'s VQA; Thomas Bachelder (who tasted for me in Quebec); and last, but not least, Deborah Benoit, who assisted me in researching and collating all the new material for this edition.

_I_NTRODUCTION

_T_welve years ago ago I wrote a book called _Vintage Canada_. It was a history of winemaking in Canada, complete with profiles of the thirty-four wineries in five provinces that existed then (including Andrew Wolf of Alberta who makes wine from frozen California grapes). The book also contained tasting notes on all the wines — still, sparkling and fortified — that were available in provincial liquor stores at the time.

While researching that book, I travelled across the country, visiting wineries, grape growers, liquor boards and government research stations, and I sampled over 600 products. Only a handful impressed me then as being of international standard and my critical assessments, I admit now, leaned towards the charitable — rather like the statements you make after sitting through a school concert in which your kids are performing. I really wanted Canadian wines to be good and I did everything I could in that book and through subsequent wine columns and magazine articles to encourage our wineries to make wines Canadians could take pride in.

Ten years later, I came back to the subject to document how the industry had changed. Pressures of the free trade agreement and GATT had radically altered the oenological landscape — geographically, financially and psychologically. Over that decade, major wineries with long histories disappeared while many others had sprung up to take their place. The success of Canadian wines at home and in overseas competitions has been unprecedented, so much so that many growers have been encouraged to take the plunge and start up wineries of their own. There is no shortage of entrepreneurs, it seems, who believe that Canada is a wine-growing country. At the time of writing there are 104 wineries in five provinces making wine from locally grown grapes or fruit (which is the focus of this book, not those operations in Quebec that bottle imported wines or other producers who bottle off-shore wines or, with the blessing of Ontario's Wine Content Act, who blend 75 percent imported wine with the local product).

Since the last edition of this book in 1993, thirty-nine wineries have opened. No excuses have to be made for Canadian wines today. They stand on their merits in the global wine world. They win prizes in international competitions. They are exported to Europe, the Far East and the United States. They appear on the wine lists of fine dining rooms — and, more importantly, Canadian consumers have begun to realise that wines of quality are at last being produced in their own backyards.

Permit me to quote myself. Ten years ago, I wrote in *Vintage Canada*:

Today, the Canadian wine industry is on the verge of producing products in the blended table wine range that can stand up against those from any wine-producing country in the world. Canada may never produce a Château Lafite, a Richebourg or a Hermitage, but a fine Chardonnay or Johannisberg Riesling is certainly within reach — as well as wines that have nothing to do with a European tradition, like Seyval Blanc, Vidal, Baco Noir and Maréchal Foch. Given our climate and the delicacy of the vines which produce the noble wines of Europe we can only hope that through clonal selection the wineries can find varieties sturdy enough to withstand winter cold and fungal diseases and, equally important, to find the right soil and microclimate in which to plant them.... It must not be forgotten that the Canadian wine industry — in terms of the production of table wines — really only began after World War II. It took the French and the Germans 2,000 years of trial and error to achieve their Lafites and Bernkasteler Doktors. With modern technology and European know-how the Californians, blessed with a better climate than Niagara or the Okanagan Valley, took 200 years to produce their excellent Cabernets and Chardonnays. Today, the Canadian wine industry is where California was in the late 1960s. We have nowhere to go but up. As long as it remembers it is a *wine* industry and not a commodities market where the bottom line is all that counts, it can win the respect and admiration of wine lovers across Canada.

Perhaps I was a little optimistic in my time frame. In ten years, we have not developed the way the Californians have. Our wineries have moved cautiously, even timidly. The second generation of small boutique operations (after Inniskillin and Château des Charmes in Ontario and the now defunct Claremont in B.C.) have become the engine, dragging the old established firms reluctantly behind them into a bright new dawn.

From tastings I have done, I am now convinced that we can make good red wines as well from the noble European varieties but only in great vintages such as 1991 or by seriously reducing yields in the vineyard in average to good years.

Ironically, what has awakened the consumers' interest in Canadian wines both at home and abroad is not Chardonnay or Riesling, Cabernet or Pinot Noir, but a luxury product as rare as it is expensive—Icewine. Icewine made in Ontario and B.C. from frozen grapes is the one wine that no winelover can resist, and we make it as well if not better than the Germans who invented it. Overseas buyers are beginning to clamour for our Icewine.

But the industry cannot sustain itself on Icewine alone. It needs a solid consumer base for its inexpensive table wines, white and red, as well as its single vineyard, vintage-dated bottlings. And, more importantly, our wineries cannot rely on an export market for their financial health. Canadians have to drink Canadian wine and have all wineries represented in all provinces. Right now we experience the ludicrous situation of having free trade with the United States but inter-provincial tariffs on our own wines. Surely, it is not beyond the wit of our politicians to allow us to have B.C. and Quebec wines in Ontario and vise versa.

And what of the future? The optimism of our young winemakers is infectious. Taste their wines blind against comparable bottles from Europe and you will be amazed by the result. There is no question now that Canada is a wine-growing country, even if the rest of the world has not woken up to that fact.

Then again, perhaps it is not a bad thing that Canadian wines have yet to be discovered. That means the best that we produce still remains within our borders for our own delectation and delight.

*I*N THE BEGINNING . . .

*"A bunch of grapes is beautiful, static and inno-
cent. It is merely a fruit. But when it is crushed it
becomes an animal, for the crushed grapes become
wine and wine has an animal life."*

William Younger, *Gods, Men and Wine*

*W*inemaking is the world's second-oldest profession. According to a
Persian legend, it was a woman who first discovered the delights of
the fermented grape. This unnamed heroine was a concubine in the harem
of King Jamsheed. Her royal master had a weakness for grapes and ordered
bunches to be stored in jars so that he could enjoy them at his table all year
round (presumably as raisins).

One of the jars began to ferment and the raisins lost their sweetness. The
king supposed that the juice was poisonous and had the container labelled
as such. One day, our unknown benefactress, who suffered from constant
migraines, decided to put herself out of her misery. Finding the jar marked
"poison," she drank deeply and immediately fell asleep. She awoke feeling
on top of the world and returned to the jar to finish it off. Summoned before
the king to explain her odd, euphoric behaviour, she confessed her misde-
meanour. Intrigued, King Jamsheed ordered a quantity of wine to be made
for the pleasure of his entire court. The fabled king is said to have lived for
700 years — the earliest testimonial we have to the salutary effects of the
fermented grape.

William Younger, in *Gods, Men and Wine,* argues that winemaking may
date back 10,000 years or more to the Magdalenian rock painters of southern France. "During the Upper Palaeolithic Age which marks the emergence
of 'modern man,' some of the conditions existed for the deliberate making
of wine, although they did not exist for the deliberate growing of grapes."

It is a pleasing thought that those primordial artists working in the bow-
els of the earth with their charcoal and vegetable dyes might have stepped

5

back to admire their work by the light of the fire, with a bowl of wine in their hands.

Certainly they would have had grapes to eat, if not to ferment, since wild vines have existed since the Tertiary Period, which dates from a million to 70 million years ago. But the first vigneron, who deliberately cultivated grapes, was Noah. According to the Book of *Genesis* (IX, 20), "Noah began to be an husbandman, and he planted a vineyard: And he drank of the wine, and was drunken; and he was uncovered in his tent." Scholars have placed that first vineyard near Erivan in Armenia, though they have yet to agree on what "uncovered" meant.

The Old Testament is replete with references to vineyards, grapes and wine. Perhaps the best-known has provided the logo for the Israeli Tourist Board — Moses' spies returning from Canaan, the land of milk and honey: "... and they came upon the Brook of Eschol and cut down from thence a branch with one cluster of grapes and they bare it between two upon a staff." (*Numbers* XII, 23.) Imagine! One bunch of grapes that required two men to carry it! Grape growers through the ages must share this same sense of hyperbole when it comes to describing the quality of their harvest!

The story of Moses' spies has its echo in the first documented discovery of grapes growing in Canada.

In the summer of 1001 A.D., Leif Ericsson set sail from Norway in a Viking longboat. According to the two sagas handed down from oral sources around 1250, Leif, a newly baptized Christian, was "a big strapping fellow, handsome to look at, thoughtful and temperate in all things." But this did not prevent him from provisioning his crew of thirty-five with beer and mead to help them survive the rigours of the journey.

The expedition sailed first to Baffin Island, which Leif named "The Country of Flat Stones," and then on to Labrador ("Land of Forests"). Historians still argue where the intrepid explorer made his final landfall on the American continent — the place he was to call "Vinland." As Samuel Eliot Morrison says in *The European Discovery of America*, "There are few local histories of seaport towns between Newfoundland and the Virginia capes which do not open with a chapter asserting 'Leif Ericsson was here!'" In the Latin translation of the sagas published by Thormodus Torfaeus at Copenhagen in 1705, the author was unequivocal in identifying Vinland as Newfoundland.

In 1960, Helga Ingstad, a Norwegian archaeologist, pinpointed Leif's landfall at L'Anse aux Meadows in northern Newfoundland. Morrison is convinced that this is the spot "where Leif Ericsson spent one winter and where members of his family founded a short-lived colony." The exact location is significant because of what the sagas tell us in the narrating of the "history" of the voyage to Vinland. According to a tale in the *Greenlanders Saga*, one member of the party — Leif's foster father, a German named Tyrker, emerged triumphantly from the woods "rolling his eyes and babbling, first in a German dialect none of his shipmates understood, then in

Norse." The crew gathered round him and the excited old man broke the news: "I found grape vines and grapes!" Leif was incredulous and not a little dubious. "Certainly," replied the German, "I was born where there is no lack of either vines or grapes."

Leif ordered his men to harvest the grapes and load them aboard along with the cargo of timber they had cut. When spring allowed the expedition to sail home again, Leif had already named the unknown country Vinland—the land of the vines.

Adam of Bremen was the first chronicler of Leif Ericsson's original voyage, and around the year 1075 he reported to the King of Denmark that Leif "spoke of an island in that (northern) ocean, discovered by many which is called WINLAND, for the reason that vines yielding the best of wine grows there wild."

Grapes growing in northern Newfoundland? Grapes that produce "the best of wine"? Certainly, today, the finest European grapes as well as hybrids flourish in the Annapolis Valley above the Bay of Fundy and the Northumberland Strait in Nova Scotia. So perhaps there is a microclimate where the hardy wild grapes might have grown around L'Anse aux Meadows in Newfoundland.

Cynics have suggested that what Leif Ericsson actually found were blueberries, wild currants, gooseberries or, possibly, the mountain cranberry. Samuel Eliot Morrison dismisses such speculation: "If it be objected that Leif Ericsson, after whooping it up in the court of King Olaf (of Norway), must have known wine and would not have been put off by a poor substitute made from berries, one may reply that, just as his father Eric (the Red) put the 'Green' in Greenland to attract settlers, so Leif put the 'Vin' in Vinland. And with such success as to throw off all Vinland-seekers for centuries!"

But it was 500 years after Ericsson before we have more evidence of grapes and winemaking in eastern Canada. In 1535, when Jacques Cartier sailed down the St. Lawrence on his second voyage to New France, he anchored off "a great island." Here Cartier found masses of wild grape vines growing up the trees. He named it Ile de Bacchus, but on reflection — thinking that this might be seem too frivolous for his masters in Paris — renamed it Île d'Orléans after the duc d'Orléans, son of his monarch, Francis I.

From this point on, the history of the grape is closely bound with the history of Canada.

The Jesuit missionaries who followed in Cartier's footsteps brought sacramental wine with them, and when they ran out they tried their hands at winemaking using the native wild grape. They recorded that the grapes were plentiful but the wine they produced (probably from *Vitis riparia*) was obviously only tolerable enough to be sipped at Mass, not to be quaffed back to warm the hearts of the settlers during the long winters.

The Jesuits may have been able to supply their own sacramental needs, but their congregation required something a little more palatable. In 1648, a certain Jacques Boisdon in Quebec City applied to the Council of New France for a licence to open the first tavern. The Council agreed and even supplied Boisdon with eight barrels of French wine, free of charge, to help him start his business. But in true bureaucratic style, they set down stringent regulations. "To prevent any unseemliness, drunkenness, blasphemy or games of chance," the inn had to be located in a public square within sight of the church, allowing the priest to be a one-man Liquor Control Board.

But the Church fathers, far from frowning on the practice of winemaking, actively encouraged it. Father Jacques Bruyas wrote in a letter dated 1668: "If one were to take the trouble to plant some vines and trees, they would yield as well as they do in France ... and (properly pruned) the grapes would be as good as those of France" — a sentiment which would be echoed down the years to our own day by every grape grower who put a plant in the ground.

If the new settlers, accustomed to the wines of France, were less than enthusiastic about the possibility of winemaking from wild grapes, the indigenous peoples of Upper Canada were untroubled by such latent wine snobbery. Indian tribes, such as the Seneca, Tuscarora and Cayuga, are believed to have offered tributes of fermented grape juice to the gods who lived at the foot of Niagara Falls. The ceremony, during which the wine was poured into the churning waters to placate the gods, was known as the "Wischgimi." The bands travelled great distances to make their offering, and as Percy Rowe suggests in *The Wines of Canada*, "It is conceivable that the journey would have been a dusty one so that the Indians were sufficiently tempted to slake their throats with a portion of the 'gifts.'"

If wild grapes like *Vitis riparia* and *Vitis labrusca* flourished in eastern Canada, it would not be until the nineteenth century when committed amateurs tried to cultivate vines for the express purpose of producing wines fit to drink. The wild *labrusca* grapes with their small berries would have produced a wine of poor quality — harsh and acidic, with a decidedly "foxy" flavour.

Father Bruyas's suggestion of planting vines had already been tried by British colonists in Virginia and the Carolinas at the instigation of Lord Delaware who, in 1619, imported French cuttings along with French vignerons to oversee their planting. The vines they planted died, unfortunately, before a commercial wine industry based on French *vinifera* grapes could be established in the new colonies. But their presence among the native varieties was enough to create new strains. Through cross-pollination with wild grapes, the first North American hybrids were created.

THE EARLY YEARS

*I*n the years to follow, the nascent Canadian wine industry in the east was to benefit from American grapes which flourished in the more conducive climate of the south. The poor performance of imported vines forced the early American winemakers to re-evaluate the native root stock. As early as 1683, William Penn called for better viticultural practices to improve the quality of the vine in the hope that "the consequence will be as good wine as any European countries of the same latitude do yield."

Some ninety years later, during the American revolution, Governor John Penn's gardener, a certain John Alexander, discovered the first accidental hybrid growing by a river near Philadelphia. He had been experimenting unsuccessfully with European varieties, and some of them survived long enough to cross with nearby wild varieties. Alexander planted a cutting and happily it took root in Governor Penn's garden. The Alexander grape became popular around 1800 as the Cape, a name which suggested South African origins.

With the blessing of President Thomas Jefferson, who had vines growing in his garden in Virginia, the Alexander enjoyed a brief moment in the sun before it was eclipsed by two new hybrids — Isabella, introduced in 1816, and Catawba, introduced in 1823.

At the same time in Ontario, a retired German soldier, Corporal Johann Schiller (variously spelled Schuler, Sheler or Sheeler, according to one of his descendants, John Scheeler of Port Lambton, Ontario) was tending his *labrusca* vines on a twenty-acre plot by the Credit River. He had built himself a house on North Dundas Street, Cooksville (now Mississauga) on land granted to him by the Crown on October 12, 1811 — Lots 9 and 17 Concession 1 (north of Dundas Street). Schiller had served with the 29th Regiment of Foot at Quebec in 1784. On his discharge from the British army, he lived in Montreal for eight years on a land grant of 400 acres there but eventually moved to Niagara where he re-applied for the same acreage in Ontario.

By 1811, Schiller, who had previous winemaking experience in the Rhine, was fermenting grapes he had grown from cuttings of wild vines and early American hybrids furnished by settlers from Pennsylvania. He made sufficient quantities to be able to service his own needs and sell to his neighbours. Johann Schiller is generally acknowledged to be the father of the Canadian wine industry.

We have no indication as to how long Schiller's winery lasted. He died five years to the day after he received his Ontario land grant. His sons, William and Michael, proceeded to sell Lot 17 in 1824, parcels of which were bought by Thomas Silverthorn who was later associated with the Canada Winegrowers Association. The Schiller property itself was bought in 1864 by Count Justin M. de Courtenay, who formed a company called the Vine Growers Association. He extended the original vineyards to forty acres of Clinton and Isabella grapes, making his Clair House label the largest in Ontario.

De Courtenay was an aggressive evangelist in the cause of Canadian wine, harrying the government of the day with letters and pamphlets to proselytize its members in support of the infant industry.

The owner of Clair House had begun his wine-producing experiences in Quebec. He was convinced that European grapes could not only grow in Lower Canada, but could outperform their Burgundian cousins in terms of the wine they produced: "It will be easily perceived the importance attached in Burgundy to their wines," wrote de Courtenay, "and there is no reason why we should not produce better ones on the borders of the St. Lawrence."

To prove his point, de Courtenay sent some bottles to the premier of Lower Canada, L.V. Sicotta, on January 15, 1863, with a covering letter:

> I have now the honour to present you with the samples of wine fur-
> nished by the cultivated wild grape, and am persuaded that, making
> allowances for the green taste which it possesses in common with
> almost all new wines, you will consider it equal to ordinary
> Burgundy which it resembles not only in flavour but in its qualities
> and colour ... The fact that a good, sound wine can be produced in
> this country, I consider has been by me practically demonstrated.

The Honorable L.V. Sicotta was not won over by such confident huck-stering, and passed the bottles over to a government consultant, a Mr. McDougall, who pronounced the wine sour.

But de Courtenay would not take this criticism of his wine lying down. He shot back a letter to Quebec City full of righteous indignation: "I deny the wine in question being sour, but admit it to be bitter in consequence of containing too much tannin." The age-old cry of the winemaker: "All it needs is bottle-age."

What Justin de Courtenay could not accomplish in Quebec he tried with more success in Ontario. He considered his Clair House of sufficient quali-ty to be exhibited in Paris in celebration of Canada's nationhood in 1867. On July 8th, the *Toronto Leader* printed the following story:

The French exposition has established the character of our Canadian wines. The jury on wines, which would naturally be composed of the best judges to be found in Europe, speak in very high terms of the wines sent from the Clair House Vineyards, Cooksville. They find in them a resemblance to the Beaujolais wine, which is known to be the best produced in France. They say of those wines that they resemble more the great French table wines than any other foreign wines they have examined, and that the fact of the wine being so *solide* as to bear the sea voyage, and the variations of heat and cold without losing anything of either its quality or limpidity, should be a question of great consideration even to our own producers.

This authoritative opinion of the quality of Ontario wine will do more than anything else that could possibly occur, at present, to bring this wine into general use ... The time will come, we hope and verily believe, when grape-growing and wine-making will be one of the principal employments of our population; and when it does come, the cause of temperance will be advanced to a degree that could be reached by no other process.

De Courtenay had been vindicated. His red wine, at an alcoholic strength of 13 percent, was the talk of Toronto. But the newspaper's predictions failed to come about. In 1878, no longer able to secure a grant from the Parliament of Upper Canada, de Courtenay was forced to close his winery.

Justin de Courtenay, the flamboyant count who dashed off letters of blistering irony to parliamentarians, quoting Pliny and Virgil, overshadowed the efforts of those stolid Ontario farmers of lesser education who laboured quietly in the background. For example, Porter Adams was shipping grapes to the Toronto market from the Queenston area in the same year that de Courtenay was shipping his wines to France. John Kilborn — as early as 1862 — won a prize of $3.00 at the Provincial Exhibition in Toronto for the "best bottles of wine made from the grape."

Kilborn owned seventeen acres of land on Ontario Street in Beamsville. In 1860, he reported to *The Canadian Agriculturist* that his wine was fetching $1.75 a gallon locally "and probably would bring in more if we asked for it. At all events it is worth four times as much as the miserable stuff sold by our merchants under the name of wine."

Winemaking in the late nineteenth century was more of a basement hobby than a business. When it was not sold through the kitchen door, it would have been available at the local drugstore. Farm wineries, such as those owned by John Kilborn and W.W. Kitchen of Grimsby, were, however, large enough to advertise their products.

Kitchen's broadsheet declared that his wines were "in use by some Hundreds of Churches for sacramental services." In addition, "It is sold by most of the principal Chemists in Canada East and West."

The problem for those early winemakers, whether they made wine for their own consumption or for profit, was the alcohol strength. The native hybrids like Catawba and Isabella were low in fructose and high in acidity so sugar had to be added to the fermentation to bring up the alcohol level. The grapes would be pressed a second time after water or sugar syrup had been added to the skins to extract every last ounce of juice.

The first growers along that Niagara Peninsula, like Porter Adams, planted their vines basically to service the fresh fruit trade. One of the best table varieties, as well as an excellent taste in jams and jellies, was the Concord grape whose flavour is unmistakable to us today as the essence of virtually all grape-flavoured products. The grape was named after the Massachusetts town were it was propagated by a man who rejoiced in the splendid name of Ephraim Wales Bull.

As a boy growing up in New York's Hudson River Valley, Bull became interested in grape growing. In 1836, he moved to Concord to pursue his hobby more vigorously — and to make wine. In his quest for a grape that would survive the New England winter better than the Isabella, he planted the seeds of some wild *labrusca* grapes. The one that succeeded best he named Concord in honour of the town where it was raised.

In 1854, Bull offered his Concord vines to nurseries at a hefty price of five dollars a vine, but the nurserymen managed to propagate the vine for themselves and Bull saw little remuneration for his gift to the North American wine industry. He died penniless in Concord's Home for the Aged in 1895. His tombstone bears the forlorn legend: "He sowed, but others reaped."

When the Concord grape was exhibited at the Massachusetts Horticultural Society, it was an instant winner. In his book *American Wines and How to Make Them*, Philip Wagner explains why: "It produces so cheaply and abundantly that it makes a dismal joke of all competition: it is virtually indifferent to climate, growing rankly in both hot and cold regions, and flourishes in practically any soil; it is immune to most of the vine diseases and thrives under neglect; it travels well and withstands storage moderately well; it does not winter kill."

The only problem is that Concord grapes make awful wine. As grape juice it can be enjoyable, or when its "foxy" taste is camouflaged as sherry or port, but as wine I'd rather drink the gum they used to stick on the label. Yet the Concord was to become the backbone of the Canadian wine industry up until the 1940s — and as the major constituent in the "Duck" range of pop wines it provided 90 percent of the company profits until the late 1970s.[1]

---

[1] Ten years after it started its grape-breeding program in 1913, the Horticultural Research Institute of Ontario at Vineland had given up using the Concord as a "parent." In 1942, the Institute stated in its report that the goal of the grape-breeding program was to produce hybrids that no longer had the *labrusca* taste characteristics and resembled more those of the European *viniferas*.

Not only did the Americans send their grapes north, they also dispatched their entrepreneurs whose presence would give the youthful industry a nudge toward the twentieth century. In the 1860s, most of the operations in Ontario were small-volume businesses, a sideline for farmers who had crops other than grapes to harvest.

In 1866, "a company of gentlemen from Kentucky," according to a letter in the *Canadian Farmer*, "who have been in the grape business for 14 years, have purchased a farm on Pelee Island and planted 30 acres this spring, and intend to plant 20 acres next spring." Pelee Island — the most southerly part of Canada, on the same latitude as northern California — stands twelve miles to the north of Kelly's Island in Lake Erie. In 1860, Catawba grapes were successfully planted there to supply the wineries at Sandusky, Ohio, one of the oldest winemaking centres in the United States. (In 1893, Brights bought Catawba from Pelee Island to produce a sweet table wine.)

The southern gentlemen were D.J. Williams, Thomas Williams and Thaddeus Smith, who formed a company called Vin Villa to create the first commercial winery on Pelee Island. Before they had built a house on their land, they excavated a wine cellar, forty feet by sixty feet and twelve feet deep, which showed that this was to be no bathtub operation.

But Vin Villa was not to be without competition. A few months after the Kentuckians acquired land on Pelee Island, two English brothers, Edward and John Wardoper, purchased fifteen acres and planted a rival vineyard. Today, the Pelee Island Vineyards boast the largest *vinifera* planting in Canada — Riesling, Gewürztraminer, Chardonnay and Pinot Noir — planted by Walter Strehn in 1980.

An enterprising grocer in Brantford named Major J.S. Hamilton bought the grapes as well as finished wine from the Pelee vineyards. Hamilton had opened his store in 1871 and in the same year was granted a royal charter to sell wine and liquor. Three years later he met Thaddeus Smith and was impressed by the yield of his vineyards (four to five tons per acre of Delaware and Catawba) and the quality of his wine. He asked Smith if he could sell Vin Villa for him in the eastern United States.

Hamilton also wanted to market these wines in Canada, and to do so he entered into an agreement with the Pelee Island growers to transfer the winemaking operation from the island to the city of Brantford.

The assets of J.S. Hamilton and Company Limited, which absorbed the Pelee Island Wine and Vineyard Company in 1909, would be sold in 1949 to London Winery, giving that company the longest pedigree in the venerable art of Canadian winemaking.

In the same decade that Major Hamilton was shipping casks of wine over from Pelee Island, some 2,000 miles away, the Oblate Fathers' tiny vineyard at their mission seven miles south of Kelowna in British Columbia's Okanagan Valley was reaching maturity. In British Columbia, as in Quebec, it was the Church that first fostered and encouraged the cultivation of the grape for winemaking.

If Justin de Courtenay moved from Quebec to Ontario to find more favourable microclimates in which to grow vines to produce better Burgundies than those of France, other English-speaking farmers remained to battle the winters. A certain Mr. Menzies of Pointe Claire, Quebec, created a vineyard "on a larger scale than usual in the province" which he called the Beaconsfield Vineyard. Two years later, he was joined by a partner but the association was brief. After a few months, Mr. Menzies was forced to publish a pamphlet warning his clients that his former associate had set up a farm a mile from his own from which the rascal had been selling American wines under the name of the Beaconsfield Vineyard.

But the lustiest child in the nation's vinicultural nursery was Ontario. From the 1860s, vineyards flourished in the Beamsville-Vineland-Grimsby area. Grape growers experimented in their own backyards to find new varieties that were disease resistant and winter hardy. The process was long and difficult. It takes at least three years for a vine to produce a commercial crop, let alone the years it takes to develop a successful crossing. So when a new variety was introduced, the effect was rather like a coronation or the arrival of a royal baby.

In 1868, in Lockport, New York, two growers created what they were to call the Niagara grape by crossing the Concord with a relatively little-known variety called the Cassady. It was to be the white wine equivalent of the unkillable purple Concord. The two growers, mindful of what had happened to Ephraim Bull, sold their vines at $1.25 a piece with a written understanding that the purchaser would return all cuttings to them so the vines could not be pirated.

In 1882, the Niagara grape was introduced to Ontario and, like the Concord, it is still with us today.

By 1890, there were forty-one commercial wineries across Canada, thirty-five of which were situated in Ontario. The great majority of these, fully two-thirds, were centred around Essex County, which in 1904 boasted 1,784 acres of vines. The pre-eminence of Essex as Canada's grape-growing centre was to last twenty years. By 1921, the grape vines had been torn out in favour of such cash crops as tobacco and soft fruit. A mere fifty acres remained, but this concentration was still greater than anywhere else in Canada.

In 1873, two years after Major James Hamilton had shaken the hand of the gentlemen from the South to confirm their business arrangement, George Barnes, a relative of grape-grower Porter Adams by marriage, started a winery at St. Catharines. With the literalness of a German wine label, he embraced every function of the company in its name so there could be no mistaking its purpose: The Ontario Grape Growing and Wine Manufacturing Company, Limited. What it lacked in imagination it made up for in longevity because it operated until 1988 as Barnes Wines.

George Barnes's vines had been in the ground one year when Thomas Bright and his partner, F.A. Shirriff, opened a winery in Toronto. In naming it they must have subconsciously realized they would have to move closer to their grape supply. They called it The Niagara Falls Wine Company and move they did, sixteen years later, in 1890, to the outskirts of the town. In 1911, they changed the name to T.G. Bright and Company.

Those years at the end of the nineteenth century showed a remarkable growth for Ontario, and for the grape-growing areas south and southwest of the province. At the turn of the century, there were some 5,000 acres under vine along the Niagara Peninsula.

However, two events were to check the new wine industry and to set it off on a path of incipient self-destruction: World War I and Prohibition.

PROHIBITION

*I*n the early days of this century, what was a small Canadian wine industry resided in Ontario. And those companies that survived into the 1900s were targets for the growing number of drum-beating temperance societies in the province, particularly in the rural areas. Some farmers refused to sell their grapes to winemakers, and by 1892, the public outcry against alcoholic beverages had reached such a crescendo that even the idea of planting more vineyards in Niagara came under scrutiny.

When World War I broke out, the government's need for industrial alcohol to make explosives synchronized with the popular sentiment for prohibition. Once the Temperance Act had been passed, the distilleries could be converted to the production of industrial alcohol for the war effort.

On September 15, 1916, the government of Sir William F. Hearst, an active Methodist layman and dedicated temperance advocate, passed the legislation known as the Ontario Temperance Act. Under its statutes all bars, clubs and liquor shops would be closed for the duration of the war. No one could sell any intoxicating liquor unless authorized to do so by the province and no one could "have, keep, give, or consume liquor except in a private dwelling house."

In 1916 and 1917, all but one of the provinces went dry. Quebec, which marches to a different drum in these matters, held out until 1919 and then proscribed the sale of liquor, but not wine or beer.

The Women's Christian Temperance Union of Ontario, the vanguard of the movement, had triumphed but political realities began to nibble away at their victory. Pressure from the strong grape growers' lobby caused the Conservative government to exempt native wines from the provisions of the act. Section 44 stated that wines made from Ontario-grown grapes could be produced by manufacturers who held permits from the Board of Licence Commissioners. This political sleight of hand was to elicit a raised eyebrow — if somewhat belated — from the editorial page of the *Toronto Telegram* (April 21, 1921): "There may be political reasons for protecting wine and banning beer. But there is no moral or social reason. There is no inherent vice in barley which does not also lodge in grapes."

17

When the Ontario Temperance Act became law, there were ten wineries in operation in the provinces. While they were able to vinify legally during Prohibition, the government saw to it that consumers had a difficult time getting hold of their wine. Each winery was allowed one store outlet and that had to be located on its premises. Customers could only buy a five-gallon quantity or its equivalent in bottles — two cases. What an extraordinary piece of double-think by a government dedicated to the proposition that people must be denied alcoholic beverages!

Another bizarre anomaly of Prohibition in Canada was that while it might have been illegal to sell liquor, it was not against the law to manufacture it. Alcohol was readily available for "sacramental, industrial, artistic, mechanical, scientific and medicinal purposes." And it was the medical profession that was to become the barman of the nation. A doctor could prescribe alcohol to a patient if he felt that patient might benefit from such "medicine." Peter Newman writes of those days in *The Bronfman Dynasty*: "As well as selling straight liquor through the drug stores to patients with doctors sympathetic enough to prescribe it, the booze was sold to processors who concocted a variety of mixtures for the drug trade, including a Dandy Bracer–Liver and Kidney Cure which, when analyzed, was found to contain a mixture of sugar, molasses, bluestone and 36 percent pure alcohol, plus a spit of tobacco juice."

Stephen Leacock summed up the social situation with the observation that "to get a drink during Prohibition it is necessary to go to the drug store ... and lean up against the counter making a gurgling sigh like apoplexy. One often sees there apoplexy cases lined up four deep."

Nevertheless, during the eleven years of Prohibition in Ontario, the only alcoholic beverage that could be sold legally was wine. The natural consequence was to spark off a mad scramble by European immigrants who had some brush with winemaking in the Old Country to get in on the act, and even those native-born Ontarians who could not tell wine from vinegar jumped on the bandwagon. Wineries were started up in basements, at the back of grocery stores and in garages — and even in the converted pig shed of a Beamsville farm!

The Board of Liquor Commissioners handed out permits with heady abandon to placate the vociferous grape growers' lobby. Between 1917 and October 31, 1927, no fewer than fifty-seven licences for new wineries were issued, in addition to the ten that were already established. The three major centres for these wineries were the Niagara Peninsula (at the source of the grapes); Toronto (as the largest urban population); and Windsor (to take advantage of the great thirst across the Detroit River).

But distance from the vineyards was of little consequence to those early wine producers. There were two successful wineries in the lakehead cities of Fort William and Port Arthur (Twin City Wine Company and Fort William Wine Co.), one at Kitchener (in the basement of Fred J. Kampmann's house), one at Belleville (John Tantardini who started in Guelph, eventually selling out to the Belleville Wine Company in 1926) and yet another in Sudbury (The Sudbury Wine Company). There were even two Toronto rabbis who made kosher wines: Rabbi M.H. Levy of Bathurst Street was granted a licence in 1921. His company was purchased in 1925 by Canada Wine Products Ltd., which in turn was swallowed by Jordan in 1938. The other was Rabbi Jacob Gordon, who manufactured Passover wine in the cellar of his home at 116 Beverly Street. In 1928, the rabbi's winery licence was purchased by the Oporto Wine Company on Danforth Avenue, which sold medicated wine. After a series of takeovers the rabbinical company — originally called the Concord Wine Co. Ltd. in 1923 — ended up as part of Château-Gai in 1978.

Only those companies that made a drinkable product survived this extraordinary era — companies like Brights who introduced the first bottling line in Canada, Jordan Wines (a company formed to take over Canadian Grape Products Ltd. in 1926), London Winery (which purchased a three-year-old licence from Giovanni Paproni in 1925) and the Turner Wine Company. This last enterprise dated back to 1885 when it was founded by a Brantford grocer, no doubt in competition with the enterprising Major J.S. Hamilton. They distributed a product known as "Turner's Tonic Bitters," which was heavy on alcohol and quinine.

As far as most winemakers were concerned there were no quality controls, no government interference and, in many cases, little of the basic knowledge of the craft. American equipment and cooperage, hastily bought by the newly formed companies, was calibrated in U.S. gallons as opposed to Imperial measurements, but this meant nothing to some unscrupulous manufacturers who were simply out to line their pockets at the expense of the public thirst. They squeezed their grapes — literally — till the pips squeaked and with added water they were getting as much as 660 gallons of wine from every tonne of grapes. (Today, the negotiated limit is 818 litres per tonne.)

Sugar was poured into the vats by the sackful during fermentation to bring up the alcohol level. If the colour wasn't right after so much dilution, there was always coal tar or vegetable dyes like cochineal to deepen it. Blocks of sulphur were pitched into the vats to kill bacteria, and one enterprising vintner even used aspirins to control his fermentation.

For all those who made wretched wine under licence, there were many countless others who did so without the bureaucratic blessing of a permissive government. Unlike moonshine whisky, homemade wine was legal and the hobbyist who had a few hundred gallons of wine could always plead that he had made it for the home consumption of his entire family rather than for selling through the back door. Few such cases ever came to court, and the government took a lenient view of new immigrants who wished to make their own wine, as evidenced when the LCBO was created in 1927. All home producers would require was a home winemaking licence, and they could produce up to 100 gallons for their own use. (Today no such permit is required.)

In spite of the abysmal quality of most wines available during the eleven-year hiatus, the mere fact of Prohibition had focused the attentions of Canadians on their domestic wine industry, and Prohibition more than anything else turned Canadians into a nation of wine drinkers. During 1920-21, Canadians consumed 221,985 gallons of domestic wine. A decade later the figure was 2,208,807 gallons — for Ontario alone! And 80 percent of it was a red port-style wine of maximum alcoholic strength made from the Concord grape.

After eleven years of social dislocation, Canada passed through the wilderness of Prohibition. Even those who were loudest in its support saw that Prohibition had failed. Sanity finally prevailed. It was seen by most conservative politicians as a victory for "British values" over "all the evils ... wished on Canada by agitators who took their ideals not from the Motherland but from that hotbed of political experiment, the American Middle West."

If the politicians could not stop the fermented juice of the forbidden fruit from finding its way down the throats of the people, at least they could regulate its use.

Eventually, province after province would adopt a form of government control over the sales and distribution of alcohol — a system which involved a state monopoly, based on the Scandinavian model, and more importantly, control over the quality of the product. The new system meant that each province would decide, individually, which wines of the world they would make available to their consumers and how much they would tax them for that privilege.

With the advent of government liquor stores, consumers now had a focus for their complaints if the wines they purchased were substandard — and they had a lot to complain about. During Prohibition, the mere idea of beating the regulations in acquiring wine made the drinker overlook its dubious quality. However, now it was legal and the government was held responsible for every bottle that tasted of vinegar, was black with sediment or contained such foreign bodies as spiders and flies. Some bottles never reached the consumer as they exploded on the liquor store shelves owing to a secondary fermentation — much to the consternation of employees, who felt as if they were working in a minefield. And the bottles themselves could be any shape. A.N. Knowles, vice-president of London Winery, recalls seeing the same label of his father's company on three or four different types of bottle. "Winery employees used to visit the junk yards," he said, "buy up boxes of old bottles, wash them out and fill them with wine. Bottles were hard to get in those days."

In Ontario, the government acted by bringing in a rudimentary quality control for the products it accepted for sale from the wineries. The new Liquor Control Board under Sir Henry Drayton, a former federal minister of finance, administered the new regulations which set a maximum of 250 gallons per tonne of grapes, limiting the amount of water that could be added to the wine. The new restrictions stressed cleanliness of operations above all and fixed the permissable level of volatile acid at 4 percent, which was still enough to make a wine taste of vinegar. (Even this generous limit was beyond the capabilities of most basement vintners.) But the bureaucrats had to move cautiously since the Depression was looming and the vocal farmers' lobby was concerned about the dropping price of grapes. King Concord had fallen as low as twelve dollars a ton.

In an effort to improve the quality of winemaking, the Board's chief analyst, Bert Bonham, suggested that the provincial Department of Health set up a winemaking school at the laboratory in the east block of Queen's Park. When the more marginal companies found their products were being refused for listing at the liquor stores, their winemakers flocked to attend. Many were new immigrants whose command of English was limited and they decided that winemaking in the New World was not for them. The courses lasted for two years, but they had the desired effect. The bathtub school of winemaking as a commercial proposition quietly died.

Encouraged by the government, viable companies such as Brights and Jordan began buying up the licences of these precarious operations lock, stock and barrel at prices as low as $5,000 to $10,000. Over the years, Brights acquired thirteen such licences, not for the wine which was generally sent to the distillers or for the equipment, but for the privilege of owning another retail store. The wineries still had their own single outlet and the government now allowed them to locate these stores away from the facility in the cities of their choice. Through this expedient, the government eventually reduced the number of Ontario wineries from fifty-one to eight.

The next problem was to rationalize the sale of tonic wines and patent medicines which were readily available over grocery store counters. Doubtful products such as Dandy Bracer–Liver and Kidney Cure were extraordinarily high in alcohol and of questionable therapeutic value. The Liquor Control Board came up with an elegant solution. The sale of medicated wines could continue, but the makers had to blend in a "certain additive." If the tonic in question were taken without reference to the stated dosage, the additive induced vomiting in the would-be patient. Needless to say, such nostrums quickly disappeared from the shelves for all time.

But the well-intentioned government did not address the fundamental question of what Ontarians were drinking. Wines made from the Catawba and Concord grapes were selling for thirty cents a bottle. They were sweet and highly alcoholic — twice the strength of European table wines. (In 1932, the government established a 20 percent by volume limit.) In an effort to help the wine industry and the growers, the Ontario government had removed the fifty-cent-a-gallon tax on wines in January 1929 to enable the Liquor Board to sell Ontario products at such a low price. These beverages were known as "Block-and-Tackle" wines — you drank a bottle, walked a block and you could tackle anybody!

Further representations from the grape growers and the wine lobby convinced the Department of National Revenue to allow the fortification of domestic wines. By adding pure grape spirit, the producers could now manufacture fortified wines. The new legislation was a godsend for the industry which could now use wine that was badly oxidized. Before, they would have had to pour it into the sewer. Now they could distil it for grape alcohol.

The Ontario grape growers, too, were happy because they could sell more grapes and doubly so when in 1931 the government banned the importation of grapes from outside the province. The Liquor Board also insisted that the wineries pay a minimum of forty dollars a ton for those they bought.

Concerned about the rocketing sales of these new fortified wines — 42 percent of all wines sold in 1933 — the government appointed a Wines Standards Committee in an attempt to wean Canadians from such heady products towards lighter wines to be drunk with meals. In its report, the committee suggested that it was the industry's responsibility to supply the marketplace with a range of "good quality light wines." It stated that, "the distribution of pamphlets fully describing the merits and low alcoholic content of table wines will unquestionably materially assist in promoting the sale of same."

But the Canadian public was not yet ready for wines of 9 percent to 12 percent alcohol; their palates had become accustomed to fortified products which were closer to whisky than wine in their alcoholic strength. It would take another twenty-five years before the industry would suddenly be caught off-guard by the demand for the style of wines consumed by the Europeans. In the meantime, port and sherry would be the mainstays of the Canadian industry, especially during the Depression when disenchantment and despair found solace in cheap alcohol.

The brand leaders at this time were Brights' Catawba sherry, (affectionately known as "Bright's Disease") and Jordan's Bran-Vin.

Without the ability to advertise or promote their products — a legacy of the Prohibition mentality — the Wine Standards Committee loftily reported that "many people in this province associate drinking of any kind of alcoholic beverage with fostering drunkeness." So the wineries struggled through the 1930s to keep their industry alive. No new winery licences were to be granted in Ontario to allow those currently operating to stay afloat.

But in those dismal years between the two world wars, a dedicated group of individuals laboured in their respective vineyards to produce wines of quality, and if this goal proved to be beyond the capabilities of the native grapes, these men were determined to find varieties that could do so.

In the early 1930s, Harry Hatch, the new owner of Brights, brought a young chemist and winemaker from Montreal to his Niagara Falls winery. A French aristocrat by birth, Viscomte Adhemar de Chaunac de Lanzac was working at Brights' Quebec plant in Lachine at the time. Nurtured on the wines of his native land, he had little time for the company's sweet "ports" and "sherries" and set about to make experimental batches of dry table wines from Catawba and Delaware grapes he found in Brights' mainly

Concord vineyards. Harry Hatch was so impressed by the results that he gave de Chaunac his head to experiment further, setting aside funds for his winemaker to buy vines from New York State to be planted in the company's experimental plot. In 1937, de Chaunac returned to France to find out more about the hybrids being experimented with there.

At the same time, the Horticultural Research Institute at Vineland was conducting similar experiments to provide the wineries with hardy varieties to resist winterkill. Patiently, the scientists at Vineland had been crossing vines to produce the magic grape free of *labrusca* flavour. William Rannie writes in *The Wines of Ontario* that the Institute planted and evaluated 57,000 seedlings between 1913 and 1928, and retained only six as "promising for table grapes and five wine making!"

World War II interrupted this quiet revolution, the fruits of which would eventually change the nation's wine-drinking habits.

Cut off from Europe during the war, the wineries retrenched. All experimentation ceased; it was enough to keep the companies going until the servicemen returned home. As members of a non-essential industry, winemakers found themselves short of bottles and were forced to recycle those they could find.

During the war, wineries were rationed by the government as to how much wine they could sell; the figure varied between 75 percent and 80 percent of their production in the base of year 1939. Wine drinkers used to line up for three hours outside the liquor stores until they opened at 10 a.m.

The Canadian wine industry marked time and waited for the peace that would signal its renaissance.

*P*OST-WORLD WAR II

*W*hen the war ended, Adhemar de Chaunac of Brights was determined to upgrade the quality of his company's table wines. In 1946, he visited France again and ordered forty European vine varieties — hybrids and such noble *viniferas* as Chardonnay (the grape of white Burgundy) and Pinot Noir (red Burgundy). The vines were planted in the spring of that year, some on their own roots, while others grafted onto a European root-stock known as Couderc 3309.

Ten varieties, including the two *vinifera*, adapted reasonably well to their new surroundings. In 1952, Harry Hatch ordered 600 acres of Concord and Niagara vines torn out between Lake Ontario and the Niagara Escarpment to make way for the new varieties. Among them was a hybrid called Seibel 9549 which would be rechristened De Chaunac in 1972 as an accolade to the Frenchman for his contribution to the Canadian wine industry.

De Chaunac also selected a list of varieties for the Horticultural Research Institute at Vineland after discussion with J.R. Van Haarlem, who was in charge of grape development at the time. These vines were planted in the spring of 1947. HRIO's initial experiments suggested that a hybrid called Chelois would be the grape of the future. It took ten years before they found that Chelois was susceptible to a disease called "dead arm."

Other commercial concerns were also experimenting. Parkdale Winery, based in Toronto, brought in vines from Hungary in 1947. Although they proved to be a "dead loss," they did have some success with Gamay Beaujolais on their test farm as well as Johannisberg Riesling and a Muscat-flavoured Couderc, which de Chaunac had brought in as well. (A young nurseryman in Niagara-on-the-Lake, Donald Ziraldo, would eventually propagate these vines for cuttings and starting in 1971 would sell them to other wineries.)

Of all the hybrids planted at Vineland, it was the Seibel 9549 — or as we know it today, De Chaunac — which would prove to be the leading commercial variety for red wines in Ontario during the 1960s and 1970s.

If Brights thought back in the 1950s that their Pinot Noir vines would give them wine to rival the best of Burgundy — as Justin de Courtenay had dreamed about — they were disappointed. The vines produced a mere ton per acre, well below commercial viability; in fact, in winemaker's parlance, "a nuisance volume."

But the initial step to plant better grapes had been taken and Brights' former director of Viticultural Research, George Hostetter (the first vintner to be awarded the Order of Canada), could justifiably claim that their 1946 experiment predated the introduction of the finest French grapes to the Eastern United States by that outspoken champion of *vinifera*, the late Dr. Constantin Frank of the Finger Lakes in New York State.

In 1955, Brights produced the first 100 percent Canadian Chardonnay from the vines de Chaunac brought back from France. Now, every Canadian winery worth its salt has a Chardonnay among its premium varietal wines.

De Chaunac also brought to Canada eighty-eight vines of a red hybrid called Maréchal Foch (a cross between Pinot Noir and Gamay). Nine years later, having propagated them and allowed them to reach maturity, Brights put on the market a wine called Canadian Burgundy in 1958, much to the disgust of the French who were unhappy that their finest wines should be impugned with such a soubriquet.

Brights shared their research willingly with the rest of the industry, and when de Chaunac retired in 1961 the wineries were nudging their growers to replant their vineyards with more acceptable hybrid varieties such as Seibel, Foch and Verdelet and, where possible, *vinifera*. They were now in a position to produce the style of products the Wine Standards Committee had called for back in 1933, only this time it was the consumers' voice they heard demanding drier wines that resembled those of France and Germany — if not in complexity and finesse, at least in alcoholic strength and without the overriding "foxy" *labrusca* taste. But old Mr. Fox would be a long time a-dying and a new craze would give him a breath of life again.

Social behaviour is governed by the law of the pendulum and wine drinking like everything else has its cycles, its fads and its fashions. In the affluent 1960s, young people became a formidable force in the marketplace and the wine companies began to take notice of this new section of society. In the late 1960s, at the request of a Detroit tavern owner, a German winemaker in Michigan created a blended sparkling wine named "Cold Duck" which immediately took off.[2] Everyone started making Cold Ducks — a 12 percent alcohol sparkling wine made from *labrusca* grapes with sugar and water added.

---

[2] There is a European tradition, convivial though unsanitary, which calls for the guests to pour their glasses into a common bowl at the end of the party. The mixture of wines of whatever hue are then sampled. This is called, in German, *Das Caulde Ende* — the cold end. The German word *Ente*, meaning "duck," very similar in sound, is a pun which gave the winemaker his name.

In 1952, when Brights purchased the Fred Marsh Wine Company, one of the products Marsh was working on was a 7 percent sparkling wine. Adehmar de Chaunac overcame the problems of instability and developed Brights' Winette which was originally sold in a thirteen-ounce pop bottle. Since it was a sparkling product, the champagne tax of $2.50 per gallon was applied. M.F. Jones of Brights argued successfully with the LCBO to lower the tax and the markup because of the product's low alcohol level. The tax per gallon was fixed at twenty-five cents.

The 7 percent "wine" was an inspiration: not only did it score Brownie points with those pressure groups who wanted to see less alcohol consumed, but it saved the company vatfuls of money. The *labrusca* grapes which were — and still are — used are the cheapest on the market. The crush is stretched with water and the excise tax is half that of table wines.

For several years, Brights had the market to themselves with Winette and Du Barry Sparkling Vin Rosé. However, out in British Columbia, Andrew Peller at Andrés was looking for a new product line and, realizing that there were high profits to be made from this style of beverage, he and his company took the plunge.

Andrés created a range of Chanté wines (as in *enchanté*) and one of these evolved as the "wine" that would create a revolution in Canadian taste — Baby Duck. At its peak, two years after its 1971 launch, one out of every twenty-four bottles of wine sold in Canada was Andrés Baby Duck.[3] The rest of the trade — and by now it was corporate business run by marketing men and Harvard-trained MBAs — scrambled to make a light sparkling wine. In consequence, a whole menagerie of pop wines descended on liquor board shelves. Their names suggested Noah's ark rather than a wine shop; Little White Duck, Luv-A-Duck, Fuddle Duck, Baby Bear, Baby Deer, Pink Flamingo, Gimli Goose and Pussycat were just some of them.

The generation of post-war Canadians may have turned their backs on the whisky-substitutes of the Depression era, but there were few Canadian wines of sufficient quality to fill the gap between the ports and sherries and the Ducks. The provincial liquor boards, seeing there were hefty profits to be made by catering to the growing demand for wine, began to increase their imports of European products until, in 1975, 3,315 imports were listed across the country as opposed to 1,875 domestic products. This posed a new problem for the indigenous wineries that had to contend with a public that knew what it didn't want from Canadian wineries and went elsewhere

---

[3] As Winston Collins wrote of the Baby Duck phenomenon: "Most Canadian grow up on soft drinks, and prefer to consume their alcoholic beverages flavoured, sweetened, carbonated, chilled, and diluted — rum and Coke, rye and ginger. Baby Duck was an easy transition from soft drinks to not-too-hard alcohol for the baby-boom generation, young people who may have been attracted to wine but were put off by its 'come-alive-for-a-dollar-five' image, or else intimidated by the overly sophisticated aura of something with an unpronounceable foreign name." (*Saturday Night*, June 1982)

for what it thought it ought to be drinking — the wines of France, Italy and Germany.

Alarmed at the influx of inexpensive wines from overseas, the grape growers and the wineries appealed to the Ontario government. In 1976, Queen's Park instituted the Ontario Wine Industry Assistance Program. The LCBO sent around a memo to all its stores saying, "Delist imported wines that are not meeting their sales quotas and thereby make room for Ontario wines.... Urge store managers and wine consultants to mention Ontario wines.... Store managers will rearrange shelf-facings and thereby make room for additional brands of Ontario wines." The government also initiated a program for the growers to help change over from *labrusca* to the more desirable hybrids and *viniferas* so that the wineries could produce European-style wines. The program provided interest-free loans for five years.

The "Big Four" wineries of Ontario — Andrés, Brights, Château-Gai and Jordan — in searching for ways to sell more of their products, began to build bottling plants and blending facilities in nongrape-growing provinces. The initial capital outlay would soon be ameliorated by a grateful province which would now list all that company's products in its stores. Their investment was welcomed because the new facilities provided local jobs. And the companies gained the added benefit of being able to manufacture wines without the regulations that restricted them in Ontario and, to a lesser extent, in British Columbia.

The mid-1970s were a watershed for the Canadian wine industry. The large companies were desperately searching for a table wine that would appeal to the nation's palate to compete with such imported blends as Black Tower, Blue Nun, Colli Albani and Donini.

Indications from south of the border suggested that Americans were drinking white wine instead of red and that the same phenomenon would happen here. The sherry and port market virtually collapsed. Diet- and health-conscious Canadians switched their allegiance from red to white, and there were hardly enough quality white hybrid grapes in the ground to satisfy the demand.

The Baby Duck drinkers had graduated to Mateus Rosé and the blended whites of Europe. Imports enjoyed a cachet on the strength of their label alone, irrespective of the quality of the wine in the bottle.

In 1976, Calona Wines in British Columbia entered the field with a wine to compete with the top-selling Black Tower called Schloss Laderheim. It looked suspiciously like a Rhine Riesling in its brown bottle and German gothic scripted label. In 1978, Château-Gai launched Alpenweiss in Ontario, the first of that company's wines to contain California grapes blended with the locally grown Seyval. The success of these two wines sent the other companies off in the direction of brand names and labels which were unashamedly European in appearance and style. The age of the packaged wine had arrived. The way the bottle looked was as important as what was in it.

The "Big Four," with their modern plants strung out across the country, not only had to contend with burgeoning imports but also with the arrival of a new source of competition — the boutique wineries. The last licence issued by the Ontario government was in 1930, but the young nurseryman, Donald Ziraldo, so impressed Major-General George Kitching, chairman of the Liquor Board of Ontario, with his concept of a cottage winery that he and his winemaker-partner Karl Kaiser were given the green light to produce 10,000 gallons of wine from the 1974 vintage. Inniskillin Wines was born that year.

A few months earlier, a Hungarian winemaker named Karl Podamer had been granted a licence to create the Podamer Champagne Company at Beamsville, Ontario (subsequently bought by Magnotta). These two small wineries were the first since the bad old days of Prohibition and paved the way for other such adventuresome entrepreneurs as Alan Eastman at Charal (now defunct), Paul Bosc at Château des Charmes, Joe Pohorly at Newark (subsequently renamed Hillebrand Estates Winery) and Enzo DeLuca and his winemaker Carlo Negri at Collio Wines in Harrow.

In British Columbia, the first estate winery, Claremont, was opened in 1979. This opened the doors for Uniacke Cellars (now CedarCreek), Sumac Ridge and Gray Monk. And in 1980 the tiny Grand Pré Winery began fermenting grapes grown on its own property near Wolfville in Nova Scotia.

These cottage enterprises were dedicated to producing labour-intensive wines of quality from *vinifera* and hybrid grapes, and would nudge the big wineries in both grape-growing provinces to follow their lead. The public, in the belief that smaller is better, snapped up the wines of Inniskillin and Château des Charmes, and over-enthusiastic nationalists held blind tastings against European products to prove that Canadian wines could hold their own in the international marketplace.

There is no question that since the early 1980s Canadian wines have improved out of all recognition to what was offered to the consuming public in the past. Tasted blind in competition against wines of similar style and character from Europe or other New World regions, they have more than held their own. Slowly, a style is evolving in Ontario and British Columbia that is unique to these growing regions and has nothing to do with California taste profiles, let alone those of France, Italy or Germany. Canadian white wines, both dry and sweet, have come of age. They have consistently won medals in international competitions. The reds are improving steadily and some Pinot Noirs, Merlots and Cabernets are very fine indeed. If, over the next ten years, our winemakers can continue to lower yields, perfect their cold fermentation techniques and their use of barrel ageing, we will have a wine industry to rival those whose products currently take up the majority of space on our restaurant wine lists and provincial liquor board racks.

ONTARIO

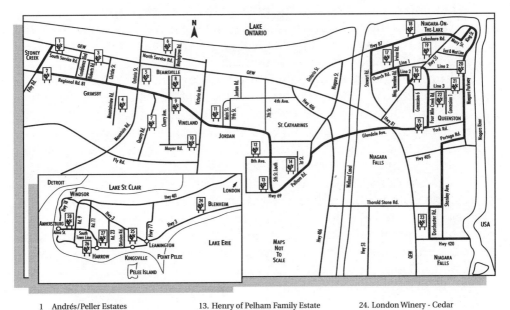

1 Andrés/Peller Estates	13. Henry of Pelham Family Estate Winery
2. Stoney Ridge Cellars	14. Wiley Brothers' Juices
3. Kittling Ridge Estate Wines & Spirits	15. Château des Charmes Wines
4. Thirty Bench Winery	16. Hille Estatse Winery
5. Magnotta Cellars	17. Stonechurch Vineyards
6. Maplegrove Vinoteca Estate Winery	18. Konzelmann Estate Winery
7. DeSousa Wine Cellars	19. Pillitteri Estate Winery
8. Willow Heights Winery	20. Reif Estate Winery
9. Lakeview Cellars Estate Winery	21. Inniskillin Wines
10. Vineland Estates Winery	22. Marynissen Estates
11. Cave Spring Cellars	23. Vincor-Niagara Cellars
12. Hernder Estate Winery	

24. London Winery - Cedar Springs Vineyard
25. Pelee Island Winery
26. Colio Wines
27. LeBlanc Estate Winery
28. D'Angelo Estate Winery

Others:

Culotta Wines
Southbrook Farms Winery
Vinoteca Premium Winery

WINE REGIONS AND WINE ROUTES OF ONTARIO

*O*ntario's vineyards, which produce over 85 percent of Canadian wine, lie in the same latitudes as Languedoc-Roussillon in Southern France, the Chianti Classico zone of Italy and Spain's Rioja region. From a geographer's perspective, the Niagara Peninsula, the north shore of Lake Erie and Pelee Island are smack in the middle of the Northern Hemisphere's wine belt. True, cities such as Hamilton and London, Ontario, may not enjoy the same climate as Cannes and Florence, but Lake Erie and Lake Ontario smooth the rough edges of our harsher weather — reflecting sunshine and storing heat

31

in the summer, acting like hot water bottles during the winter — making it possible to grow wine grapes of quality in Ontario.

Today there are 15,000 acres of vines in the province, down from the 24,000 that existed prior to the Free Trade Agreement with the United States. That political reality, coupled with a GATT (now the World Trade Organization) ruling in 1988, has radically changed the Ontario wine industry — ironically, for the better — although at the time winery executives and farmers joined in a collective tearing of hair, convinced that the end of the world was at hand.

In Ontario, politics and wine go hand in hand, and to appreciate the dramatic change in the style and quality of its products we have to understand the history involved. The year 1988 will go down in the annals as a watershed year for Ontario wine. On September 1st of that year, the Ministry of Agriculture and Food revamped The Wine Content Act. Under pressure from the estate wineries, the government banned the use of *labrusca* grapes (native North American varieties such as Concord and Niagara) in table wines. The government also lowered the amount of wine that could be made from a tonne of grapes from 1,022 litres to 818 (products at the upper limit owed as much to the local reservoir as they did the vineyard) and allowed the wineries to raise the amount of imported wine they could use in any one of their own blended products from 30 percent to 70 percent. (Today, the figure is 75 percent and it could soon become 100 percent.) In order to protect the growers, the wineries were committed to buy a minimum 25,500 tonnes of Ontario grapes each year for twelve years, starting with the 1988 harvest.

But from the wineries' viewpoint, if they were forced to purchase expensive local grapes and then compete on a level playing field with international giants such as Ernest & Julio Gallo (who annually makes two and a half times the amount of wine all Canadians consume in one year), they had to have some break on the price of the raw material.

The formula arrived at was typically Canadian: it's called the Grape Price Support Program. It takes the average price per tonne grown in California and relates it to the same grape or its equivalent variety grown in Ontario. For example, no Seyval Blanc is grown in California, but the equivalent varieties are Chenin Blanc and French Colombard. The average laid-in cost per tonne of Chenin Blanc or French Colombard delivered in Ontario when the regulation was set was $381; the Ontario Grape Growers Marketing Board price for Seyval Blanc that year was $661 per tonne. Under the program, the wineries paid the landed California price and the government gave the difference to the grower in the form of a transition subsidy that decreases with the years and will be eliminated in the year 2000.

However, even these "reforms" were not going to turn the industry around by themselves. Apart from personal pride, there was no real incentive to make quality wines since the Ontario government cushioned the local industry against foreign imports with a markup differential of 65 percent (and that included the wines of British Columbia as well as those of Europe and the New World). Spurred on by the deal that Ottawa was cooking up with Washington that would give preferential treatment to California wines in Canadian markets, exasperated members of the European Community ruled that provincial liquor boards contravened GATT regulations by implementing discriminatory markups against their wines. Under the Free Trade Agreement, the markup on American wines was cut by half on January 1, 1990 and the remaining tariff was phased down to parity with Canadian wines over the following five years (seven for VQA wines). Under the GATT deal that International Trade Minister John Crosbie's team brought back from Brussels in December 1988, the preferential markup given to Canadian products against European and Australian products was to be phased out entirely over a period of seven years for blended wines and ten years for wines made from 100 percent Canadian-grown grapes. This distinction is significant because it gave the growers and the wineries an economic incentive to concentrate on purely Canadian wines. (The growers had asked for a fifteen-year phase-down period. At the time of writing, Canadian blended wines are now on the same level as imports; VQA wines will be phased down to parity by 1998.)

Given the harsh reality of foreign competition and Canadians' traditional indifference to the locally grown product, farmers were faced with the prospect of unwanted grapes. To ease the burden, the federal and provincial governments stepped in with a hefty financial assistance package to the tune of $156 million. Fifty million dollars of amount was earmarked for the contentious vineyard "pull-out" program. In order to compete in the global wine world, the Ontario industry had to downsize. Some 7,000 acres of unwanted *labrusca* and hybrid vines were pulled (in B.C., under a similar program, nearly one-third of the vineyards were ripped out). The scheme, however well intentioned, basically rewarded failure. Those growers who had insisted on maintaining *labrusca* vineyards when there was no call for those grapes (the government bought any surplus so they always had a market for them) received fat cheques to cease and desist, while more committed farmers who had struggled to create Chardonnay, Riesling, Pinot Noir and Cabernet Sauvignon vineyards got no support at all.

The most significant occurrence in 1988 was the creation of the Vintners Quality Alliance. The VQA is an Ontario appellation system which has also been embraced by the B.C. wine industry. Negotiations are currently underway with Nova Scotia and Quebec to bring these regions under the umbrella.

Every wine growing region around the world has its own appellation system which is a set of minimum production standards followed by a bureaucratic testing for type. The VQA rules are designed to establish conditions to create quality wines although as yet they do not address the concerns of grape yields per acre or the amount of wine produced from a given number of vines.

Eventually, the geographic designations of Niagara Peninsula and Lake Erie North Shore will be fragmented into smaller sub-zones, just as Bordeaux is broken down into communes such as St-Émilion, Pauillac, Graves, etc. There is a case, for instance, for wines grown on the bench of the Niagara Escarpment to be differentiated from those grown on the lakeshore plain since their taste profiles are perceptibly different.

There can be no question that the banning of *labrusca* and the creation of the VQA have been the two major factors that have signalled a dramatic leap forward for the quality of Ontario wines. Exposing the industry to global competition has also positively affected the thinking of winery executives. They soon realized that they could not compete with the economies of scale practised by the major Californian houses when it comes to house blends. But they could compete with varietal wines of quality — a situation that fits nicely with the current consumer preferences for less but better.

One interesting sidelight on the phoenix-like rebirth of the Ontario wine industry is the subtle shift of power from the large commercial wineries — Andrés, Brights, Cartier and London — to the new kids on the block. Since the inception of the Vintners Quality Alliance, the philosophies and marketing strategies of the major estate wineries — Inniskillin, Château des Charmes and Hillebrand — have become the motivating force of the industry. These enterprises, which had all started as cottage wineries in the middle and late 1970s, became the engine for the industry, fuelled by aggressive competition from smaller, newer companies such as Cave Spring Cellars, Vineland Estates, Reif, Henry of Pelham, Konzelmann and Stoney Ridge. Their voices are the ones that people are listening to and it is their wines that began to turn up on restaurant wine lists. The large commercial concerns, in an effort not to be left behind, jumped on the VQA bandwagon and started to produce wines of sufficient quality to merit the appellation. As well, very recently, Andrés' prestige label, Peller Estates, won a Grand Gold medal at Vinitaly in Verona, for winemaker Barry Poag's 1993 Chardonnay Sur Lie.

It's one thing to produce better products, but quite another to convince jaded consumers with long memories that Ontario wines can now rival some of the best white wines around the world, both in the dry and sweet categories. For years the wineries had taken an apologetic stance, dressing their products in labels that suggested that they came from a castle on the Rhine or a château in Bordeaux rather than an industrial park in Niagara-on-the-Lake, Oakville or Woodbridge, Ontario. Since 1988, all that has changed. When the dust of free trade settled, the wineries repositioned themselves to withstand the cold blast of competition. Niche marketing became the watchword of the industry and a new self-confidence was born.

Somehow the message had to be gotten out, but after years of vilification and consumer neglect, the industry had forgotten how to blow its own horn. In 1991, a $5-million government-financed advertising campaign was undertaken to convince Ontario consumers to try the wines again. "We're ready when you are" was the ambiguous copy line. Two television commercials and a series of print ads had the desired effect because in that fiscal year sales of VQA wines rose 1.1 percent while imports fell 3.8 percent. (According to VQA's executive director, Peter Gamble, that increase in market share translates into over 750,000 bottles sold at a value of $5 million.) These figures become more significant when you realize that in the three previous years Ontario wine sales had declined by 7.5 percent each year! Now VQA wine sales have sky-rocketed thanks mainly to the presence of 240 winery stores throughout the province, in addition to the over 600 LCBO outlets.

Ontario's wine industry is over 130 years old and it has finally come of age. At international competitions in Europe and the United States, wines from the Niagara Peninsula, Lake Erie North Shore and Pelee Island are winning gold medals, much to the astonishment of the organizers.

Wine is about grapes, soil and sunshine, rain and wind. That's what makes an Australian Chardonnay taste different from one grown in northern Italy. And there will be subtle differences too within each region. Slowly, the differing regional styles of Ontario's three designated growing areas are beginning to emerge. Grape growers are become aware of what their *terroir* (the total microclimate within a vineyard given its soil, drainage, exposure to sun, wind factors, etc.) will deliver and what grape varieties they should plant in which plots of ground.

The Ontario Wine Council's export program has forced producers to look beyond their own vineyards to see where they fit into the global wine world. This new perspective has helped them define what their wines should taste like. The acceptance that Ontario is a cool climate area like Champagne, Chablis and New Zealand has tempered the winemakers' quest for the highly extractive wines that the climates of California or Australia can deliver. The style of Ontario wines is more European than New World — elegant rather than bold.

Where there was industry doubt and low self-esteem from years of consumer neglect, there is now conviction and confidence that Ontario deserves its measure of space in the reference books. The commercial producers no longer invoke the names and images of European wines and vineyards on their labels; they all want to be perceived as small Ontario wineries. Witness Brights' Sawmill Creek line, Andrés' Peller Estate label and Cartier's Jackson-Triggs bottlings. The purchase of Inniskillin by Cartier (and that conglomerate by Brights to consolidate as Vincor) and Hillebrand's merger with Andrés show how eager the major companies are to get on the premium Ontario wine bandwagon; buying estate wineries was the fastest way for the big companies to secure a significant slice of the most rapidly growing segment of the market, namely VQA wines.

And then there is Icewine. Without even realizing it, Canada has reinvented the concept of Icewine. Now the largest producer of this winter nectar, Ontario and B.C. producers have made Icewines from the hybrid Vidal grape that are instantly drinkable from the moment they are bottled. Even those made from the traditional Riesling differ in taste profile from their German counterparts. The amazing fact is that Ontario has been able to accomplish in ten years what took the Europeans 200 years to achieve on a sometime basis — namely, to produce a consistent Icewine of quality year after year.

Ontario Wineries

Andrés Wines

P.O. Box 10550
697 South Service Road
Winona, Ontario
L8E 5S4

Telephone: (905) 643-4131
            1-800-263-2170
Fax: (905) 643-4944

Andrew Peller was fifty-eight when he founded Andrés Wines in Port Moody, B.C. in 1961. He would have opened up in Ontario, but provincial bureaucrats turned down his winery licence application because of his flagrant beer advertising on radio under the guise of selling his ice. (Under the Peller name, he owned a brewery and an ice factory.) After an early success, facilities in Calgary and Truro, N.S. were opened to get listings in those provinces, but business reversals forced Andrew's son, Dr. Joseph Peller, to take over the financial reins of the company. In 1969, Andrés bought their winery in Ontario, and five years later purchased a winery in St-Hyacinthe, Que. followed by the Rouge Valley Winery in Morris, Man.

The mid-1970s was Andrés era with the success of Baby Duck followed by the German-sounding Hochtaler. But the company got left behind in the *vinifera* revolution when the small wineries began to dictate public taste. It was not until 1991 that the company realized that the Andrés name — synonymous with Baby Duck — was not going to sell Chardonnay and Riesling, so it introduced the Peller Estates label to market its varietals which conform to VQA regulations. In 1991, Andrés made its first Icewine and limited amounts of Cabernet Sauvignon.

In July 1994, Andrés purchased Hillebrand Wines to remain competitive with Brights, who had merged a year earlier with Cartier-Inniskillin.

Winemaker: Barry Poag

Production: 750,000 cases

Average tonnage crushed: 6,000

Annual tonnage purchased: 3,000

Winemaking philosophy: "Ensure the offering of a wide selection of quality wines to address the wants and needs of the wine consumer, from their 'good value' everyday wine selection to their premium varietal wines."

Wines: **LCBO**: *White*—Domaine D'Or, Domaine D'Or Chardonnay, Domaine D'Or Superieur, Grand Canadian Chablis, Hochtaler, Hochtaler Dry, Peller Estates French Cross**, Peller Estates Chardonnay*

Red—Domaine D'Or, Domaine D'Or Superieur, Peller Estates Cabernet, Peller Estates Proprietors' Reserve

Sparkling—(Charmat process) Canadian Champagne Dry*, Blush Champagne, Kurhauser Trocken Sekt; (7% sparklers) Baby Champagne, Baby Duck, Baby Duck White, Chante Blanc, Moody Blue, Sangria, Spumante

Peller Estates label white—Chardonnay Sur Lie**, Dry Riesling*, Vidal*, Muscat Ottonel*, Vidal Icewine**

Red—Botticelli, Cellar Reserve Dry, Domaine D'Or Cabernet

Own stores: *White*—Auberge, Boisseau Blanc, Botticelli, Cellar Reserve, Cellar Reserve Dinner, Cellar Reserve Dry, Hochtaler Riesling, Wintergarten

Sherries: Almond Cream, Club House Gold, Medium Dry, Regency Fine Old, Golden Cream

Specialty products: Madrigal Dessert NV; (under licence) Stone's Ginger Wine, Bulmer's Strongbow Cider

Wine Stores: 102 Wine Shoppes
Ajax: Food City, 955 Westney Rd. South

Loblaws, 125 Harewood Ave. North
Aurora: Food City, 15278 Yonge St.
Barrie: 279 Yonge St. South
Barrie (North): Zehrs, 201 Cundles Rd. East
Bramalea: Miracle Mart (Highway 7 & Dixie Rd.)
Brampton: Dominion Store, 277 Vodden St.
    Food City Conestoga Square Plaza
    Food City MacKay Plaza
    Kingspoint Plaza, 370 Main St. West
    Loblaws, 295 Queen St. East
    Westbram Food City (400 Queen St. West)
Burlington: Burlingwood Centre, 2400 Guelph Line
    Lakeside Shopping Village, 5353 Lakeshore Rd.
    Walkers Place, 3305 Upper Middle Rd.
    Supercentre, 2025 Guelph Line
Cambridge: Zehrs, Highway 8 at Highway 97
    Zehrs, 180 Holiday Inn
Collingwood: Blue Mountain Mall, 55 Mountain Rd.
    Loblaws, 12 Hurontario St.
Dundas: Miracle Ultra Mart, 119 Osler Drive
East York: Food City, 1015 Broadview Ave.
    Loblaws, 11 Redway Rd.
Etobicoke: Loblaws, 245 Dixon Rd.
    Sherway Gardens, 25 The West Mall
    Shipp Centre, 3300 Bloor St. West
Gloucester: Loblaws, 1224 Place d'Orleans
Guelph: Zehrs, 297 Eramosa Rd.
    Zehrs, Hartsland Plaza, 160 Kortright Rd. West
    Zehrs, Willow West Mall
Hamilton: Food City, 1565 Barton St. East
    Fortinos, 75 Centennial Parkway North
    Fortinos, 50 Dundurn St. South
    Fortinos, 65 Mall Road
    Lloyd D. Jackson Square, 2 King St. West
    Westdale Village, 1018 King St. West
Kanata: IGA, 111 - 4th Avenue
    Loblaws, 700 Eagleson Rd.
Kingston: Cataraqui Town Centre: 945 Gardiners Rd.
Kitchener: Highland Hills Mall, 46-875 Highland Rd. West
    Zehrs, 700 Strasburg
    Zehrs HiWay Market, 1375 Weber St. East
London: A&P, 395 Wellington Rd. South
    A&P, Adelaide Centre
    A&P, Byron Village, 1244 Commissioners St.
    Loblaws, 7 Baseline Rd.

Oakridge Mall, 1201 Oxford St. West
Sebastians, 539 Richmond St.
Zehrs, Treasure Island Plaza
Mississauga: A&P, 1240 Eglinton Ave. West
A&P, 2550 Hurontario St.
A&P, King Ten Plaza
Clarkson Village, 1865 Lakeshore Rd. West
Food City, 4040 Creditview Rd.
Food City, 6040 Glen Erin Dr.
Food City, Deer Run Plaza
Loblaws, 250 Lakeshore Rd. West
Loblaws, 925 Rathburn Rd. East
Miracle Mart, 1151 Dundas St. West
South Common, 2150 Burnhamthorpe Rd. West
Nepean: Loblaws, 1460 Merivale Rd.
Newmarket: The Newmarket Place, 17725 Yonge St. North
Niagara-on-the-Lake: Hillebrand Winery, RR #2, Highway 55
Oakville: 131 Lakeshore Rd. East
Abbey Plaza, 1500 Upper Middle Rd. West
Food City, Maple Grove Plaza
Orangeville: Zehrs, Heritage Mall, 54-4th Ave
Orleans: Orleans Gardens, 1615 Orleans Blvd.
Oshawa: A&P, 285 Taunton Rd. East
Loblaws, 1300 King St. East
Ottawa: Hunt Club Centre, 2-3320 McCarthy Rd.
Rideau Centre, 50 Rideau St.
Southgate Shopping Centre, 2515 Bank St.
Owen Sound: Heritage Place, 1350 - 16th St. East
IGA, 915 Tenth St. West
Peterborough: Food City, 900 Lansdowne St.
Loblaws, 661 Lansdowne St.
Peterborough Square, #9, 360 George St. N.
St. Catharines: A&P, 149 Hartzel Rd.
A&P, 285 Geneva St.
A&P, Midtown Plaza, 126 Welland Ave.
Food Terminal, 318 Ontario St.
IGA, 111 - 4th Ave.
Port Plaza, 600 Ontario St.
Zellers, 366 Bunting Rd.
St. Thomas: Zehrs, 295 Wellington St.
Scarborough: 1880 Eglinton Ave. East
Markington Square, 3227 Eglinton Ave. East
Miracle Mart, 5085 Sheppard Ave.
Simcoe: Sobey's, 470 Norfolk St. South
Stoney Creek: Fortinos, Fiesta Mall, 102 Highway 8

Toronto: 1689 Bayview Ave.
   Bloor West Village, 2273 Bloor West
   Food City, 2490 Gerrard St. East
   Forest Hill, 446 Spadina Rd.
   Pusateri's, 1539 Avenue Rd.
   Queen St. Market, 238 Queen St. West
   The Beaches, 2144 Queen St. East
Vanier: Loblaws, 100 McArthur
Waterloo: 450 Erb St. West
   585 Weber St. North
   Zehrs, Beechwood Plaza
Welland: Seaway Mall, 800 Niagara St. North
Whitby: Loblaws, 3050 Garden St.
Willowdale: 4775 Yonge St.
   Loblaws, 3555 Don Mills Rd.

Winery store hours: Monday to Friday, 10 am-5 pm; Saturday and Sunday, 12 pm-5 pm

Winery tours/tastings: During store hours: Every day—$1.95 per person. Introductory tasting with cheese and crackers: $3.95. Vintner's Choice - $7.95. Classic Selection - $10.95. Gold Medal Event - $13.95

Brights Wines

(See under Vincor International, page 90)

Cartier Wines & Beverages

(See under Vincor International, page 90)

Cave Spring Cellars

3836 Main Street   Telephone: (905) 562-3581
Jordan, Ontario   Fax: (905) 562-3232
L0R 1S0

Cave Spring is a model for what a small Ontario winery should be. The company produces a limited number of wines, but each has a style and quality that expresses what the region is capable of growing. The "farm on the bench" is owned by Len Pennachetti, who went into partnership with winemaker Angelo Pavan in 1986. The winery and store are located seven km away in an old stone building in Jordan that used to be an apple warehouse dating back to 1870. In 1978, Len planted the original twelve acres of vines.

Cave Spring is one of the few small wineries in that it only uses *vinifera* grapes for its products. All grapes are sourced from the Beamsville Bench of the Niagara Escarpment located between Twenty Mile Creek and Thirty Mile Creek. The principals are so dedicated to the Bench as "Ontario's finest growing microclimate" that they have called their newsletter *Benchmarks*.

The company buys sixteen new barrels for each vintage. Angelo uses a rotary vacuum filter to get the cleanest possible juice from the lees.

The winery's restaurant, On The Twenty, is certainly worth a detour (905) 562-7313. A hotel is currently under construction across the street from the restaurant and winery.

Winemakers: Angelo Pavan and Robert Summers

Acreage: 94

Soil: Moderately well-drained clay loam soil of the Benchland. A steep north-facing slope affords good natural water drainage and excellent air drainage. Close proximity to the Escarpment gives a relatively high concentration of mineral deposits from erosion which add complexity as trace elements in the wine.

Grape varieties: Chardonnay, Riesling, Gamay, Pinot Noir, Cabernet Sauvignon, Cabernet Franc, Merlot

Production: 33,000 cases

Average tonnage crushed: 465

Winemaking philosophy: "One hundred percent *Vitis vinifera* to produce only premium varietal wines. No house wines produced. Minimal intervention in the winemaking process with fining on juice only, never on finished wines. Filtration is kept to an absolute minimum with diatomaceous earth filtration only prior to bottling. No pad filtration."

Wines: **LCBO**: *White*—Chardonnay Beamsville Bench*, Dry Riesling**, Off-Dry Riesling*

Red—Gamay*

Own store: *White*—Chardonnay Reserve**, Chardonnay Musqué, Riesling Reserve*, Late Harvest Riesling, Indian Summer Riesling**, Riesling Icewine**, Gewürztraminer*

Red—Pinot Noir, Cabernet/Merlot*

Rosé—Gamay Rosé*

Store hours: Monday to Saturday, 10 am-5 pm; Sunday, 12 pm-5 pm

Tours: Yes (call for times)

Public tastings: During store hours

Central Valley Wines

98 Crockford Blvd.   Telephone/fax: (416) 752-1616
Toronto, Ontario
M1R 3C3

After nine years of operation, Central Valley Grapes and Juices became Central Valley Wines in May 1992 when Simon Di Liddo decided to make wine from the raw material he tankered in from Lodi, California. He had a loyal following of Italian home winemakers, many from his native town of Monte Leone (Foggia) near Naples, who now buy his wines which he sells either in 16-litre plastic containers or 750-ml bottles. His wines bear varietal labels but are blends with 25 percent to 30 percent Ontario wines. In the past three years, production has tripled, embracing products from California, Italy, South America, Oregon and Washington at budget prices. His winery is a 9,000-sq.-ft. facility that used to be a metal factory in an industrial area of Scarborough, Ont.

The wines are fermented in sixteen stainless-steel tanks, and fifteen oak barrels are used for aging. Simon says he will blend in terms of sweetness and acidity according to customer requests.

Winemaker: Simon Di Liddo

Production: 105,000 litres

Winemaking philosophy: "Selling great tasting bulk wine at an affordable price for everyday people."

Wines: **Own store only**: *White*—Chardonnay, Chenin Blanc, Chablis, Sauvignon Blanc, French Colombard, Johannisberg Riesling

Red—Ruby Cabernet, Cabernet Sauvignon, Zinfandel, Montepulciano, Pinot Noir, Rosé

Store hours: Monday to Friday, 9 am-6 pm; Saturday, 9 am-5 pm

Tours: Available on request

Public tastings: During store hours

Château des Charmes Wines

1025 York Road
Niagara-on-the-Lake, Ontario
L0S 1J0

Telephone: (905) 262-4219
Fax:　　　　(905) 262-5548

Paul Bosc trained at the University of Dijon and made wine in Algeria before emigrating to Canada. A stint as winemaker with Château-Gai convinced him that there was an opportunity to make fine wines in Niagara, so in 1978 he opened his own winery with its sixty-acre vineyard with lawyer Rodger Gordon as a partner. Paul did much to convince the industry that the future lay in *vinifera* varieties and his early Rieslings and Chardonnays were a model for other wineries.

His winemaking style is totally Burgundian, especially in his penchant for the difficult Aligoté grape and his insistence in making a Gamay Nouveau every year (the best in Ontario). He also makes the one of the best champagne method sparkling wine in Canada.

Paul's wife Andree, and his sons Paul Jr. and Pierre-Jean, are very active in the company. The black-labelled Estate refers to the original farm (now a warehouse) while Paul Bosc Estate refers to the property purchased in St. Davids in 1983 with its dramatic 35,000-sq.ft. French château. The Boscs own a ninety-three-acre vineyard on St. David's Bench. Paul Sr. will not submit hybrids for the VQA designation. He uses Allier oak barrels for his range of Chardonnays and reds.

Winemaker: Paul Bosc, Sr. and Pierre-Jean Bosc

Acreage: Château des Charmes Estate—60 acres (Chardonnay, Riesling, Gamay, Pinot Noir, Aligoté, Auxerrois

Soil: Four different soil types, 70 percent sandy loam, some clay. Paul Bosc Estate Vineyard—60 acres (35 planted): Chardonnay, Pinot Noir, Gamay, Riesling, Cabernet Sauvignon, Cabernet Franc, Merlot.

Vineyard features extensive under-drainage. St. David's Bench vineyard—93 acres (84 planted): Chardonnay, Pinot Noir, Gamay, Aligoté, Sauvignon Blanc, Viognier, Savagnin, Cabernet Franc, Merlot. Heavily under-drained **Grape varieties**: Chardonnay, Riesling, Pinot Noir, Gamay, Aligoté, Cabernet Sauvignon, Cabernet Franc, Merlot

Production: 70,000 cases

Average tonnage crushed: 900

Annual tonnage purchased: 200 (approximately)

Winemaking philosophy: "The Boscs produce wines which are the closest to the French style by virtue of their heritage (fifth- and sixth-generation French winegrowers) and education. Paul Bosc's experience in Burgundy has allowed him to enjoy his greatest success with those varieties (Chardonnay, Pinot Noir, Gamay, Aligoté) and he has produced a range of styles (Champagne, Nouveau, Blanc de Noir, dry whites, dry reds) with these varieties."

Wines: **LCBO**: *White*—Seyval Blanc, Gamay Noir, Gamay Blanc, Chardonnay*, Estate Chardonnay**, Cour Blanc, Aligoté, Sauvignon Blanc, Riesling**

Red—Cour Rouge, Gamay Noir, Pinot Noir*, Cabernet Sauvignon

Sparkling—Canadian Champagne Sec**

Own stores: *White*—Paul Bosc Estate Chardonnay**, Auxerrois*, Gewürztraminer**, Riesling Icewine**, Late Harvest Riesling**

Red—Estate Pinot Noir*, Paul Bosc Estate Merlot**, Paul Bosc Estate Cabernet Franc**, Paul Bosc Estate Cabernet Sauvignon**, Paul Bosc Estate Cabernet**

Sparkling—Canadian Champagne Brut**

Stores: (4)—At the winery
Oakville: 216 Lakeshore Rd. East
Ottawa: Minto Place, Laurier Ave. at Lyon St.
Toronto: Minto Place, 655 Bay St.

Store hours: Monday to Sunday, 10 am-6 pm

Public tastings: During store hours

Tours: Seven days a week: 11 am, noon, 1 pm, 2 pm, 3 pm, 4 pm

MAJOR

Colio Wines of Canada

1 Colio Drive
P.O. Box 372
Harrow, Ontario
N0R 1G0

Telephone: (519) 738-2241
Fax: (519) 738-3070

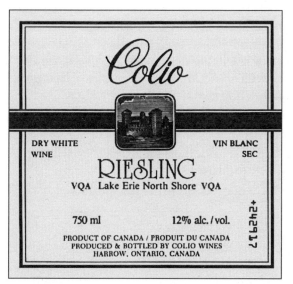

Colio, as its name suggests, was founded by a group of Italian businessmen in 1978. They brought over a winemaker from Trentino Alto-Adige, Carlo Negri, for their first crush in 1980. The style of wines from the beginning was unrepentantly commercial, but Carlo's natural ability has given them a flair generally lacking in competitively priced brand-name wines. The winery is located in the village of Harrow and its exterior belies the extend of the investment in stainless steel within.

In March 1992, Colio purchased the vineyard acreage of the former Kingsville Estate Winery first planted in 1983.

Carlo not only produces Icewine but has gone back to his roots to produce a wine he first called Vin Santo and then Vin de Curé (made from grapes dried in a greenhouse). Colio is the only winery to use grapes from all three of Ontario's designated viticultural areas in its blends. Carlo also uses American oak.

Two of his wines are sold in a British supermarket chain as North Shore White (Vidal) and North Shore Red (Baco Noir, Villard Noir and Maréchal Foch).

Winemaker: Carlo Negri

Acreage: 100 (90 acres currently in production)

Grape varieties: Riesling-Traminer, Riesling, Cabernet Franc, Gamay Noir, Pinot Gris, Chardonnay, Vidal and other French hybrids

Production: 110,000 cases

Average tonnage crushed: 1,100

Annual tonnage purchased: 700

Winemaking philosophy: "To produce dry wines which not only are Italian in style but also coincide with all major wine-producing countries. To be proud of the entire production, not only of the small percentage of the production that would be written up from wine tastings. All the wines Colio enters in wine tastings and competitions are produced in quantities available to the public, mostly through general listings."

Wines: LCBO: *White*—Bianco Secco, Extra Dry, Riesling Dry*, Riesling-Traminer**, Pinot Gris*, Vidal, Blanc de Noir*, Oak Aged Classic Chardonnay, VQA Chardonnay*, Riesling Italico*

Red—Cabernet Franc*, Maréchal Foch*, Rosso Secco, Gamay Noir, Oak Aged Classic Merlot

Sparkling—Chateau D'Or Canadian Champagne* (Charmat process), Spumante* (Charmat process)

Winery stores: *White*—Bianco (semi-dry), Chablise, Castle Cellar White, Riserva Bianco

Red—Castle Cellar Red, Riserva Rosso

Other: Vin de Curé*, Icewine**, Port, Sherry, Dry Sherry, Vino Cucina Bianco (white cooking wine), Vino Cucina Rosso (red cooking wine)

Non-alcoholic: *Sparkling*—St. Tropez White, St. Tropez Red, St. Tropez Peach

Stores (14): At the winery
Bright's Grove: 2600 Lakeshore Rd.
London: 1166 Commissioner's Rd.
   630 Richmond St.
Nepean: 250 Greenbank Rd.
Newmarket: 16655 Yonge St.
Oakville: 125 Cross Avenue, Trafalgar Village
Port Colborne: Port Colborne Mall, 287 West Side Rd.
Tecumseh: 13300 Tecumseh Rd.
Toronto: 1971 Queen St. East
Waterloo: Westmount Plaza, 50 Westmount Rd.
Whitby: 3570 Brock St. North (Delville Produce)
Windsor: A&P, 6740 Wyandotte St.

Store hours: Monday to Saturday: 10 am-5 pm. Open Sundays, May to October, 12 am-5 pm

Winery tours: Monday to Friday at 1 pm, 2 pm, 3 pm. Saturdays 12 am until 4 pm, every hour. Bus tours welcome by appointment. Admission free.

Public tastings: During store hours from 11 am-5 pm

Culotta Wines

1185 North Service Road East	Telephone: (905) 844-7912
Oakville, Ontario	Fax: (905) 844-2228
L6H 1A7	

In 1984, Peter Culotta officially turned the California grape business he inherited from his father into a winery. He had incorporated the company five years before and 1983 was his first vintage. Culotta's location between Toronto and Niagara-on-the-Lake (opposite the Ford plant on the Queen Elizabeth Way) hints at the industrial nature of the enterprise. The original Columbus labels suggested the Italian style of the wines made by a German winemaker, Rudi Müller, who had worked for Château-Gai, Andrés and Barnes. The late Bob Claremont took over the winemaking in 1987 until his untimely death in 1994.

The style of the company is geared towards easy-drinking table wines, using imported juice to flatter Ontario grapes. The first production of Vidal Icewine was in 1991. Some wines are aged in "Yugoslavian oak ovals—off premises." The wine for their "champagne" is sent to Montravin in Beamsville, Ont. for secondary fermentation by the Charmat process.

Culotta has purchased a fourteen-acre site in the Grimsby Bench for their own future plantings and is concentrating now on VQA wines.

Winemaker: Kim Culotta

Grapes bought in: Approximately 60 percent of Culotta's grape requirement is imported either as juice or finished wine. The rest is Ontario product.

Production: 30,000 cases

Winemaking philosophy: "The philosophy of Culotta is to produce an affordable everyday wine in the style and character enjoyed by our European ancestors. It is also our goal to enhance our image and reputation by utilizing the expanded availability of premium off-shore varieties to complement superior Ontario hybrids and limited local *viniferas*."

Wines: **LCBO**: *White*—Chablis, RMS *Segwun* Dry White

Red—RMS Segwun Red

Own stores: *White*—Dry White, Seyval Blanc, Gewürztraminer, Chardonnay, Barrel-Fermented Chardonnay, Riesling, Muscat/Riesling, Vidal, Vidal Icewine**

Sparkling—Champagne

Red—De Chaunac/Foch, Petite Sirah, Merlot, Maréchal Foch, Cabernet Sauvignon*, Cabernet Franc

Stores:
At the winery
Burlington: The Barn, 2075 Fairview St.
Collingwood: Royal City Centre, 275 First St.
Hamilton: The Barn, 2371 Barton St. East
Oakridges: Foodland, 13075 Yonge St.
Toronto: 40 St. Regis Cres., Downsview
        The Wine Store, 90 Caledonia Park Rd.

Store hours: 9 am-6 pm

Culotta store hours: Sundays, 12 pm-5 pm

D'Angelo Estate Winery

5141 Concession 5, RR #4   Telephone: (519) 736-7959
Amherstberg, Ontario   Fax: (519) 736-1912
N9V 2Y9

Salvatore D'Angelo planted his vineyard in 1983. As an accomplished amateur winemaker, his ambition was to open his own winery — which he did

seven years later. Located south of Windsor and just east of Amherstberg in the heart of Essex County, the winery bears the Lake Erie North Shore appellation. Only grapes grown on the estate are used in Sal's wines, which are vinted in his temperature-controlled fermenting room. In the vineyard, he uses a unique fourteen-wire trellising system to provide the ripeness and exposure to air contact he seeks. He also sells fresh juice to home winemakers.

Sal's art labels, historic and contemporary, are some of the most appealing in Ontario.

Winemaker: Salvatore D'Angelo

Acreage: 13

Soil: Clay loam; vineyard at the centre of Essex County, surrounded by Lake St. Clair and Lake Erie. Well drained, with breezes off Lake Erie six km away.

Grape varieties: Chardonnay, Riesling, Pinot Blanc, Seyval Blanc, Vidal, Cabernet Sauvignon, Pinot Noir, Merlot, Gamay, Maréchal Foch, Cabernet Franc

Production: 2,000 cases

Average tonnage crushed: 100

Winemaking philosophy: "To produce the best wines from our own vineyards. We make wine the old-fashioned way. We grow it."

Wines: **LCBO:** Vidal, Vidal Icewine*

Own store: *White*—Seyval Blanc, Riesling, Chardonnay**, Pinot Blanc, Gamay Blanc de Noir, Premium Select Late Harvest Riesling*, Vidal Icewine*

Red—Maréchal Foch**, Pinot Noir, Merlot, Cabernet Sauvignon, Cabernet-Merlot**, Gamay Rosé

Store hours: *May to December*: 10 am-6 pm, seven days a week; *January to April*: Thursday to Sunday, 11 am-5 pm

Tours: Yes

Public tastings: During store hours

De Sousa Cellars

3753 Quarry Road   Telephone: (905) 563-7269
Beamsville, Ontario
L0R 1B0

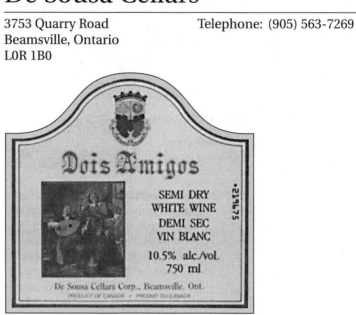

John and Mary De Sousa are Canadian farmers who remember the wines of their native Portugal. In 1987, they decided to turn the grapes they grew high on the Bench of the Niagara Escarpment into Portuguese-style wines. They hired Dieter Guttler, formerly a partner and winemaker at Vineland Estates, to produce a red and a white under the Dois Amigos label. All the wines are aged in oak in the traditional Portuguese manner.

Winemakers: John De Sousa, Sr. and John De Sousa, Jr.
Wines: Dois Amigos white (Vidal, Riesling and Chardonnay)
Dois Amigos red (De Chaunac, Maréchal Foch and Pinot Noir)

Domaine Vagners

1973 Four Mile Creek Rd., RR #3 Telephone: (905) 468-7296
Niagara-on-the-Lake, Ontario
L0S 1J0

DOMAINE VAGNERS

1993
RIESLING • LATE HARVEST
WHITE WINE • VIN BLANC

9.9% alc./vol.   375 ml
Product of Canada   Produit du Canada

DOM VAGNERS WINERY • NIAGARA-ON-THE-LAKE, ONTARIO

"I may be Canada's smallest winery and may remain so," says Martin Vagners, who started his operation "to make a good red wine" in 1994 in a converted barn. An executive for Scott Laboratories for many years, and an experienced taster and wine judge, he is determined to grow only the top *vinifera* (except Chardonnay, "because everyone else has it").

Martin planted his tiny vineyard in 1990 and made his first crush three years later. He ages his wines in reshaved French oak barrels and uses a minimum of chemicals. Ultimately, he plans to make a champagne method sparkler.

Winemaker: Martin A. Vagners

Acreage: 3

Soil: Sandy, well drained, about 2 km from the lake

Grape varieties: Merlot, Cabernet Franc, Cabernet Sauvignon, Riesling, Pinot Gris, Gewürztraminer, Pinot Noir

Average tonnage crushed: For 1995, "expecting six-plus tons"

Production: 1994—1000 litres; 1995—2000-plus litres. "Max out at about 10,000 litres."

Winemaking philosophy: "Country wines, handcrafted for early enjoyment. Our grapes are 100 percent hand-picked at the correct time, therefore no SO_2 is required. The wines are lightly filtered, slightly bruised. Basically, I realize we cannot make a Bordeaux château-style red wine, but we can make an early drinking, fruity Loire (Chinon) type. I feel that a blend of 60 percent Merlot, 30 percent Cabernet Franc and 10 percent Cabernet Sauvignon for me will work, whereas 60 percent Cabernet Sauvignon, 30 percent Cabernet Franc and 10 percent Merlot will not."

Winery store: *White*—Riesling Late Harvest, Pinot Gris, Pinot Blanc
Red—Cabernet Franc, Merlot, Proprietors' Blend (Bordeaux blend)
Tours: By appointment
Public tastings: None

Henry of Pelham

1469 Pelham Road, RR #1	Telephone: (905) 684-8423
St. Catharines, Ontario	Fax: (905) 684-8444
L2R 6P7	

Empire Loyalist Henry of Pelham, whose lugubrious hand-drawn features grace the winery's labels, is an ancestor of the Speck family, owners of this historic property. Henry's father, Nicholas Smith, was a bugle boy in the Revolutionary War of 1776. The graveyard next to the winery attests to the fact that the property has been in the Smith family in an uninterrupted line.

The modern, well-equipped winery, located on the Bench of the Escarpment, is housed behind the ancient coaching inn (1842) with its atmospheric cellars — now the tasting room — wine shop and cooperage storage. When the late Paul and Bobbi Speck and their three sons took over the property in 1988, there was already a twenty-acre vineyard which had been planted seventy-five years ago. They have planted fifty-five more acres of vines with a further 100 acres at their disposal.

Winemaker: Ron Giesbrecht

Acreage: 75

Soil: Heavy clay/loam soil called Smithville Till Clay, high in calcerous content which contributes to low yields. Good air drainage and water run off. Lower humidity than the lakeshore below and marginally higher heat accumulation.

Grape varieties: Chardonnay, Riesling, Cabernet Sauvignon, Baco Noir, Seyval Blanc, Gamay Noir

Production: 25,000 cases

Average tonnage crushed: 330

Annual tonnage purchased: 180 (mainly from the Bench)

Winemaking philosophy: "To provide handcrafted wines which mirror the qualities and potential of our unique conditions in Niagara, and in particular the Niagara Bench. Our philosophy of winemaking embraces innovation, enabling the creation of what tradition and Nature have inspired."

Wines: **LCBO**: *White*—Vidal*, Riesling*, Chardonnay, Proprietors' Reserve Chardonnay**, Proprietors' Reserve Riesling*

Red—Loyalist House Red*, Baco Noir**

Own store: *White*—Seyval Blanc, Riesling Icewine**, Barrel Fermented Chardonnay*, Sauvignon Blanc, Late Harvest Sauvignon Blanc, Late Harvest Vidal

Red—Merlot, Pinot Noir, Blanc de Pinot Noir, Cabernet Sauvignon

Rosé—Cabernet Franc Rosé

Store hours: 10 am-6 pm, seven days a week

Tours: Yes

Public tastings: During store hours

Hernder Estate Wines

1607 8th Avenue   Telephone: (905) 684-3300
St. Catharines, Ontario   Fax: (905) 684-3303
L2R 6P7

In 1987, Fred Hernder purchased an old Victorian barn which was being used to house cattle. The Hernder family renovated it and turned it into a winery and a juice plant with a capacity of nearly 600,000 litres, as well as a winery store, tour room and lately a restaurant. They produced their first wines in 1991 (Dry and Semi-Dry Vidal) and for the next vintage hired Ray Cornell as winemaker for an expanded production of *vinifera* varietals, including Riesling, Chardonnay and Cabernet Franc. The following year Ray added Cabernet Sauvignon, Merlot and two Icewines to the portfolio — a Riesling and a Riesling-Vidal blend.

Winemaker: Ray Cornell

Grape varieties: "We are currently planting approximately 30,000 vines a year to include the following varieties: Cabernet Franc, Cabernet Sauvignon, Merlot, Baco Noir; Gewürztraminer, Pinot Gris, Chardonnay, Chardonnay Musqué, Riesling, Muscat Ottonel, Morio Muscat, Seyval Blanc, Vidal (future plantings will include Gamay, Pinot Noir)."

Production: 5,500 cases

Average tonnage crushed: 150 for wine (271 for the juice operation)

Winemaking philosophy: "We do not import any foreign wine for blending. We will ultimately be 95 percent self-supporting in grapes and so can offer the public wines which begin life in vineyards that are carefully monitored by the Hernders themselves, as good wines begin in the vineyards. Will only offer wines that are true to their type."

Wines: **LCBO/Vintages**: *White*—Dry Vidal, Chardonnay

Winery store: *White*—Riesling, Proprietors' Reserve Riesling*, Semi-Dry Vidal, Seyval Blanc, Riesling Icewine**

Red—Cabernet Franc, Cabernet-Merlot

Store hours: Monday to Friday: 9 am-5 pm; weekends: 11 am-5 pm

Public tastings: During store hours; fifty cents per wine. Icewines: $2.50

Tours: 1:30 pm and 3:30 pm. Pre-booked tours, nominal charge. Bus tours and groups of 10 or more by appointment.

Hillebrand Estates

RR #2, Highway 55　　　　　Telephone: (905) 468-3201
Niagara-on-the-Lake, Ontario　Fax:　　　　(905) 468-4789
L0S 1J0

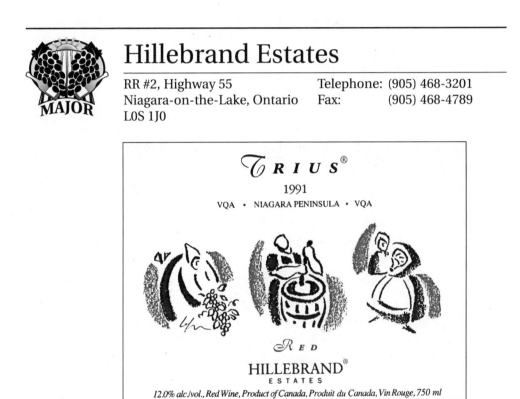

Joe Pohorly created a winery in 1979 called Newark, but three years later debt problems forced him to sell to Underberg, the giant Swiss bitters company which held a controlling interest in Peter Mielzynski, the Toronto-based wine and spirit importers. The name was changed to Hillebrand Estates.

The company's winemaking expertise was evident in early brands such as Schloss Hillebrand and the initial Rieslings, and no winery in Canada has grown as quickly as Hillebrand, thanks to the injection of capital from Switzerland. Hillebrand's equipment and facilities are the envy of their colleagues. In 1990, the company built a new building to house the offices above a bottling line which is itself over a new sparkling wine cellar for its Mounier label. In July 1994, Underberg sold its 100 percent interest in Hillebrand Estates to Andrés Wines of Winona.

Hillebrand, although large, concentrates on quality in its varietals, especially Chardonnay (24,000 cases), Cabernet and Riesling, of which their are a bewildering number of labels.

Heavy emphasis is placed on barrel fermenting and ageing with oak from Nevers, Voges, Tronçais and Allier as well as American.

Winemaker: Jean-Laurent Groux (known as "J-L")

Acreage: 30

Soil: Clay

Grape varieties: Chardonnay, Riesling, Pinot Noir, Pinot Gris, Cabernet Franc

Production: 340,000 cases

Average tonnage crushed: 3,000

Annual tonnage purchased: 900

Winemaking philosophy: "Our philosophy in making wine is to respect the fruit that Mother Nature has given us. We associate art and technology to produce varietal wines with distinctive character from the finest vineyards of the Niagara Peninsula."

Wines: **LCBO**: *White*—Chardonnay*, Riesling**, Pinot Gris*, Muscat Reserve*, Gewürztraminer, Vidal, Cuvée 1812, Chablis, Brulé Blanc, Schloss Hillebrand

Red—Gamay Noir*, Maréchal Foch, Cuvée 1812, Brulé Rouge

Vintages: *White*—Trius Chardonnay*, Trius Riesling Dry*, Collectors' Choice Chardonnay*, Late Harvest Vidal*, Icewine**

Red—Collectors' Choice Cabernet*, Trius Red**

Cuvée 1812 Burgundy, Maréchal Foch

Sparkling—Mounier Brut**, Canadian Champagne*

Own stores: Seyval Blanc, Sauvignon Blanc and Pinot Noir Rosé

Specialty wines: Olde Town Sherry Cream and Dry Sherry (winery's retail stores only)

Stores: At the winery
  Ajax: Loblaws, 125 Harwood Ave. North
  Barrie: Allendale Plaza, 279 Yonge St. South
  Brampton: Kingspoint Plaza, 370 Main St. North
      Loblaws, 295 Queen St. East
  Burlington: Burlingwood Centre, 2400 Guelph Line
      Lakeside Shopping Village, 5353 Lakeshore Rd.
      Walkers Place, 3305 Upper Middle Rd.
  East York: Loblaws, 11 Redway Rd.
  Etobicoke: Loblaws, 245 Dixon Rd.
      Shipp Centre, 3300 Bloor St. West
  Gloucester: Loblaws, 1224 Place D'Orleans
  Hamilton: Westdale Village, 1018 King St. West

Kanata: Loblaws, 700 Eagleson Rd.
　　Van Leeuwen Centre, 420 Hazeldean Rd.
Kingston: Cataraqui Town Centre, 945 Gardiners Rd.
Kitchener: Highland Hills Mall, 46-875 Highland Rd.
London: Loblaws, 7 Baseline Rd.
　　Oakridge Mall, 1201 Oxford St. West
　　Sebastian's, 539 Richmond St.
Mississauga: Clarkson Village, 1865 Lakeshore Rd. West
　　Loblaws, 250 Lakeshore Rd. East
　　Loblaws, 925 Rathburn Rd. East
　　South Common Mall, 2150 Burnhamthorpe Rd. West
Nepean: Loblaws, 1460 Merivale Rd.
Newmarket: Newmarket Place, 17725 Yonge St. North
　　The New Marketplace, 155 Yonge St. North
Oakville: 131 Lakeshore Rd. East
　　Abbey Plaza, 1500 Upper Middle Rd. West
Orleans: 1615 Orleans Blvd.
Oshawa: Loblaws, 1300 King St. East
Ottawa: Hunt Club Centre, 2 - 3320 McCarthy Rd.
　　Rideau Centre, 50 Rideau St.
　　Southgate Shopping Centre, 2515 Bank St.
Peterborough: Loblaws, 661 Lansdowne St.
　　Peterborough Square, 360 George St. North
St. Catharines: IGA, 111 - 4th Ave.
　　Port Plaza, 600 Ontario St.
Scarborough: Markington Square, 3227 Eglinton Ave. East
　　Super Centre, 1880 Eglinton Ave. East
Toronto: 1689 Bayview Ave.
　　2144 Queen St. East
　　446 Spadina Rd.
　　Bloor West Village, 2273 Bloor St. West
　　Pusateri's, 1539 Avenue Rd.
　　Queen St. Market, 238 Queen St. West
　　The Beaches, 2144 Queen St. East
Vanier: Loblaws, 100 McArthur Rd
Waterloo: 585 Weber St. North
Welland: Seaway Mall, 800 Niagara St. North
Whitby: Loblaws, 3050 Garden St.
Willowdale: Loblaws, 3555 Don Mills Rd.

Winery tours (one hour): Seven days a week, twelve months a year: 11 am, 1 pm, 3 pm and 4 pm. Additional tours on weekends during the summer and fall harvest. Deluxe private tours for groups. Catering on request.

Public tastings: During store hours, 10 am-6 pm

MAJOR

Inniskillin Wines Inc.

RR #1, Line 3 at the Niagara Parkway
Niagara-on-the-Lake, Ontario
L0S 1J0
(See also Vincor International, page 90)

Telephone:
Administration: (905) 468-2187
Fax: (905) 468-5355
Tour & Retail: (905) 468-3554, ext. 4
Fax: (905) 468-7501

To Donald Ziraldo and Karl Kaiser must go the credit for rejuvenating the
Ontario wine industry at a time when it could easily have foundered in the
swamps of *labrusca*. They received their boutique winery licence — a new
concept in 1975 when the industry was dominated by large commercial
wineries ferociously competing with Baby Duck-style products and imita-
tion Liebfraumlich — and they determined to make only quality wines. For
a decade it was an uphill battle, but they have earned their place in the sun
with a range of single vineyard Chardonnays, Pinot Noir, Cabernet
Sauvignon and Vidal Icewine. And along the way they have raised the profile of Ontario wines in Canada and around the world.

The tireless Donald Ziraldo was the prime mover in setting up the
Vintners Quality Alliance, Canada's appellation system, and lobbying the
provincial government to create a wine route through the Peninsula.
Inniskillin's 1989 Vidal Icewine won a gold award at Vinexpo in 1991, the first
such international accolade and one that has drawn global attention to
Ontario as a wine region.

The winery itself, beautifully sited just off the Niagara Parkway, has a California look and feel. The Brae Burn barn, which acts as the store and champagne loft, is well worth a visit.

Given Karl Kaiser's Austrian background, you'd expect to find Grüner Veltliner and Zweigeltrebe in the vineyard — and you do. Each year he brings in forty to eighty new barrels from France.

In 1992, Inniskillin merged with Cartier Wines, and a year later that new conglomerate was taken over by Brights and was renamed Vincor International. Inniskillin continues to operate independently and is now making wine in British Columbia as well as in Ontario. The partners have an agreement with the Burgundy shipper Jaffelin to create a Pinot Noir and a Chardonnay — a selection of their best barrels — to be marketed under the name *Alliance*.

Winemaker: Karl Kaiser

Acreage: 60

Soil: Medium light to medium heavy sandy loam with some clay

Grape varieties: Pinot Noir, Gamay, Cabernet Sauvignon, Cabernet Franc, Merlot, Zweigeltrebe, Maréchal Foch, Baco Noir, Leon Millot, Chambourcin, de Chaunac; Chardonnay, Riesling, Gewürztraminer, Vidal, Seyval Blanc, Pinot Grigio, Pinot Blanc, Grüner Veltliner, Auxerrois

Production: 150,000 - 200,000 cases

Average tonnage crushed: 1,500 - 2,000

Average tonnage purchased: "Insignificant, only in short crop years."

Winemaking philosophy: "Our basic philosophy of expanding varietal planting in Ontario has not changed since 1974. In winemaking, our goal is to establish a style for whites that will be remembered for their balance and finesse, offering the appropriate flavours for our region's cool autumn climate."

Wines: LCBO: *White*—Auxerrois, Brae Blanc, Braeburn, Chardonnay*, Chardonnay Reserve*, Gamay Blanc, Gewürztraminer*, Late Harvest Riesling*, Vidal*, Late Harvest Vidal, Proprietors' Reserve Riesling/Chardonnay, Riesling, Late Harvest Riesling, Seyval Blanc

Red—Brae Rouge, Gamay Noir, Maréchal Foch*, Pinot Noir, Cabernet Franc, Proprietors' Reserve Cabernet Sauvignon/Zweigeltrebe

Sparkling—L'Allemand (Riesling, Charmat process)

Winery stores: *White*—Single vineyard Chardonnays (Schuele*, Seeger*, Klose**, Butler's Grant*), Riesling Reserve*, Pinot Grigio, Pinot Blanc, Grüner Veltliner, Vidal Icewine** (the most decorated Canadian wine), Duchess, Sauvignon Blanc, Melon, Welschriesling

Red—Pinot Noir Reserve**, Cabernet Sauvignon Klose Vineyard*, Cabernet Franc/Merlot*, Merlot, Merlot/Cabernet Sauvignon, Petite Syrah, Zweigeltrebe, Maréchal Foch*, Baco Noir

Sparkling—Canadian Champagne

Specialty wine: Fleur d'Ontario* (Pineau de Charentes style—Vidal and grape spirit)

Stores (4): At the winery
   Toronto: 142 Davenport (Retail and Education Centre)
   Marché, 42 Yonge St., BCE Place
   Ottawa: 11 Metcalfe St.

Winery store hours: Open daily. *Winter*: November to April, 10 am-5 pm. *Summer*: May to October, 10 am-6 pm. Closed for major holidays.)

Tours: Guided: *June to October*: Saturday and Sunday, 10:30 am and 2.30 pm. Monday to Friday: 2:30 pm. *November to May*: 2:30 pm only. Saturday and Sunday, 2:30 pm. Self-guided tours: year round during store hours.

Tastings: Fifty cents per serving. *November to April*: 11 am-4:30 pm. *May to October*: 11 am-5:30 pm.

Kittling Ridge Estate Wines & Spirits

297 South Service Road	Telephone: (905) 945-9225
Grimsby, Ontario	(416) 777-6300
L3M 4E9	Fax: (905) 945-4330

Kittling Ridge is the phoenix risen from the ashes of the old Rieder Distillery (founded in 1970 by Otto Rieder). The bird analogy is apt because "kittling" is a term used for migratory birds as they soar on circling updraughts, a sight common on the Niagara Escarpment at Grimsby where the facility is located. John Hall and his two silent partners officially opened their winery-distillery in July 1994, although it started operations in 1992 and boasts Ontario's first on-premise spirits store. Apart from grapes brought in for its varietal wines (aged in American and French oak), Kittling Ridge also purchases quantities of Niagara tender fruit — strawberries, cherries, plums, pears and apples — for its distillates. It also created a new category — "fortified Icewine" — much to the chagrin of the VQA. Kittling Ridge also produces Canadian whisky, rum, vodka, brandy, eaux-de-vie, bitters and liqueurs.

The facility has a buffet-style dining room for private group functions.

Winemaker: Jamie Macfarlane (formerly with Brights)

Production: 32,000 cases

Annual tonnage purchased: 448 (1994)

Winemaking philosophy: "A passion for creativity, taste and satisfaction."

Wines: **LCBO**: *White*—Sauvignon Blanc, Chardonnay Proprietors' Cuvée
Red—Cabernet Sauvignon

Winery store: *White*—Riesling (off-dry), Icewine, Dry Reserve
(Coming soon: Gewürztraminer, Late Harvest Vidal)

Red—Dry Reserve (Coming soon: Merlot, Pinot Noir, Cabernet Franc, Gamay)

Sparkling—Classic Canadian Champagne (Charmat process)

Fortified—Icewine & Brandy*, Icewine & Eaux-de-vie, Icewine Grappa (coming soon: Chardonnay Grappa, Muscat Grappa)

Boutique hours: Monday to Saturday, 10 am-5 pm; Sunday, 12 pm-5 pm

Tours: *May to October*: Tuesday to Saturday, 11 am-2 pm. Sunday, 1 pm-3 pm (call ahead to confirm dates and times)

Konzelmann Winery

RR #3, Lakeshore Road   Telephone: (905) 935-2866
Niagara-on-the-Lake, Ontario   Fax: (905) 935-2864
L0N 1J0

Herbert Konzelmann's family has been making wine in Württemberg since 1893, and a reproduction of the entrance to that winery can be seen on his Ontario labels. An oenology graduate from Weinsberg in Germany, Herbert ran the family facility for twenty-five years before visiting Canada on a hunting trip in 1980. He was so impressed by the potential of winemaking in Niagara that he took soil samples home with him in margarine containers and had them analyzed. Four years later he was back to purchase his forty-acre estate that backs onto Lake Ontario. He planted 32,000 vines and took his first crop off in the 1986 vintage, producing nine different varietals.

His Germanic winemaking style manages to coax subtle perfumes from his grapes, particularly Riesling, Chardonnay and Gewürztraminer. While he uses Allier, Nevers and Jugoslavian oak, especially for Chardonnay, his best results are from stainless steel, according to his own traditions. Herbert's Icewine is one of Canada's best.

In the German style, he believes in sweet reserve, back-blending fresh grape juice to the finished wines.

Winemaker: Herbert Konzelmann

Acreage: 40

Soil: Clay, sand. Ideal microclimate because of the proximity of the lake. Winds dry the vines, inhibiting fungus growth.

Grape varieties: Riesling, Chardonnay, Pinot Blanc, Gewürztraminer, Riesling-Traminer, Geisenheim 311, Vidal, Pinot Noir, Gamay, Zweigelt, Cabernet Sauvignon, Cabernet Franc, Merlot

Production: 80,000 cases

Average tonnage crushed: 130

Annual tonnage purchased: 30

Winemaking philosophy: "Konzelmann stands for quality."

Wines: **LCBO**: Golden Vintage, Johannisberg Riesling (Sugar Code 1*) and (Sugar Code 2*), Chardonnay, Pinot Blanc, Pinot Noir*

Own store: *White*—Late Harvest Riesling Dry, Chardonnay Reserve*, Late Harvest Vidal*, Late Harvest Riesling Medium Dry*, Gewürztraminer*, Pinot Noir Rosé, Peach Wine, Riesling-Traminer Icewine**, Vidal Icewine**, Select Late Harvest Vidal**

Sparkling—Canadian Riesling Champagne

Red—Pinot Noir (1), Gamay Noir, Baco Noir Late Harvest, Zweigelt Late Harvest

Store hours: Monday to Saturday, 10 am-6 pm; Sunday, 12:30 pm- 5:50 pm. *January to March*: Wednesday to Saturday, 10 am-6 pm

Public tastings: During store hours

Tours: By arrangement

Lakeview Cellars Estate Winery

RR #1, 4037 Cherry Avenue   Telephone/fax: (905) 562-5685
Vineland, Ontario
L0R 2C0

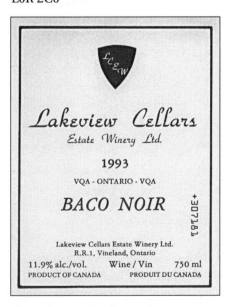

Grower Eddy Gurinskas was a dedicated home winemaker who consistent-ly won medals at national and international amateur competitions, especially for his Vidal Icewine. In 1991, he and his wife Lorraine followed in the footsteps of their friend John Marynissen in turning from grape grower to commercial winemaker when Lakeview Cellars got the second farm winery licence issued in Ontario.

From the start, Eddy's intention has been to bottle single vineyard wines with barrel aging for his Chardonnay, Cabernet Sauvignon and Baco Noir. Currently, he has thirty-six French and American oak *barriques*. The winery is a newly constructed barn with a gambrel roof.

Winemaker: Eddy Gurinskas

Acreage: 13

Soil: The vineyard is located on the first plateau of the Niagara Escarpment, better known as "The Bench," approximately 3 km from Lake Ontario. The air drainage is very effective in the summer and provides considerable protection from extreme cold in winter. Soils are heavy clay loam.

Grape varieties: Cabernet Sauvignon, Chardonnay, Pinot Gris, Baco Noir, Vidal, Riesling, Welschriesling, Merlot

Production: 2,600 cases

Average tonnage crushed: 35

Grapes bought in: Nil

Winemaking philosophy: "Our aspirations are to make wine using only 100 percent Ontario grapes that are locally grown. We intend to cap our production at 5,000 cases with sales of our wines through our winery store along with limited sales through the LCBO."

Wines: LCBO and Vintages: Chardonnay**, Vidal*, Pinot Gris*, Riesling*, Vidal Icewine**, Cabernet Sauvignon**

Own store: Chardonnay Reserve, Welschriesling, Late Harvest Riesling, Late Harvest Vidal, Baco Noir**

Store hours: Monday to Sunday, 10 am-5:30 pm

Tours: Yes

Public tastings: During store hours (free)

LeBlanc Estate Winery

4716-4th Concession, RR #2   Telephone: (519) 738-9228
Harrow, Ontario   Fax: (519) 738-2609
N0R 1G0

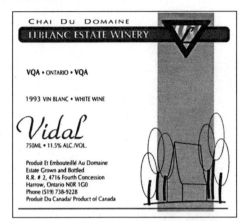

In 1984, Alphonse and Monique LeBlanc planted their vineyard just north of Harrow. Their son Pierre and his wife Lyse got their winery licence in 1993, although Lyse (from Papineau, Que.) began fermenting in 1992, and even made an Icewine. They started with a single American oak barrel.

Winemaker: Lyse LeBlanc

Acreage: 22

Soil: Mostly clay, typical Lake Erie North Shore climate—higher heat units than Niagara, but colder winters.

Grape varieties: Pinot Blanc, Riesling, Seyval, Vidal (experimental plantings of Cabernet Sauvignon, Pinot Gris, Geisenheim, Merlot)

Average tonnage crushed: 30

Annual tonnage purchased: 5

Production: 1,200 cases

Winemaking philosophy: "To produce a wine that mirrors the quality of the grapes and the distinctive *gout de terroir*. We believe this to be achieved by merely guiding the grapes along to their natural conclusion."

Wines: **Own store**: *White*—Vidal*, Riesling, Pinot Blanc, Gewürztraminer, Chardonnay, Vidal Icewine*

Red—Cabernet (30 percent Cabernet Sauvignon, 70 percent Cabernet Franc), Pinot Noir

Rosé—Chant d'Eté*

Store hours: *May to October*: Daily, noon-5 pm. *November to April*: By appointment.

Public tastings: During store hours

Tours: On request, large groups by reservation

London Winery

560 Wharncliffe Road South   Telephone: (519) 686-8431
London, Ontario   Fax: (519) 686-2829
N6J 2N5

London Winery was founded by the Knowles brothers in 1925 and is still in the family. A traditional company, specializing in ports and sherries, mead (the only Canadian producer) and other sweet dessert wines, it also makes a range of *vinifera* table wines as well as Icewine and VQA products. London boasts Canada's oldest wine, St. Augustine Communion, a sweet red of 16 percent alcohol that dates back to the time when Vin Villa on Pelee Island first made it in the 1870s.

For all its atmosphere of history and conservatism, London does have some impressive achievements in the technological advance of the Canadian wine industry. The company was the first to introduce the process for making flor sherry (invented by Ralph Crowther at Vineland's Horticultural Research Institute), the first to put on the market sherry in a decanter with a ground glass stopper (London Cream), and the first to use the millipore filter.

Of special note is the 225,000-litre barrel solera-ageing cellar for the company's premium sherries and ports. London does a healthy export business to the northeastern United States.

The Scottish winemaker, Jim Patience, lives up to his name. He's been making wines with the company for thirty years. Varietal wines are sold under the Cedar Springs label, from their vineyard in Blenheim.

Winemakers: Jim Patience and Peter Knowles

Acreage: 130 (sixty miles west of London at Cedar Springs, established in 1984)

Soil: Fox gravel loam, situated half a mile from Lake Erie

Grape varieties: Riesling, Chardonnay, Merlot, Vidal, Seyval Blanc, Vivant, 23-512

Production: 300,000 cases

Average tonnage crushed: 1,800

Annual tonnage purchased: 1,050

Winemaking philosophy: "To address all segments of the winemarket (i.e., Sherry, Port, Vermouth, Blended Table Wines, Premium VQA Varietals, Sparkling Wines, Champagnes, Fruit Wines, Honey Wine). To produce premium quality products in all categories and thereby provide excellent value to the wine consumer. To bring the fullness of the fruit to an unforgettable tasting experience."

Wines: **LCBO**: *Fortified*—XXX Sherry, Westminster Sherry, Supreme Sherry, Cream Sherry, Pale Dry Sherry, Golden Cream Sherry*, Sweet Vermouth*, Dry Vermouth*, XX Port

White—Chablis, Cuvée Superieur, Late Harvest Vidal, Cedar Springs Reserve White

Red—Red St. Augustine Communion Wine, Baco Noir, Cuvée Superieur Red, Cedar Springs Proprietors' Reserve Baco Noir*, Proprietors' Reserve Maréchal Foch, Proprietors' Reserve Red

Sparkling—Bella Spumante, Spumante Bianco

7 percent alcohol—Cold Duck, L'Oiseau Bleu, O'Brien's

Own stores: Icewine**, Late Harvest Vidal, North Shore Estates Premium Selection White, Vinroi White

Cedar Springs label red—Global Cabernet Sauvignon, Global Chardonnay, Proprietors' Reserve Chardonnay, Proprietors' Reserve De Chaunac, Proprietors' Reserve Gamay Noir, Proprietors' Reserve Pinot Noir, Proprietors' Reserve Merlot, Proprietors' Reserve Riesling, Proprietors' Reserve Vidal

Other: Cream Port, Edelmere, Honey Wine, Pink Flamingo, White Champagne, Pink Champagne, Peach Wine, Strawberry Wine, Cherry Wine, Ancient Mead Honey Wine, Creme d'Or Sherry, Cuvée d'Or, Night Moves, Summer Cooler, Chilly Willy Wine Cooler, Pink Flamingo Wine Cooler

Stores:
Blenheim: R.R. #1
Brockville: 2399 Parkdale Ave.
Cornwall: 31 Ninth St. East
Hamilton: 15 King William St.
    665 Upper James St.

Kitchener: 1405 Ottawa St. North
London: 155 Clarke Side Rd.
    509 Commissioners Rd. West
    115 Dundas St.
    1401 Ernest Ave.
    1275 Highbury Ave.
    130 King St.
    1299 Oxford St. East
    540 Wharncliffe Rd. South (Tour Centre)
Orleans: 100 Place d'Orleans Dr.
Ottawa: 296 Bank St.
    1309 Carling Ave.
    1670 Heron Rd.
St. Thomas: 417 Wellington St.
Sarnia: 500 Exmouth St.
    600 Murphy St.
Sault Ste. Marie: 50 Great Northern Rd.
    248 Northern Ave. East
Sudbury: 1485 LaSalle Blvd.
    1933 Regent St. South
Thunder Bay: 1020 Dawson Rd.
    660 Harbour Expressway
        425 North Edwards St.
Timmins: 654 Algonquin Blvd. East
Toronto: 1548 Bloor St. West
    700 Lawrence Ave. West (North York)
    250 The East Mall
Windsor: 880 Goyeau St.
    7201 Tecumseh Rd. East

Public tastings: At retail stores (hours vary). Blenheim: Monday to Saturday, 10 am-6 pm; Sundays, noon-6 pm

Tours: Winery tour by reservation. Vineyard tour (Blenheim) call (519) 676-8008.

Magnotta Winery

MAJOR

100 Cidermill Avenue	Telephone: (905) 738-9463
Vaughan, Ontario	Toll free: 1-800-461-WINE
L4K 4L9	Fax: (905) 738-5551

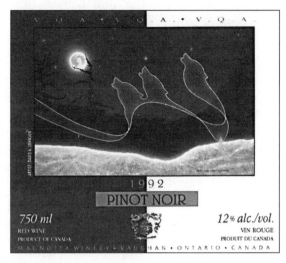

Gabe and Rosanna Magnotta used to be in the juice business, supplying Toronto's Italian community and other interested home winemakers with imported juice. In 1990, they opened a winery in a business park in Vaughan, having purchased the stock of the defunct Charal winery in Blenheim. Taking advantage of the Ontario Wine Content Act (which then allowed 70 percent off-shore material to be blended with Ontario wines), their Argentinian winemaker produced a range of very inexpensive table wines for the ethnic community. Much of the imported juice is sourced from Argentina and Chile or from Delicato Vineyards in California's San Joaquin Valley, as well as from Italy, Washington State and Oregon. In 1994, the Magnottas purchased the Montravin winery (including 80,000 bottles of Podamer sparkling wine) and renamed it Magnotta Cellars. They also acquired seventy-two acres of vineyard in the Niagara Peninsula to concentrate on VQA wines. Their art labels are some of the most attractive in Canada.

The winery uses sixty French and American *barriques* (Chardonnay and reds) and made its first Vidal Icewine in 1991. Only the Icewine is sold through the LCBO; all other wines are sold through Magnotta's three stores. In spite of this, the winery is the fifth largest in Ontario. In 1995, Gabe Magnotta bought the Northumberland Brewery in Brighton, Ont. and relocated it in an 8,000-sq.-ft. facility in Scarborough to obtain another winery licence.

A new 50,000-sq.-ft. facility is on the drawing board on a three-acre site at the junction of Highways 7 and 400. Plans include a winery, a microbrewery and a distillery. At the time of writing, Magnotta intends to go public.

Winemakers: Alejandro DeMiguel and Bela Varga

Production: 130,000 cases

Average tonnage crushed: 70

Annual tonnage purchased: 1,500

Winemaking philosophy: "Affordable excellence. To make world- class wines available to the consumer as inexpensively as possible."

Wines: **Own stores**: *VQA wines/White*—Chardonnay*, Chardonnay Oak-Aged*, French Blend White, Vidal, Riesling Dry*, Riesling Medium Dry*, Riesling Dry Lenko Vineyard*, Auxerrois, Vidal Icewine**, Riesling Icewine**, Late Harvest Vidal*, Select Late Harvest Vidal*, Riesling Select Late Harvest*

Red—Cabernet/Merlot*, Pinot Noir*

Off-shore blends with Ontario wine: *White*—Del Paese White, The Art of Blending White*, Chardonnay, Sauvignon Blanc, Semillon/Chardonnay Special Reserve, Pinot Gris Special Reserve, Fumé Blanc Special Reserve*, Chardonnay Special Reserve*, Chardonnay Limited Edition*

Red—French Blend Red, Del Paese Red*, The Art of Blending Red*, Burgundy, Cabernet Sauvignon, Cabernet Sauvignon Oak-Aged, Cabernet Sauvignon Riserva, Merlot Riserva, Cabernet Franc Special Reserve*, Merlot Special Reserve*, Cabernet Sauvigon Special Reserve*, Pinot Noir Limited Edition*, Cabernet/Merlot Limited Edition*, Merlot Limited Edition**, Cabernet Sauvignon Limited Edition**, Pinot Noir Limited Edition**

International Series: *White*—(Italy) Verdicchio, Tocai Friulano, Pinot Grigio*, Chardonnay Riserva*, Sauvignon Blanc Riserva*; (California) French Colombard, Chenin Blanc*, White Zinfandel; (Washington) Semillon/Chardonnay, Riesling Dry, Riesling Medium Dry, Gewürztraminer*; (Chile) Semillon, Sauvignon Blanc, Chardonnay

Red—(Italy) Montepulciano d'Abruzzo, Merlot, Cabernet Franc; (California) Barbera, Zinfandel; (Washington) Cabernet Sauvignon Riserva*; (Chile) Cabernet Sauvignon*, Merlot*, Malbec; (Oregon) Pinot Noir*

Rosé—(Washington) Cabernet Rosé

Sparkling—Podamer Brut*, Podamer Tres Sec, Podamer Cuvée Spéciale, Podamer Blanc de Blancs, Podamer Brut Blanc de Blancs, Spumante SiSi

Stores (3): On winery premises: Monday to Wednesday, 9 am-6 pm; Thursday to Friday, 9 am-7 pm; Saturday, 9 am-5 pm; Sunday, 11 am-4 pm

Mississauga: 2555 Dixie Rd.: Monday to Wednesday, 10 am-6 pm; Thursday to Friday, 10 am-7 pm; Saturday, 10 am-5 pm

Beamsville: 4701 Ontario St.: Monday to Wednesday, 10 am-6 pm; Thursday to Friday, 11 am-7 pm; Saturday, 10 am-5 pm; Sunday, 11 am-4 pm

Tours: Yes

Public tastings: During store hours

Maple Grove Estate Winery

4063 North Service Road   Telephone: (905) 562-7415
Beamsville, Ontario   Fax: (905) 865-8208
L0R 1B0
(See also Vinoteca, page 99)

Having established themselves at Vinoteca in Woodbridge as the first winery north of Toronto since Prohibition, Giovanni (Johnny) Follegot and his wife Rosanna bought a property in 1994 at the foot of the Niagara escarpment to make VQA wines. The winery, according to Johnny, is a "miniature operation intended to grow slowly along with the production of grapes from the estate, producing exclusively 100 percent Ontario wines, particularly reds" — a sentiment that reflects the predilection of his native Veneto.

Winemaker: Giovanni (Johnny) Follegot

Grape varieties: Chardonnay, Riesling, Pinot Noir, Cabernet Sauvignon

Winemaking philosophy: "My philosophy is quite simple, grow grapes the best way I know how, transform each into a unique, characteristic Ontario wine experience and improve along the way."

Wines: **Winery store**: Chardonnay, Riesling, Pinot Noir, Cabernet Sauvignon, Trillium White and Red (a blend of Ontario wines), Icewine

Store hours: Weekends, 10 am-6 pm

Public tastings: Yes

Tours: Yes

Marynissen Estates

RR #6, 1208 Concession #1   Telephone: (905) 468-7270
Niagara-on-the-Lake, Ontario   Fax: (905) 468-5784
L0S 1J0

As an amateur winemaker, grower John Marynissen has a cabinet full of trophies for his Chardonnays, Rieslings, Cabernet Sauvignons and Icewines won in national and international competitions. His family talked him into creating Ontario's first farmgate winery, and with some backing from Tony Doyle (who used to own Willowbank — the stock was sold to Brights and the equipment went to Marynissen's barn), he started his own operation in 1990. A farmer for over forty years, he sources his fruit from his two vineyards located between the Niagara Escarpment and the Lake. Marynissen's Chardonnay, planted in the mid-1970s, and his Cabernet (1978) are some of the oldest in the Niagara region.

John is a believer in carbonic maceration for Ontario reds and favours the use of oak for fermenting and ageing. He currently uses Tronçais, Allier, Nevers and some American oak.

Winemaker: John Marynissen

Acreage: 70

Soil: Lot 31, sandy loam; Lot 66, more stoney, loam and gravel. The vineyards are protected from the more extreme air currents near the Lake and from the Escarpment.

Grape varieties: Chardonnay, Riesling, Gewürztraminer, Cabernet Sauvignon, Cabernet Franc, Merlot, Gamay Noir, Vidal (recently planted — Petite Sirah and Malbec)

Production: 9,000 cases

Average tonnage crushed: 180

Winemaking philosophy: "We emphasize working with nature and producing wines as natural as possible. Growing all of our grapes for wine production here gives us an advantage in that we cut back our yields in order to produce a more concentrated premium grape and wine. We also use crop control depending on the weather, etc."

Wines: **LCBO/Vintages**: *White*—Chardonnay, Vidal Icewine**

Red—Cabernet Sauvignon*

Winery store: *White*—Riesling, Riesling Icewine*, Chardonnay Barrel Fermented*, Gewürztraminer*, Cabernet Sauvignon Blanc de Noir, Vidal*, Vidal Winter Wine (second pressing of Icewine), Sauvignon Blanc

Red—Merlot*, Cabernet Sauvignon*, Cabernet/Merlot*, Riesling Icewine*

Store hours: *November to April*: 10 am-5 pm (Sundays, 11 am-5 pm).

May to October: 10 am-6 pm (Sundays, 11 am-6 pm)

Tours: Yes—group tours of 15 or more by appointment only ($2 per person)

Public tastings: Boutique hours, fifty cents per sample

Milan Wineries

911 Matheson Boulevard East	Telephone: (905) 602-7835
Mississauga, Ontario	Fax: (905) 602-7836
L4W 2V3	

Previously known as Lauro & Burden Fine Wines (founded in 1992, a 3,000-sq.-ft. facility in a commercial/industrial zone), the winery was bought in 1994 by Alberto Milan who ran a imported grape juice company named Vin Bon. Alberto was trained in oenology at the University of Conegliano in Italy and he intends to expand the production space and upgrade the product line "to include more wine types, grape varieties, sources and vintages — as well as oak-aged 'Riservas.'" The wines, a blend of imported material with Ontario grapes, are aged in French and American oak and sold at bargain prices.

Winemaker: Alberto Milan
Production: 16,000 cases
Average tonnage crushed: 75
Annual tonnage purchased: 225
Winemaking philosophy: "To provide wines of interest at interesting prices."
Wines: Own store: *White*—House White (Soave style), Biancalina, Chardonnay (Washington)
Red—House Wine, Cabernet Sauvignon
Rosé—Rosalina
Sparkling—M&M Spumante
Specialty wine—Marsala
Store hours: 10 am-6 pm daily
Tours: Yes
Public tastings: During store hours

Ocala Orchards Farm Winery

971 High Point Road, (RR #2)   Telephone: (905) 985-9924
Port Perry, Ontario   Fax: (905) 985-7794
L9L 1B3

Irwin and Alissa Smith's farm winery (founded in 1995) is currently outside the VQA's designated wine-growing regions, located as it is five minutes south of Port Perry in the heart of Scugog Township. The winery is housed in a turn of the century dairy barn complete with timber beams, board floors and oak doors, surrounded by orchards and a young vineyard planted in 1992. They currently make two white wines, Chardonnay (aged in French oak from 1995 vintage) and an off-dry Riesling and a range of fruit wines from their orchards. They plan to produce a Gamay and — from Niagara grapes — a Cabernet/Merlot blend this harvest (1995). Irwin intends to make an Icewine from their own vineyard in 1997 and a champagne method sparkling apple.

Winemaker: Irwin Smith

Acreage: 6 (vineyard), 20 (orchard)

Varieties: Chardonnay, Riesling, Vidal, Seyval, Gamay, Auxerrois, Gewürztraminer

Production: 400 cases (1994), 2,000 projected

Average tonnage crushed: (grapes and orchard fruit) 15 tons

Annual tonnage purchased: 5 tons

Winemaking philosophy: "To produce appealing wines from orchard fruit as well as grapes. As a young winery we will grow slowly while paying close attention to quality and customer approval of new wines."

Wines: **Own store**: *White*—Chardonnay barrel aged, Riesling

Fruit—(apple wines) MacIntosh, red Delicious, Spartan*, Idared, Empire*; (cherry wine) Montmorency*

Specialty wines: Iced dessert wines—Golden Apple, Golden Pear*

Store hours: Monday to Saturday 10 am-5:30 pm, Sunday noon-5 pm

Tours: Yes

Public tasting: Yes

Pelee Island Winery

455 Highway #18 East	Telephone: (519) 733-6551
Kingsville, Ontario	Fax: (519) 733-6553
N9Y 2K5	

Pelee Island Wine Pavilion (on Pelee Island)
Telephone: (519) 724-2469   Fax: (519) 724-2507

In 1980, Austrian winemaker Walter Strehn planted Chardonnay and Riesling and other German varietals on the island, the first such planting

since the 1860s and 1870s when Canada's first commercial winery, called Vin Villa, was founded on the island. Vineyards here are the most southerly in Canada enjoying the longest growing season and most heat units. The cottage-style crushing facility (built in 1984) is on the mainland but there is now a newly opened tasting pavilion on the vineyard site complete with restaurant and picnic facilities, petting zoo and playground.

Walter Schmoranz, a German winemaker, took over the winery in 1986. The barrel cellar tasting room is worth the long drive to Kingsville — and so are the wines.

Walter Strehn produced Ontario's first Icewine in 1983 and Walter Schmoranz made Ontario's first red Icewine in 1989 (from Lemberger and Blaufränkisch). Through the Opimian Society, Pelee Island offers a range of wines blended with California and Oregon fruit (from the William Hill winery). The vineyards on the island and at Kingsville are the most extensive *vinifera* plantings of any estate winery.

Winemaker: Walter Schmoranz

Acreage: 480

Soil: Limestone bedrock close to surface, Toledo clay and sandy loam; moderating effect of Lake Erie

Grape varieties: Chardonnay, Riesling, Gewürztraminer, Zweigelt, Vidal, Riesling Italico, Gamay, Pinot Noir, Scheurebe, Merlot, Cabernet Franc, Cabernet Sauvignon, Pinot Gris, Sauvignon Blanc

Production: 75,000 cases

Average tonnage crushed: 750 - 1,100

Annual tonnage purchased: 300 (Niagara)

Winemaking philosophy: "Our winemaking philosophy is to combine our extensive oenological and viticultural skills with our significant estate vineyards located in the most favoured climatic grape-growing region to produce quality wines as unique as the appellation of Pelee Island."

Wines: LCBO: *White*—Blanc de Blanc, Chardonnay, Ducks Unlimited Chardonnay, Hulda's Rock Chardonnay, Pelee Island Dry, Gewürztraminer, Pinot Gris, Riesling Dry, Riesling Italico, Riesling Late Harvest, Scheurebe*, Vin Villa

Red—Country Red*, Ducks Unlimited Gamay Noir, Fenian's Cuvée*, Pinot Noir*, Pelee Island Rouge

Sparkling—Battle of Lake Erie

Own stores: *White*—Chardonnay *barrique*, Vidal Icewine*

Stores: At the winery and one on Pelee Island (West Dock for tax free export sales) and one in Kingsville

Store hours: *April to December 31*: Monday to Saturday, 9 am-5 pm; Sunday, 11 am-5 pm. *January 1 to March 31*: Monday to Saturday, 9 am-5 pm

Public tastings: During store hours

Tours: Saturdays only. *January to March*: Monday to Saturday, 9 am-6 pm
Tours: Noon, 2 pm, 4 pm
Pelee Island Wine Pavilion (on Pelee Island): *May 1 to Canadian Thanksgiving,* open 7 days a week. Tour times are coordinated with the arrival of the ferry.

Pillitteri Estates Winery

1696 Highway 55	Telephone: (905) 468-3147
Niagara-on-the-Lake, Ontario	Fax: (905) 468-0398
L0S 1J0	

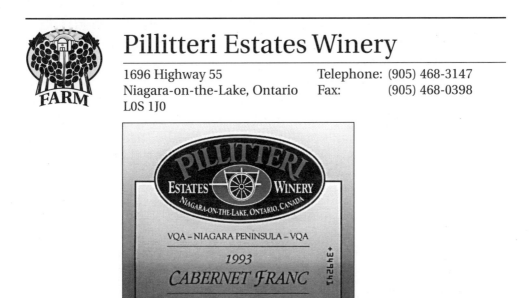

It is, to say the least, unusual for a winery owner to be a federal member of parliament, but that's the case of Gary Pillitteri who launched his winery on June 5, 1993.

Gary emigrated to Canada from Sicily in 1948. A longtime grower and former Grape King, Gary was an amateur winemaker of distinction who won gold medals for his Icewine. The operation is very much a family affair involving his son Charles, son-in-law Jamie Slingerland who manages the vineyard and his own grape and fruit farm, daughters Connie and Lucy and her husband Helmut Friesen. The winemaking is in the hands of Joseph Will, a graduate of Australia's Roseworthy wine school, an experience which has led him to experiment with barrel-fermented and barrel-aged Seyval Blanc.

The modern barnlike facility on the highway into Niagara- on-the-Lake features a wine garden, farm market, bakery, greenhouse and tasting room, as well as a hospitality room that can accommodate 150 people.

Winemaker: Joseph Will
Acreage: 37
Soil: Winery farm — sand; Line A farm — sand and clay.

Grape varieties: Riesling, Chardonnay, Sauvignon Blanc, Vidal; Pinot Noir, Cabernet Sauvignon, Merlot

Production: 10,000 cases

Average tonnage crushed: 135

Annual tonnage purchased: 85

Winemaking philosophy: "Our approach is to produce quality wines that emphasize the fruit characteristics of our varieties and the climate of this cooler growing region. For certain wines, such as Chardonnay and Cabernet Sauvignon, we include some oak barrel ageing to complement the fruit flavours."

Wines: **LCBO/Vintages**: *White*—Seyval Blanc Oak Aged*, Chardonnay Oak Aged*, Riesling Semi-Dry*, Select Late Harvest Vidal**

Red—Cabernet Sauvignon*

Winery store: *White*—Chardonnay, Chardonnay Oak Fermented, Seyval Blanc Oak Fermented*, Riesling Dry, Vidal Dry, Vidal Semi Dry, Vidal Sweet Reserve, Select Late Harvest Vidal*, Chariot White, Vidal Icewine**

Red—Cabernet Franc, Pinot Noir, Carretto Rosso Secco, Chariot Red

Tours: Yes

Public tastings: Yes

Quai Du Vin Estate Winery

RR #5   Telephone: (519) 775-2216
St. Thomas, Ontario
N5P 3S9

Roberto Quai, like Jim Warren of Stoney Ridge and John Marynissen, was an accomplished prize-winning amateur winemaker who went professional. He created his small winery in 1988 with the determination to keep his operation small so that he could control all of its aspects. His father, Redi, had planted the vineyard twenty years ago. The winery itself is spartan and its unique philosophy of offering a twenty-five-cent return deposit on bottles may be the future of an industry that is becoming more environment-conscious. (It's also a good marketing ploy to keep customers coming back.)

When asked if he used any special winemaking equipment in his bijou operation, Roberto replied: "Big feet." No oak barrels or stainless-steel tanks; all the wines are made in polyethylene tanks. He also makes limited amounts of "port" and "sherry."

Winemaker: Robert Quai

Acreage: 20

Soil: Clay-loam, gravel base. Highest point in Elgin County, 5 km from Lake Erie.

Grape varieties: Vidal, Chardonnay, Aurore, Seyve-Villard 23-512, Riesling, De Chaunac

Production: 5,000 cases

Average tonnage crushed: 36.6

Annual tonnage purchased: 16

Winemaking philosophy: "To produce good quality wine at reasonable prices. Simple winemaking techniques, no sophisticated equipment. Low overheads, no employees — 'profit driven.'"

Wines: **Winery store only**: Aurore (Semi-Dry), Riesling Semi-Dry, Late Harvest Riesling, New York Muscat Blush, Chardonnay, SV 23-512; De Chaunac

Store hours: Tuesday to Saturday, 10 am-5 pm; Sunday, 1 pm-5 pm (closed Monday)

Tours: Yes (no set hours)

Public tastings: Yes (no set hours)

Reif Estate Winery

RR #1   Telephone: (905) 468-7738
Niagara Parkway   Fax: (905) 468-5878
Niagara-on-the-Lake, Ontario
L0S 1J0

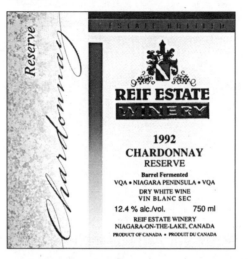

Ewald Reif purchased his vineyard on the Niagara Parkway in 1977, uprooting *labrusca* and hybrids in favour of Riesling, Chardonnay, Gewürztraminer, Kerner and Gamay. Five years later he started his winery. The equipment was sent from his brother's winery in Neustadt. His nephew Klaus (a thirteenth-generation vintner who trained at Geisenheim in Germany) took over the winemaking duties in 1987 and Ewald looks after the vineyards. Klaus has brought in the most modern winemaking equipment and pays particular attention to the health of the grapes delivered to the winery, all of which come from the estate.

The winemaking style is Germanic, using large old oak barrels and back-blending off-dry and late harvest wines with sweet reserve, but of late more emphasis has been put on stainless steel and aging in barrique in the underground cellar. Reif, a neighbour of Inniskillin, is beautifully situated on the Niagara Parkway. Wines are exported to the U.S. and the Orient.

Winemaker: Klaus Reif and Roberto DiDomenico

Acreage: 135

Soil: Sand and loam. The moderating effects of Lake Ontario and the
  Niagara River provide the vineyards with optimum growing conditions.

Grape varieties: Riesling, Chardonnay, Gewürztraminer, Vidal, Seyval
  Blanc, Kerner, Cabernet Sauvignon, Merlot, Pinot Noir, Gamay (from
  1996 Pinot Gris, Sauvignon Blanc; Zinfandel)

Production: 25,000 cases

Average tonnage crushed: 300

Winemaking philosophy: "A combination of tradition, technology and art to produce the finest wines our vineyards can make because we believe winemaking starts with the grape."

Wines: **LCBO/Vintages**: *White*—Chardonnay*, Riesling Dry*, Riesling Medium Dry, Seyval Blanc*, Vidal*, Premium Dry White, Gewürztraminer Dry, Vidal Select Harvest*, Vidal Icewine**, Chardonnay Reserve**

Red—Pinot Noir*

Winery store: *White*—Riesling-Trollinger, Vidal Late Harvest, Gewürztraminer Off Dry, Riesling Late Harvest, Riesling Icewine

Red—Cabernet Sauvignon, Cabernet Franc*, Pinot Off Dry, Baco Noir*, Premium Dry Red

Specialty wines: Vidal Select Harvest Dry, Eye of the Partridge, Gamay Quartz, Riesling Kabinett

Store hours: *Winter*: 10 am-5 pm; *Summer*: 10 am-6 pm

Tours: *June 1 to August 31*: 1:30 pm daily. (Donation of $1 per person to Kidney Foundation.) Pre-booked tours: Minimum 10 people—$15 flat fee plus $1 per person

Public tastings: Yes, year round during business hours

Southbrook Farms Winery

1061 Major McKenzie Drive   Telephone: (905) 832-2548
Maple, Ontario   Fax: (905) 832-9811
L0J 1E0

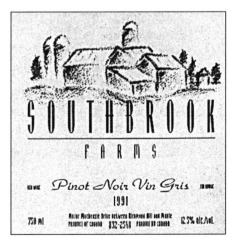

Southbrook Farms is a farm winery with a difference. There are no vineyards, but the Redelmeier family trucks in grapes from Niagara (mainly from the Reif estate) and vinifies them in an old barn. Brian Croser from

Petaluma in Australia helped the family to set up the operation and gave consulting assistance in the first crush (1991). That operation was carried out at the Reif winery. Now the company vinifies at the farm as well as buying in finished wines from California.

Half the wines are 100 percent Ontario (Southbrook Farm Winery label) and the other half are blends using California fruit (Southbrook Blends). The winery purchased twenty French and ten American oak barrels.

During the summer months, "picnic facilities and food" are provided.

Winemaker: Derek Barnett

Production: 5,000 cases

Average tonnage crushed (imported): 75

Winemaking philosophy: "Fruit focused wines with superior texture and complexity. Interfere as little as possible or necessary and let time and nature work their magic as much and as often as possible. Extended aging both in barrel and bottle allow wine the chance to develop complex flavours. Yeast fermentation and malo-lactic fermentation are controlled carefully to ensure bold clean flavours."

Wines: **Own store only**: *Southbrook Farm Winery label/VQA white*— Chardonnay, Barrel Fermented Chardonnay*, Riesling Dry*, Riesling Medium Dry*, White House Wine

Red—Pinot Noir Vin Gris**

Southbrook Blends label white—Chardonnay (70 percent Californian)

Red—Cabernet Sauvignon* (70 percent Paso Robles/30 percent Ontario), Cabernet/Merlot* (75 percent Alexander Valley Cabernet/25 percent Ontario Merlot), Red House (California Gamay/Niagara Baco Noir)

Specialty wines—Fortified fruit wines: Framboise**, Framboise Noir, Framboise d'Or, Cassis*

Store hours: *May 15 to Christmas*: daily, 9 am-7 pm; *January 1 to May 15*: Friday, Saturday, Sunday, 11 am-5 pm

Tours: Available on request. Regularly throughout the summer months.

Public tastings: Yes, during store hours. Donations for local charities in lieu of tasting charge.

Stonechurch Vineyards

1270 Irvine Road, RR #5   Telephone: (905) 935-3535
Niagara-on-the-Lake, Ontario   Fax: (905) 646-8892
L0S 1J0

The winery was founded in 1989 as the first of the new wave of small farm-gate enterprises, but the Hunse family had been growing grapes for twenty years before making the leap into a commercial operation. Lambert and Grace Hunse have farmed Stonechurch for thirty-five years. They now own 200 acres of fruit trees and vines in parcels near Lake Ontario and the Welland Canal. Their son Rick, who looks after the vineyard part of the operation, leans towards organic growing and is a believer in leaf removal to improve the microclimate around the grape clusters to allow maximum sun penetration and good air circulation.

Stonechurch make Canada's most expensive barrel-fermented Chardonnay. The winery uses new Nevers, Allier, Tronçais and American oak. They also make a champagne method sparkler from Pinot Noir. In spite of its size, the company exports to Japan, Taiwan and Holland.

Winemaker: Sandrine Bourcier-Epp

Acreage: 100

Soil: Ranging from hard-pan clay to silt to gravel.

Grape varieties: Vidal, Seyval Blanc, Baco Noir, Gewürztraminer, Riesling, Chardonnay, Morio-Muscat, Pinot Noir, Cabernet Franc

Production: 40,000 cases

Average tonnage crushed: 600

Annual tonnage purchased: 200

Winemaking philosophy: "My goal is to respect and maintain the quality and character of the grape during the wine making process. Despite my French background and training, I wish to develop unique Ontario wines that have their own appeal."

Wines: **LCBO/Vintages**: *White*—Seyval Blanc, Vidal, Vidal Icewine*, Chardonnay, Gewürztraminer, Morio-Muscat

Red—Cabernet-Merlot

Own store: *White*—Barrel-fermented Chardonnay, Vidal-Chardonnay, Riesling

Red—Cabernet Sauvignon, Merlot, Pinot Noir

Store hours: *May to September:* Monday to Saturday, 10 am-6 pm; *October to April*: Monday to Saturday, 10 am-5 pm

Tours: Daily at 2 pm (private tours and vineyard excursions by appointment)

Public tastings: During store hours

Stoney Ridge Cellars

1468 Highway 8 (at Fifty Road)	Telephone: (905) 643-4508
Winona, Ontario	Fax: (905) 643-0933
L8E 5K9	

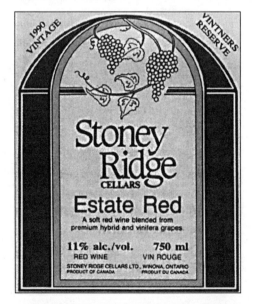

Jim Warren was a gifted and highly successful amateur winemaker (and high school teacher) before he took the commercial plunge in 1985 with two partners. The original winery was located at Vinemount on the Escarpment in a tin shed the size of a bungalow. In 1990, he went into partnership with

Murray Puddicombe, a grower at the base of the Escarpment in Winona. A spanking new facility was built that houses the store, a fruit market and a second storey balcony restaurant.

Jim has a unique winemaking style that produces opulent, aromatic and sometimes exotic wines with ripe fruit flavours. He believes in small-lot crushing and cold-settling his juice. He uses French and American small oak. A testimony to his skills is the number of medals his wines have won, especially his single vineyard Chardonnays in competition with leading labels from France, California and Australia. His reds are some of the best in Canada. For such a small winery, he makes an amazing range of products (up to fifty wines!), including the specialty port-style Passion and Jasmine and a range of fruit wines. The winery has recently opened the courtyard cafe and offers hayrides and a petting zoo for children.

Winemaker: Jim Warren

Acreage: 200 under Murray Puddicombe ("We purchase from several other Bench and Niagara area growers.")

Grape varieties: Seyval Blanc, Vidal, Chardonnay, Riesling, Cabernet Sauvignon, Maréchal Foch, Chambourcin

Production: 20,000 - 25,000 cases

Average tonnage crushed: 225

Annual tonnage purchased: 60 percent (approximately)

Winemaking philosophy: "I like to produce wines with abundant flavour and bouquet — wines that are top quality yet very appealing, well balanced and honest to the grape variety. In a word — well balanced, varietal character, good fruit."

Wines: LCBO: *White*—Seyval Blanc**, Vidal*, Bench Chardonnay**, Riesling*, Riesling/Traminer*, Gewürztraminer**, Estate White* *Red*—Estate Red*, Cabernet-Merlot**, Pinot Noir*, Romance*

Vintages: *White*—Chardonnay Eastman Vineyard**, Chardonnay Lenko Vineyard**, Chardonnay Reserve**, Riesling Plekan Vineyard*

Red—Merlot Reserve**

Winery store: *White*—Muscat Blanc*, Gamay Blanc*, Estate Riesling Dry*, Colombard*

Red—Gamay Noir, Maréchal Foch, Zinfandel, Cabernet Sauvignon**, Cabernet Franc**, Cabernet Reserve, Renaissance (Rhône-style blend)

Specialty: Late Harvest Riesling, Jasmine, Passion, Vidal Icewine**, Gewürztraminer Icewine**, Late Harvest Botrytis Sauvignon/Semillon, Ambrosia (port style); *Rosé*—Grenache

Store hours: Daily 10 am-5 pm

Public tastings: 11 am-2 pm

Tours: By appointment

Sunnybrook Farm Estate Winery

1425 Lakeshore Road
RR #3   Telephone: (905) 468-1122
Niagara-on-the-Lake, Ontario   Fax: (905) 468-1068
L0S 1J0

Gerald and Vivien Goertz have been longtime fruit growers in Niagara (and yes, they do have a daughter named Rebecca). While they dabbled in turning their fruit into wine, it wasn't until a vicious hailstorm in 1992 left them with eighty tons of bruised and unsalable peaches that they turned winemaking into a proper business. The next fall they got their winery licence in time to open for Christmas. They are now Ontario's only estate winery specializing in fruit wines. They grow peaches, cherries, pears, plums, apricots and apples. They also make their fruit version of Icewine — an artificially frozen fermented fruit salad of most of the above. All fruit wines range in alcohol from 10 percent to 11.5 percent by volume.

Winemakers: Gerald Goertz and Rebecca Goertz

Production: 5,700 cases (1995)

Winemaking philosophy: "Make high-quality fruit wines from Niagara fruit. If allergic to compounds found in grape skins, you may be able to enjoy fruit wine."

Winery store: Empire (apple), Golden Delicious (apple)*, Montmorency (cherry), Redhaven (peach), Bartlett (pear), Damson* (plum), Apricot, Summer Cherry, Summer Peach*, Bosc (pear), Winter Peach**, Winter Cherry*, Winter Pear*, Winter Apple*, Winter Apricot*

Store hours: *January to April*: Wednesday to Saturday, 10 am-5 pm; Sunday, 1 pm-5 pm. *May to December*: Monday to Saturday, 10 am-6 pm; Sunday, 1 pm-5 pm

Tours: No

Public tastings: During store hours (twenty-five cents). Winter fruit wines ($1)

Thirty Bench Vineyard & Winery

4281 Mountainview Road
Beamsville, Ontario
L0R 1B0

Telephone: (905) 563-1698
Fax: (905) 388-6271

THIRTY BENCH

RIESLING
ICE WINE

1992

Grown, Produced and Bottled by Commonty
Vineyard and Winery, Beamsville, Ontario

11% alc./vol.   375 ml

Product of Canada / Produit du Canada

Thirty Bench, Ontario's newest boutique winery, is "a limited partnership of twenty-odd people," led by a team of four gifted amateur winemakers: Dr. Tom Muckle, Yorgos Papageorgiu, Frank Zeritsch and Deborah Paskus, who also manages the vineyard. Tom Muckle helped to start Cave Spring with Len Pennachetti.

The name of the winery speaks to the acreage and its location. The first crush was 1994 but the original idea goes back to 1980 when the group's French Oak vineyard was planted with Riesling. The artisanal winery is located in the vineyard and, according to Tom, "only wines judged satisfactory to ourselves will be sold to the public." Anything considered "not good enough" will be sold in bulk to other wineries for blending. To this end, the quartet will rely on rigorous bunch thinning and late harvesting. The emphasis is on Riesling in a range of styles, although they also make barrel-fermented Chardonnay from grapes bought from a Bench grower, Steve Kocsis. French and air-cured American oak barrels are used. A restaurant is planned.

Winemakers: Tom Muckle, Yorgos Papageorgiou, Frank Zeritsch and
    Deborah Paskus

Acreage: 30

Soil: Beamsville Bench, plus limestone clay-loam. "The driest vineyard on
    the bench."

Grape varieties: Riesling, Cabernet Franc, Cabernet Sauvignon, Pinot Noir,
    Scheurebe, Merlot, Pinot Meunier, Gewürztraminer

Production: 1,000 cases (1994)

Average tonnage crushed: 31 (1994)

Annual tonnage purchased: 2 tonnes (1994 only)

Winemaking philosophy: "Geography, small scale and meticulous attention to detail are necessary for wine quality and character."

Winery store: *White*—Table Riesling, Riesling Auslese, Riesling BA, Riesling Icewine, Chardonnay

Red—Cabernet blend

Store hours: Saturday and Sunday, 10 am-5 pm

Public tastings: During store hours

Tours: Yes, on weekends during store hours; at other times by appointment

---

Vincor International Inc.

6611 Edwards Blvd.   Telephone: (905) 564-6900
Mississuaga, Ontario   1-800-265-9463
L5T 2H8   Fax: (905) 564-6909

Vincor International is the sixth-largest winery in North America, consisting of Brights, Cartier and Inniskillin. The company itself does not own any vineyards, but contracts approximately 300 acres of grapes. The corporate products cover the whole gamut of wines and low-alcohol beverages, from Spumante Bambino, L'Ambiance, President Canadian Champagne to the single vineyard Chardonnays and Cabernet Sauvignons of Inniskillin. The Jackson-Triggs and Sawmill Creek labels are also part of the portfolio.

Since 1993, when Brights bought the Cartier-Inniskillin company and became Vincor International, each winery has remained autonomous with its own series of labels. For details, see the entries for Brights, Cartier (Ontario and B.C.) and Inniskillin.

The company operates three large facilities in Niagara Falls, Ont., Oliver, B.C., and St. Hyacinthe, Que., as well as a smaller plant in Scoudouc, N.B. Apart from the stores at the various facilities, the company owns the Wine Rack chain of stores, numbering 130 outlets.

Ajax: Harwood Mall
Barrie: Sobeys, 500 Bayfield Ave.
Belleville: Zellers, 530 Dundee St. West
    Quinté Mall
Brampton: Shoppers' World, Highway #10 & Steeles Ave.
Brantford*: Lynden Park Mall, 84 Lynden Rd.
Burlington: A&P, Burlington Mall
    Ultra-Mart, 3385 Fairview St.
Cambridge: John Galt Centre
    Knobhill, 35 Pinebush Rd.
Chatham: Chatham Centre
Cobourg: Northumberland Mall
Cornwall: Eastcourt Mall
Etobicoke: 201 Lloyd Manor Rd.
Georgetown*: Northview Centre
Grimsby: Sobeys, 44 Livingstone Ave.
Guelph: Bullfrog Mall
    Sobeys, Silvercreek Parkway
    Stone Road Mall
Hamilton/Stoney Creek: A&P Centre Mall
    A&P, King at Longwood
    A&P, 2500 Barton St. East
    Eastgate Square
    Limeridge Mall
Kingston: Herbie's
    Kingston Shopping Centre
Kitchener: 95 King St. West
    Dutch Boy, 1111 Weber St.
    Fairview Park Mall
London: A&P, Sherwood Forest Mall
    Argyle Mall
    First London Centre
    Masonville Place
    White Oaks Mall
    Wonderland Mall
Markham: Ultra-Mart, Markville Shopping Centre
Midland: Mountainview Mall
Milton: 55 Ontario St. South
Mississauga: Central Parkway

Dominion Store, Meadowvale Town Centre
Eaton Sheridan Place
Knobhill, 1250 South Service Rd.
Miracle, Iona Place
Miracle, Westwood Mall
Square One Shopping Centre
Ultra-Mart, 4557 Hurontario St.
Zellers, 3100 Dixie Rd.
Nepean: Bayview Shopping Centre
Merivale Mall
Newmarket: Upper Canada Mall, 17600 Yonge St.
Sobeys, 17730 Leslie St.
Niagara Falls: 6709 Victoria Ave.
A&P, 6770 McLeod South
Winery, 4887 Dorchester Rd.
Zellers, 6777 Morrison
North Bay: Northgate Square, 1500 Fisher St.
Zellers, 1899 Algonquin
North York: York Gate Mall, 1 York Gate Blvd.
Oakville: A&P, Oakville Town Centre
Bronté Village
Ultra-Mart, 1011 Upper Middle Rd.
Orillia: Orillia Square Mall
Oshawa: Knobhill, 500 Howard Ave.
Midtown Mall, 200 John St.
Ottawa: 700 George Street
Billings Bridge Shopping Centre
Carlingwood Mall
Gloucester Centre
Lincoln Heights Galleria
Price Club, Gloucester
Zellers, 1162 Cyrville Rd.
Pembroke: West End Mall
Peterborough: Portage Place Shopping Centre
Zellers, 250 Lansdowne St. West
Pickering: Supercentre, 1792 Liverpool Rd.
St. Catharines: A&P, Fairview Mall
The Pen, 221 Glendale Ave.
Price Club
Scarborough: Bridlewood Mall, 2900 Warden Ave.
Cedarbrae Mall, 3495 Lawrence Ave. East
Dominion, 255 Morningside Ave.
Malvern Town Centre, 31 Tapscott Rd.
Ultra-Mart, 355 Bamburgh Circle
Woodside Square, 1571 Sandhurst Circle

Zellers, 2850 Lawrence Ave. East
Stratford: Sobey's, Queensland Plaza
Sudbury: New Sudbury Centre
Thornhill: Thornhill Square, 300-302 John St. East
Ultra-Mart, Shops on Steeles & 404
Ultra-Mart, 800 Steeles West
Toronto (Yonge St. & East): 103 Cosburn Ave. (at Pape Ave.)
403 Parliament St.
77 Wellesley St. East
2447 Yonge St. (at Erskine)
Shoppers World, 3003 Danforth Ave.
Loblaws, 17 Leslie St.
Toronto (Yonge St. & West): 746 King St. West
560 Queen St. West
1354 Queen St. West
946 Yonge St. (at McMurrich)
Honest Ed's, 681 Bloor West
Knobhill, 22 Lansdowne Ave.
Waterloo: A&P, Northtown, 325 Thorold Rd.
Zellers, 70 Bridgeport Rd. East
Whitby: Whitby Mall, 1615 Dundas St. East
Windsor: A&P, Devonshire Mall
Central Mall, 3669 Tecumseh Rd.
N&D, 1349 Grand Marais Road
N&D, Eastowne Plaza
Zehrmart, Malden Village Shopping Centre
Woodbridge: Price Club, Vaughan
Woodstock*: Zellers, 645 Dundas St.

Store hours: All stores open from noon-5 pm on Sundays (except those marked with an asterisk)

Brights Wines

P.O. Box 510   Telephone: (905) 358-7141
4887 Dorchester Road   Fax: (905) 358-7750
Niagara Falls, Ontario
L2E 6V4

MAJOR

With the demise of Barnes, Brights became Ontario's oldest winery, dating back to 1874 when it was called The Niagara Falls Wine Company and operated out of Toronto! As Canada's largest winery (after acquiring Jordan), it has a long and distinguished history, especially in its research and development of grape varieties suitable for Ontario winters. Thanks to its long-time oneologist Adhemar de Chaunac, who worked for the company from the late 1930s to the early 1960s, Brights was the first company to produce a non-*labrusca* table wine (Manor St. Davids Claret from Chelois grapes), the first *vinifera* varietal (Chardonnay 1956), the first 7 percent sparkling wine (long before Baby Duck uttered its first quack), the first bottle-fermented sparkling wine (Brights President 1949), the first "champagne" made exclusively from Chardonnay grapes, and the first Canadian sherry to be made by the Spanish method using flor yeasts and the solera system.

The company has a huge portfolio of products yet still manages to produce small parcels of VQA varietal wines and Vidal Icewine of high quality. Their Sawmill Creek label takes advantage of the Wine Content Act which allows for the blending of up to 75 percent off-shore material into Ontario wines.

In 1991, Brights underwent a $10-million expansion of its Niagara Falls plant to consolidate all its winemaking operations under one roof. In 1993, Brights merged with Cartier-Inniskillin to create North America's eighth-largest winery conglomerate, operating in Ontario and British Columbia.

Winemaker: Mira Ananicz

Average tonnage crushed (imported): 10,000

Winemaking philosophy: "Quality, yesterday, today and tomorrow."

Wines: **LCBO**: *White*—Entre-Lacs Chardonnay**, White House, Dry White House, House Chablis, Maria Christina White, Maria Christina Dry White, Maria Christina Light White, Entre-Lacs White, Toscano White, Manor St. Davids Medium Dry, Sauterne, Vidal

Sawmill Creek label white—Chardonnay (Yugoslavia/Ontario), Sauvignon Blanc (Washington/Ontario)*, Dry Riesling (Washington/Ontario), Reserve White

Red—Cresta Roja, House Red, Dry House Red, Maria Christina Red, Entre-Lacs Red, Toscano Red, Baco Noir*

Sawmill Creek label red—Merlot-Baco, Cabernet-Baco

Sparkling—Instant Romance, Spumante Bambino, President Canadian Champagne, President Pink Champagne, President Brut; Valley Crackling Rosé

Sherry: Cream, Pale Dry Select, President, '74 Sherry, Dry, '67 Sherry, Branvin, Sippin'

Port: President, '74

Specialty wines: Durouget, Dry Vermouth, Sacramental

Ciders: Growers Extra Dry

Own stores: *White*—Riesling, Gewürztraminer**, Vidal**, Vidal Icewine**, Sawmill Creek Sauvignon-Riesling, Sawmill Creek Sauvignon-Chardonnay, President's Choice, Chairman's Choice

Red—Cabernet Franc*, Late Harvest Baco Noir*, Merlot**, Cabernet Sauvignon**

Stores: See Vincor above

Tours: *May 1 to October 31*: Monday to Saturday, 10:30 am/2 pm/3:30 pm; Sunday, 2 pm/3:30 pm. *November 1 to April 30*: Monday to Friday, 2 pm; Saturday and Sunday, 2 pm/3:30 pm (group tours for 20 or more on request)

Cartier Wines & Beverages

P.O. Box 510   Telephone: (905) 358-7141
4887 Dorchester Road   Fax: (905) 358-7750
Niagara Falls, Ontario
L2E 6V4

In 1989, the management team of Château-Gai and its sister winery Casabello in British Columbia bought out the enterprise (including the holding company Ridout Wines) from Labatts and renamed it Cartier Wines & Beverages. Château-Gai (originally Parkdale Wines of Toronto) was one of the companies Labatts took over in 1973. The new owners — Rick Thorpe, Don Triggs, former winemaker Allan Jackson, Allan George and Peter Granger — styled their operation as "the largest employee-owned manufacturer and marketer of wine and modern adult beverages."

As a large commercial winery existing since 1928, Château-Gai had placed most of its emphasis on blended brand-name table wines and had introduced Canada's first wine cooler as well as the first wines in tetrapaks and a wine-based cream liqueur. Jackson and Triggs brought out a premium line of wines in 1992 under their own Jackson-Triggs label.

In 1991, Cartier bought into Inniskillin and two years later merged with Brights to become Vincor International.

The company's "Wine Rack" stores have now become part of the Vincor chain of stores under The Wine Rack name).

Winemakers: Mira Ananicz and Susan Szwec

Production: 1,000,000 cases (wine and wine-based drinks)

Average tonnage crushed: 6,250 (all grapes are bought in on long-term contracts)

Winemaking philosophy: "Wines of exceptional quality and value."

Wines: **LCBO**: *White*—Adagio, Heritage Estates Chablis, L'Ambiance, Alpenweiss, Alpenweiss Dry, Alpenweiss Light, Capistro Dry, Capistro Light, Gala Dry, L'Escapade, San Gabriel, Sauterne, Vintner's Choice (French), Vintner's Choice German)

Jackson-Triggs label white—Chardonnay

Red—Heritage Estates Burgundy, L'Ambiance*

Jackson-Triggs label—Cabernet Sauvignon

Blush—Capistro Grenache Baco

Sparkling (all Charmat process)—Alpenweiss, Spumante

Bianco, Imperial Dry

Own stores: *White*—Capistro Chenin Vidal, Antoine Bonet, Santa Isabela Sauvignon Blanc

Jackson-Triggs label white—Chardonnay*, Reserve Chardonnay, Chenin Blanc, Johannisberg Riesling, Gewürztraminer*, Pinot Grigio, Vidal Icewine**

Red—Santa Isabela Cabernet Sauvignon

Jackson-Triggs label—Cabernet Franc, Merlot**, Reserve Cabernet Sauvignon*

Fortified wines: Sherries—Hallmark Cream, Heritage Very Pale Dry, Imperial, Private

Ports—Concord, Private Stock

Vineland Estates Wines

RR #1, 3620 Moyer Road   Telephone: (905) 562-7088
Vineland, Ontario   Fax: (905) 562-3071
L0R 2C0

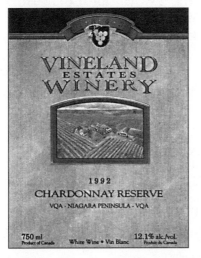

In 1992, John Howard, a former board member of the Canon Company, purchased the winery from Hermann Weis. Weis's family owns a winery in the

Mosel called St. Urban as well as Germany's largest private grape vine nursery. In 1979, in order to crack the Canadian market for his virus-free vines he bought, with other partners, two fifty-acre vineyards in Vineland, subsequently called St. Urban and St. Hilarius.

Their first commercial crop of Riesling was vinified by Barnes in 1982. Two years later, winemaker Dieter Guttler opened his own winery, named Vineland Estates, using grapes from these vineyards. Ownership of the winery passed to Hermann Weis in 1987, who took on as his partner a dynamic, young British Columbia winemaker Allan Schmidt. (Allan's father Lloyd, a viticulturist, had been a partner in B.C.'s Sumac Ridge winery.)

Set on the bench of the Niagara Escarpment, Vineland Estates is the most picturesquely situated winery in Ontario with its 1845 farmhouse (now the tasting room and boutique wine shop), small bed-and-breakfast cottage on the edge of the vineyard, and Ontario's first winedeck serving light bistro-style lunches. A newly restored 1857 stone carriage house is the venue for winemaker dinners and catered events.

The emphasis here is on Riesling, although much care is given to the barrel-femented Chardonnays (new Allier and Nevers oak) and Icewine.

Winemaker: Allan Schmidt

Acreage: 50 acres on site, 90 acres on Quarry Road — all bench vineyards

Soil: Gently sloping vineyards, clay loam soil, well drained, rolling hills

Grape varieties: Riesling, Chardonnay, Pinot Noir, Cabernet, Seyval Blanc, Gewürztraminer, Vidal (Icewine), Chardonnay Musqué, Merlot (newly planted)

Production: 18,000 cases

Average tonnage crushed: 200

Annual tonnage purchased: 15 - 18

Winemaking philosophy: "Riesling not overripe. Cool fermentations giving slightly higher acidity than normal."

Wines: **LCBO**: *White*—Dry Riesling**, Riesling Semi-Dry*, Vintners Select Dry, Vidal Icewine**

Own store: *White*—Riesling Reserve, Select Late Harvest Riesling, Chardonnay*, Chardonnay Estate, Chardonnay Reserve*, Chardonnay Musqué, Gewürztraminer, Seyval Blanc

Red—Pinot Noir, Cabernet, Carriage House Red

Store hours: Weekdays, 10 am-5:30 pm. Saturday and Sunday, 11 am-5:30 pm. *January to April*: Weekdays, 10 am-5 pm; weekends, 11 am- 5 pm

Public tastings: During store hours

Tours: Daily at 11 am, 1 pm, 3 pm (May 24th weekend through October 31)

Vinoteca Inc.

61 Caster Avenue   Telephone: (905) 856-5700
Woodbridge, Ontario   Fax: (905) 856-8208
L4L 5Z2

Vinoteca

VQA NIAGARA PENINSULA VQA

Cabernet Sauvignon
93 X7

RED WINE / VIN ROUGE
750 ml - 12% alc./vol.
PRODUCT OF CANADA / PRODUIT DU CANADA
VINOTECA INC., WOODBRIDGE, ONTARIO

Giovanni (Johnny) Follegot and his wife Rosanna, natives of Veneto in northern Italy, began by importing grape juice for the Italian community to make their own wine. Their company, Fruitland Juices, still sells a variety of imported juices for home winemakers from the Woodbridge facility and one in Hamilton (905-389-9311).

In 1989, the Follegots set up a fermenting operation in a Woodbridge industrial park, using Ontario grapes trucked in from the Niagara Peninsula and imported juice. The winery produces VQA wines and off-shore blends.

French and American oak barrels are used and the winery began making small batches of Icewine in 1990. In 1992, an Italian-style sparkling wine was produced using the Classico method.

Vinoteca wines are only available at the winery. See also Maple Grove, page 73.

Winemaker: Giovanni Follegot

Production: 3,000 cases (1992 figures)

Average tonnage crushed (brought in): 50 (1992 figures)

Winemaking philosophy: "Our total dedication and hard work has enabled us to produce valid wines that are well accepted by consumers, whose use is mainly to complement their meals. With confidence we are able to progress and improve our wines to reach the highest standards."

Wines: **Winery store only**: *White*—Albino (white blend), Pinot Bianco, Sauvignon Blanc, Chardonnay*, Riesling, Vidal Icewine*, Dolcetto (a white!), Bag In Box White Table Wine

Red—Gaio (red blend), Pinot Noir*, Cabernet Sauvignon**, Merlot, Bag In Box Red Table Wine

Store hours: 9 am-6 pm

Tours: Yes

Public tastings: During store hours

Willow Heights

4679 Cherry Avenue   Telephone/fax: (905) 562-4945
Beamsville, Ontario
L0R 1B0

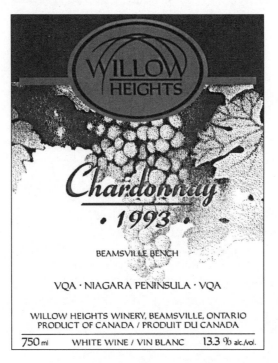

Ron and Avis Speranzini opened Willow Heights in Beamsville in 1994. Ron was a basement winemaker for twelve years who won many awards for his wines in amateur competitions. He studied oenology through university home-learning programs for five years and paid his dues by working the crush at local wineries in the peninsula. Like Jim Warren of Stoney Ridge and John Marynissen of Marynissen Estates before him, Ron made the leap from amateur to professional and he set his sights high. In the spring of 1994, with a local grower, he planted two red varieties rarely seen in Niagara

— Syrah, the grape of the Northern Rhône, and Zinfandel, the pride of California. He intends to produce other varieties such as Viognier as they become available from growers. Ron uses French and American oak.

Winemaker: Ron Speranzini

Acreage: 15 (leased)

Grape varieties: Chardonnay, Riesling, Seyval Blanc, Zinfandel, Syrah

Production: 1,000 cases

Average tonnage crushed: 10 to 15

Annual tonnage purchased: 50 percent of total production

Winemaking philosophy: "To produce the highest quality wines possible bearing the VQA trademark. This can only be achieved through the dedicated co-operation between the grower and vintner throughout the harvest year. We intend to produce wines which are distinctive to the *terroir* of the Niagara Peninsula."

Wines: **LCBO/Vintages**: Chardonnay*

Own store: *White*—Chardonnay Reserve**, Riesling, Riesling Icewine**

Red—Pinot Noir*

Store hours: Winter months on weekends only. Spring to Fall, 7 days a week

Tours: Yes

Public tastings: During store hours

BRITISH COLUMBIA

1 Vancouver Island
2 Fraser Valley
3 Similkameen
4 Okanagan

WINE REGIONS OF BRITISH COLUMBIA

*I*n general terms, British Columbia differs from Ontario in climate soil and grape varieties. It differs also in its basic approach to what constitutes a B.C. wine. While Ontario wineries, large and small, can blend up to 75 percent off-shore material into their wines (which appear without the VQA appellation), B.C.'s major wineries can bottle 100 percent off-shore products — in addition to the VQA wines they produce — while the estate and farm wineries are restricted to grapes grown in the designated viticultural areas of the province.

Ontario's wine industry is much older than that of B.C., and is still largely based on hybrids although impressive strides are being made in the planting of *vinifera*. The B.C. industry, developed comparatively recently, established itself on French hybrids and Riesling, and only since 1989 did it covert on a large scale to other *vinifera* varieties. Not only are the grape varieties of the two provinces different, but the flavours of the same varieties can vary dramatically because of the vast differences in growing conditions. Ontario never experiences the intense heat, low humidity and cool nights of the desert summer; and the Okanagan, situated as it is on a latitude roughly equivalent to Timmins, enjoys significantly more hours of sunshine during summer days. While Ontario is continuing to move to *vinifera* vines, the movement in the smaller British Columbia industry has been dramatic. The hundreds of acres of hybrid vines representing two-thirds of the total acreage that vanished in the 1988-89 pull-out program prompted by GATT and Free Trade have now been largely replaced by *vinifera* varieties including Chardonnay, Gewürztraminer, Pinot Auxerrois, Pinot Blanc, Pinot Gris, Pinot Noir, Merlot, Cabernet Franc, Cabernet Sauvignon and even Syrah and Sauvignon Blanc.

According to Dave Gamble, editor of *British Columbia Wine Trails* magazine, Okanagan and Similkameen Valley wines tend to be highly flavoured, fruity and full-bodied with good acidity, especially the German-style white; these resemble their counterparts from the Rhine rather than the softer California taste profile. A much greater range in character is evident in the Chardonnay and Pinot Blancs which, since 1993, have included softer styles with more complexity from barrel-ageing, lees contact and malolactic fermentation.

B.C. interior red hybrids are usually vinted in a fruity style, while red *viniferas* emulate Bordeaux and Burgundy with the use of barrel-ageing and malolactic fermentation.

"Wines from the new regions in the Fraser Valley and Vancouver Island," says David, "tend to have a much softer style, with delicate fruity whites and lighter but complex Pinot Noir, reflecting their cooler and more humid growing conditions."

The wine industry in B.C. did not really start until the 1930s. While the combined insanity of Prohibition and the Depression almost destroyed the Ontario wineries, ironically it provided the impetus for the birth of B.C. commercial winemaking in the Okanagan and Similkameen River valleys when *labrusca* varieties such as Campbell, Concord, Diamond, Patricia, Sheridan, Bath and Delaware were first planted.

The story goes back to the 1860s when Father Charles Pandosy planted a few vines at the Oblate Fathers' Mission, built seven miles south of Kelowna. But the farmers who followed were more interested in fruit crops such as apples, peaches and apricots than in grapes. The first commercial vineyard in the province was planted by W.J. Wilcox some fifty-five miles north of Kelowna, at Salmon Arm. This three-quarter-acre plot yielded such Ontario varieties such as Concord, Niagara, Delaware and Agawam for the table trade. Six years later, Jim Creighton planted a small vineyard in Penticton, an area which would ultimately prove to be one of the best sites for grape growing along the shore of Okanagan.

The narrow serpentine lake, carved out by prehistoric glaciers, stretches north for over 100 kilometres and the land rises steeply from the water on either side. Technically, the area is a desert since there is little rainfall (the southern end of the lake around Oliver gets no more than six inches of precipitation a year). In terms of latitude, the Okanagan Valley is in the same belt as the Champagne region of France and the Rheingau of Germany — a fact which seduced many pioneers into believing that they could produce wines to rival the great Rieslings and sparkling Chardonnays — but the climate is very different from Europe. During the summer days, the Okanagan vines experience tremendous heat, and at night the temperature dips dramatically. Intense sunlight builds up the grape sugars and the freezing nights do not allow the acids to metabolize, so the berries have very high acid readings. Because of the lack of rainfall, the vineyards have to be irrigated during the growing season.

The Okanagan experiences long, mild autumns, as does northern Germany, but by mid-October the temperature has fallen to a point where the grapes will no longer mature and they will have to be harvested. On the plus side, British Columbian summers, like those in California, are consistent and predictable, which ensures an even quality of grape from year to year. In spite of fluctuating temperatures, there are pockets along the valley's southern slopes that protect the vines from the killing frost that rolls down the lake from October on, and the body of water ameliorates the air temperature on the coldest nights. Many of these microclimates have been identified by infrared aerial photography, through a program conducted by the Summerland Research Station in conjunction with the provincial government. Without the advantage of such technology, the early grape growers could only plant their vines, sit back and pray.

The first wines in British Columbia were not made from grapes at all, but from loganberries which flourished in southern Victoria Island on the Saanich Peninsula. They rejoiced in such names as Slinger's Logan and Logana. But a few inspired souls turned their attentions to wine grapes. Peter Casero of Kelowna was a grape-growing pioneer in the 1920s, and in 1926 a farmer by the name of Jesse Willard Hughes, encouraged by the Hungarian oenologist Dr. Eugene Rittich, bought a forty-five-acre vineyard in Kelowna near the Oblate Fathers' Mission and planted vines that had been locally propagated. He also purchased a twenty-acre site on Black Mountain. The larger vineyard near Kelowna prospered to such an extent that four years later wines made from these grapes were vinified at the Growers' Wine Company in Victoria. Encouraged by his success, Hughes was to expand his vineyard to 300 acres, but the experiment at Black Mountain proved a disaster since the vines were wiped out by winter kill.

Rittich, however, was convinced that grapes could be grown on Black Mountain. It was just a question of finding the right variety and employing the correct viticultural practices to prevent winter kill. As the first champion of *vinifera* grapes in the province, he experimented with forty-four varieties on this site and one in the barren Oliver region. In 1930, he is said to have imported from Hungary a winter-hardy vine which would revolutionize the B.C. wine industry and provide the basis for its future development — a grape that became known as the Okanagan Riesling.[1]

In the same year Rittich was hired as the winemaker for the Growers' Wine Company, which had previously specialized in loganberry wine. A freak of nature was to give the fledging industry the boost it needed. Successive abundant harvests of apples caused a glut on the market and many farmers were forced to tear out their orchards and plant grapes instead. Growers' Wine Company was paying $100 a ton for grapes (compared to $65 a ton in Ontario) while apples were left rotting under the trees. "A cent a pound or on the ground" was the farmers' anguished cry. "A dollar a box or on the rocks."

At the height of the Depression in 1932, an immigrant Italian winemaker named Guiseppe Ghezzi came to Kelowna with the idea of creating a winery to use the worthless apple crop.

The idea had also occurred to a local hardware store owner, William Andrew Cecil Bennett, who had discussed just such a possibility with his neighbour on Kelowna's main street, an Italian grocer named Pasquale "Cap" Capozzi. Both men were teetotallers, but they joined with Ghezzi to form a company called Domestic Wines and By-Products. The company would manufacture not only wines but a whole gamut of products including "apple cider ... brandy, alcohol, spirits of all kinds, fruit juices, soft drinks, fruit concentrates, jelly jams, pickles, vinegar, tomato paste, tomato catsup, tomato juice and by-products of every kind." The debonair Guiseppe Ghezzi stayed long enough to set up the winery before emigrating to California where he established a "champagne" plant.

Bennett and Capozzi set about raising money to finance their new operation. At a time when soup kitchens meant more to the public than wineries, they began selling shares in the company for one dollar. They raised $4,500, and although they were undercapitalized, they bought fermenting tanks and other equipment to begin this multifaceted business. In September 1932, they took up residence in an old rented building on

---

[1] There is some controversy over the provenance of Okanagan Riesling. There are those who suggest that it is a Seyve Villard hybrid variety or a clone of Sauvignon Blanc. Lloyd Schmidt, a long-time grower in B.C. and now a consultant to vineyards in Ontario and Nova Scotia, traced the variety to a Hungarian grower named Teleki who had a grape-breeding program near Oliver in the 1930s.

Kelowna's Smith Avenue. The following year they hired Guiseppe Ghezzi's son Carlo as winemaker to complete their staff of eight employees. Their initial production included four apple-based wines — Okay Red, Okay Clear, Okay Port and Okay Champagne. But the products were far from "okay." Even the company's official history records that the wines "were a bitter disappointment. Many bottles refermented on liquor store shelves and had to be thrown out. Liquor stores were reluctant to stock the ill-famed domestic wines and people were reluctant to buy them." Sales in the company's first full year of operation were a disaster, amounting to a mere few thousand dollars.

After three years of ineffectual competition against the genuine wines of the Growers' Company, Bennett and Capozzi realized that B.C. consumers just did not want apple wines. They switched to grapes which they bought in California, and soon Growers' and the Victoria Wineries on Vancouver Island did likewise, perpetuating the fiction of making domestic wines by using whatever local grapes were available.

With the change of style the former apple winery needed a change of name, and in 1936 the directors chose a phonetic spelling of the Indian place name where the company was born: Calona Wines Limited. Okay Clear apple wine became Calona Clear grape "wine," a white semi-sweet product whose label read ominously "When Fully Mature: About 28% Proof Spirit".

In 1940, W.A.C. Bennett left Calona to pursue a career in politics. One year later he was elected to the B.C. parliament and he sold his shares to Capozzi. When he became premier of the province in 1952, he took a serious look at the wine industry he had helped to create. If the wineries were to sell their products through the government-controlled liquor stores, then they should do their part in promoting the grape-growing sector, he argued. In 1960, the B.C. government passed a law stating that wines vinified in the province had to contain a minimum percentage of locally grown grapes. Since there were only 585 acres under vines in the Okanagan Valley, that figure was set at 25 percent. To encourage the planting of new vineyards, the Liquor Board stated that the quota would rise to 50 percent in 1962 and 65 percent by 1965.

Farmers in the Okanagan Valley began planting French and American hybrids (Okanagan Riesling, De Chaunac, Maréchal Foch, Verdelet, Rougeon, Chelois and Baco Noir) with a vengeance and within four years the total acreage had risen by 400 percent.

In 1961, Andrew Peller built Andrés' spanking new winery at Port Moody; six years later a company called Southern Okanagan Wines of Penticton opened for business, but it soon changed its name to Casabello. At the same time, the beautifully situated Mission Hill Winery was built on a ridge overlooking Okanagan Lake at Westbank. This facility was acquired in 1969 by the ebullient construction king and brewer, Ben Ginter, who promptly renamed it with characteristic flamboyance (if little understanding of consumer sophistication) Uncle Ben's Gourmet Winery. He also put a portrait of himself on his labels. Among the products Ginter was to market were such items as Fuddle Duck and Hot Goose.

In 1973, the Growers' Wine Cooperative, which had merged with Victoria Wineries and changed its name to Castle Wines, was acquired from Imperial Tobacco by Carling O'Keefe. Another corporate name change was in store. Castle Wines became Ste-Michelle Wines — a subsidiary of Jordan and Ste-Michelle Cellars Ltd. — in 1974.

The company had long outgrown its facility in Victoria and looked to the mainland to build a modern winery to service the growing demand in the province for table wines. Four years later, it began building at Surrey just south of Vancouver and opened its operation in April 1978.

From 1974 to 1979, growers turned their attention to grape varieties imported from California and Washington. Experimental plantings of Cabernet Sauvignon, Merlot, Chenin Blanc, Gewürztraminer, White and Grey Riesling, Semillon and Chardonnay were evaluated at eighteen sites throughout the Okanagan. In 1975, George Heiss brought in Auxerrois, Pinot Gris and Gewürztraminer from France to plant in his Okanagan Centre vineyard.

In March 1977, the B.C. Ministry of Consumer and Corporate Affairs, responding to a strong lobby from the wineries and grape growers, announced a new liquor policy "to recognize the health and social costs caused by the abuse of alcohol on the one hand and consumer demand for better products, better prices and better premises in which to have a drink, on the other hand." The thrust of the new legislation was to encourage the consumption of wine, both imported and domestic, at the expense of hard liquor and beer.

To help the provincially based wineries compete with low-cost imports, the government lowered the markup on table wines from 66 percent to 46 percent (at the same time reducing imports from 117 percent to 100 percent markup).[2] To give their products a sales boost, B.C. wineries were allowed to open a retail store on their premises, and under the aegis of the federal and provincial Ministries of Agriculture a five-year grape-growing program was introduced, at a cost of $133,000, to upgrade the quality of the grapes they had to use. The program was directed by world-famous viticulturist, the late Dr. Helmut Becker, then head of the Research Institute of Grape Breeding and Grape Propagation at Geisenheim in Germany. At the invitation of Andrés Wines, Dr. Becker selected twenty-seven European varieties for testing in B.C. soil.

Two three-acre plots were chosen for the experiment — a southern site on light, sandy soil near Oliver, and a northern site in the heavier soil at Okanagan Mission. The first wines made from these grapes were vinified by

---

2 As a further incentive to the wineries, the government relented over its ban on TV advertising and on October 1, 1992, the companies were allowed to promote their products on air.

the Summerland Research Station in 1980. The most promising varietals turned out to be Auxerrois, Ehrenfelser, Pinot Blanc, Bacchus, Gewürztraminer, Müller-Thurgau, Schonburger and Scheurebe.

Looking south to the Napa and Sonoma Valleys of California, the B.C. government realized that there was great tourist potential for a thriving wine industry in the beautiful Okanagan Valley setting. After years of bureaucratic foot-shuffling, the politicians finally agreed to the creation of cottage or estate wineries; the first in the field was Claremont. In 1979, the late Bob Claremont took over a facility built by Marion John who had planted vineyards on a steep slope just north of Peachland nineteen years earlier. John's first wines were made and bottled at Mission Hill Winery, but Claremont, who had worked as a winemaker at Calona as well as at Jordan's Ontario plant, set up a crusher, fermentation tanks and a bottling line, and began to vinify B.C.'s first estate-bottled wines in 1979.

The B.C. Liquor Control and Licensing Branch, not knowing how to deal with the novel enterprise, hastily introduced regulations which both encouraged and inhibited the new winery. To be an estate winery, the company had to cultivate twenty acres of vines and could only make a maximum of 30,000 gallons. (This is now 40,000 gallons for the domestic market and the estate wineries can exceed this figure if they export the product.) All the grapes used in the wine had to be grown in the province and 50 percent of these had to come from Claremont's own vineyards. The winery was allowed to open a retail store on its premises and could sell directly to licensees without having to pay the government's markup. Claremont could sell two products through the specialty liquor stores only, but these would only carry the then markup of 15 percent.

Within the next three years, Bob Claremont was joined by four other small producers in the Okanagan — Sumac Ridge, Vinitera (which went into receivership in 1982), Uniacke Cellars (now CedarCreek), Gray Monk, and in the spring of 1983, Divino Wines in Oliver. In those early days, there was a feeling of camaraderie among the operators of these small wineries and they helped each other out when they could by sharing facilities and equipment, such as hand-labelling machines or storing one or other's wines. They were the pioneers of a new phase of B.C.'s growing wine industry. While the estate wineries still co-operate among themselves, most are well established enough to have their own equipment.

Meanwhile, Uncle Ben's Gourmet Wines, suffering the consequences of marketing dubious wines, fell foul of the banks and re-emerged briefly under the name of Golden Valley Wines. However, its reincarnation did not help its balance sheet; thanks to union animosity following troubles at Ginter's Red Deer Brewery, Gintner was forced to sell and the company was bought in 1981 by Anthony Von Mandl's Mark Anthony group, a successful Vancouver-based firm of wine importers, who immediately restored its original name of Mission Hill and began a massive reorganization.

The last commercial winery to open in B.C. was Brights, who built a spectacular modern winery in 1981 on Inkameep Indian Band land to ferment grapes grown on the Band's adjacent Inkameep Vineyards. The building alone cost $2 million and was funded by development money from the provincial and federal governments. Brights invested $3.5 million in equipment for the new facility.

In 1994, Brights merged with Cartier-Inniskillin to form Vincor International, and for economies of scale the company enlarged this facility for its combined winemaking operations.

When the first edition of this book was published in 1993 there were twenty-four wineries in the province. Two years later there are thirty-eight with six more provisionally licensed and expected to be operational during the year. At least six more are expected to apply for licenses.

The B.C. industry is structured into three winery classifications:

Farm wineries — Owners must have a minimum of four acres of vines and can make up to 10,000 gallons of wine from B.C. grapes. Their wines (all VQA) must be sold from their own store on the property or directly to restaurants.

Bella Vista, Blue Grouse, Carriage House, Chateau Wolff, Cherry Point, Crowsnest, Gersighel Wineberg, Hillside Cellars, House of Rose, Kettle Valley, Lang Vineyards, Nichol Vineyards, Scherzinger Vineyards, Tinhorn Creek, Venturi-Schulze, Vigneti Zanatta and Wild Goose Vineyards.

Estate wineries — Owners must have at least twenty acres of vines and can make up to 40,000 gallons of wine from B.C. grapes (all VQA) for domestic sale through their own wine shop, licensed outlets and BCLDB stores.

Blue Mountain, CedarCreek, Chateau Ste. Clair, Divino, Domaine Combret, Domaine de Chaberton, Gehringer Bros., Gray Monk, Hainle, LeComte, St. Hubertus, St. Laszlo, Sumac Ridge, Summerhill and Quails' Gate.

Major wineries — Up until 1995, major wineries were obligated to purchase all available B.C. grapes, but were also permitted to import grapes and wine. The five major wineries in the province — Vincor International (Brights-Cartier-Inniskillin), Mission Hill, Calona, Andrés and Okanagan Vineyards (the smallest of the "majors" and the only one to have its own estate vineyards) — have all developed strong VQA programs using 100 percent B.C. grapes. In addition, they continue to produce larger volumes of blended domestic and imported products as well as bottling 100 percent off-shore wines which are sold under the regional or country name in BCLDB stores.

Six more wineries are expected to open their doors in 1995 and the boom will not stop there. Why this sudden explosion of wineries in British Columbia? One factor is that from 1995 the majors no longer have to buy all the grapes grown in the province and some of the growers found that, while there was a strong market for *vinifera* varieties, it was difficult to sell their hybrids. In order to do so, they opened their own farm wineries and utilized both their *vinifera* and hybrids themselves.

Another reason is the planting of vineyards in prime sites between Oliver and Osoyoos. This area had first been redeveloped by established wineries with new *vinifera* plantings and then new enthusiasts with entrepreneurial skills bought up adjacent blocks and began to plant with the idea of starting up their own wineries. Several of these are now ready for their first crush in 1995.

Currently, the regulations governing the B.C. grape and wine industry are being completely overhauled by a committee of government and industry members. Their proposals due before the end of 1995 could radically change the rules by which farm, estate and major wineries operate.

Meanwhile, the momentum and upbeat confidence of the B.C. wine industry has ensured the survival of grape growing in the province — a situation that could not have been foretold in 1988. Before that watershed year, there were 3,400 acres of vines in the ground. By 1991, thanks to the pressures of GATT and Free Trade, the industry was forced to downsize to 1,500 acres.

After the pull-out program, replanting with desirable *vinifera* varieties and the creation of new vineyards increased the total surface to an estimated 2,100 acres at the beginning of 1995. The speed of further replanting has been slowed as growers await the arrival of imported cultivars from France, currently held up by a virus controversy between the Canadian and French bureaucracies.

In 1995, a new vine census is expected (the last was done in 1988), so there is no exact figure as to what is in the ground. However, John Vielvoye, a provincial grape specialist with B.C.'s Ministry of Agriculture, gave the following estimate of the top twelve cultivars planted since 1988, based on plant importation and local production:

Pinot Noir - 20 percent
Chardonnay - 16 percent
Merlot - 13 percent
Pinot Blanc - 7 percent
Cabernet Sauvignon - 5 percent
Ehrenfelser - 6 percent
Pinot Gris - 6 percent
Auxerrois - 5 percent
Gewürztraminer - 4 percent
Gamay Noir - 4 percent
Riesling - 3 percent
Others - 11 percent.

British Columbia Wineries

Andrés Wines (B.C.) Ltd.

2120 Vintner Street
Port Moody, B.C.
V3H 1W8

Telephone: (604) 937-3411
Fax: (604) 937-5487

Andrés Wines began operating in Vancouver's western suburb of Port Moody in 1961 and opened wineries within a year in Nova Scotia and Alberta, followed quickly by Quebec, Manitoba and Ontario. Although the commercial heart has now shifted to the Winona plant in Ontario, the Port Moody facility is the historic soul of the company. This winery on Vintner Street was built when Andrew Peller could not acquire a going concern at the price he wanted. The original winemaker, Wallace Pohl, like the equipment, came from

California. Early bottlings used California grapes which increased their price in the marketplace against wines of other B.C. houses. The public equated the expense with higher quality and bought Andrés' products to such a degree that Andrew Peller expanded quickly into other provinces. The growth took its toll on the founder's health so his son, Dr. Joe Peller, gave up his medical practice to run the company. Now his son John is at the helm.

In the 1970s, on advice from Dr. Helmut Becker of the Geisenheim Institute, Andrés developed 300 acres of French hybrid and *vinifera* vines on Indian land near Oliver, called Inkameep Vineyards. Andrés has made a commitment to VQA wines in B.C. with 90 percent of its contracted vineyards acreage being *vinifera*. A recent investment of $1 million in new equipment is beginning to show in the quality of the wines.

The company markets a variety of wines under different labels corresponding to the grape source: Franciscan California, Gold Coast (Australia), Santa Anna (Chile), Di Conti (Italy) and Dumons Cuvée Blanc (France) and Peller Estates for its VQA varietal wines.

The Domaine D'Or Chardonnay is a blend of several wine regions — Australia, California and Chile.

Winemakers: Laurent Dal'Zovo and Tony Vlcek

Acreage: 200 contracted

Production: 500,000 cases

Average tonnage crushed: 950

Winemaking philosophy: "Andrés Wines produces good quality for good value, without compromise. Our philosophy in making wine is to associate art and technology."

Wines: **LDB**: *Peller Estates label white*: Pinot Blanc, Ehrenfelser**, Dry Riesling**, Müller-Thurgau, Grand Reserve, Chardonnay, Late Harvest Ehrenfelser**, Ehrenfelser Icewine**, Proprietors' Reserve

White—Cellar Reserve House, Cellar Reserve Dry, Clos Du Lac, Domaine D'Or, Domaine D'Or Chardonnay, Domaine D'Or Dry, Hochtaler, Hochtaler Dry, Hochtaler Gold Riesling, Hochtaler Light, Similkameen Superior, Similkameen Chablis, Souvenance Blanc de Blancs, Stone's Green Ginger (under licence)

Franciscan California label white: California Chablis, Dry California Chablis

Gold Coast label white: Chardonnay, Semillon/Chardonnay, Vintage Reserve; Dumons Cuvée Blanc, Santa Anna Semillon/Chardonnay, Di Conti Bianco

Sparkling: Baby Duck, Baby Champagne, Kurhauser Trocken Sekt, Richelieu Champagne, Sparkling Hochtaler

Red—Peller Estates Cabernet, Peller Estates Proprietors' Reserve, Similkameen Superior, Domaine D'Or, Domaine D'Or Dry, Cellar Reserve Dry, Gold Coast Cabernet/Shiraz, Gold Coast Vintage Reserve, Franciscan Californian Burgundy, Santa Anna Cabernet Sauvignon, Di Conti Rosso

Sherries: Almond Cream, Golden Cream, Medium Dry

Winery store: *White*—VQA Showcase Peller Estates: Chardonnay, Pinot
  Blanc*, Bacchus*, Müller-Thurgau*, Siegerrebe*
Red—VQA Showcase Peller Estates Merlot*, Pinot Noir
Fortified: Port
Store hours: Tuesday to Friday, 9 am-5 pm; Saturday, 11 am-4:30 pm
Tours: Saturday at 2 pm or by appointment
Public tastings: During store hours

Bella Vista Vineyards

3111 Agnew Road	Telephone: (604) 558-0770
Vernon, B.C.	Fax: (604) 542-1221
V1T 5J8	

Larry Passmore's large colonial style winery on three floors, finished in 1994,
is the most northerly in the Okanagan (thus on the continent), edging out
the long-established Gray Monk for this distinction. An amateur winemaker, Larry and his wife Christine started up a U-brew store in his native
Vernon. The couple bought the Bella Vista farm with its fifteen-acre vineyard in 1991 and invited a group of local friends to buy minority shares in
the enterprise. The first crush was in 1993. Eight acres are currently under
vine after the pull-out program, including mature Maréchal Foch, Seyval
Blanc, Okanagan Riesling and a variety called Himrod.

Winemaker: Larry Passmore (consultant Gary Strachan)
Acreage: 8
Grape varieties: Maréchal Foch, Seyval Blanc, Okanagan Riesling, Himrod
  (to come, Auxerrois, Gewürztraminer, Pinot Noir, Pinot Meunier)
Production: 2,000 cases
***Wines*: Own store**: *Red*—Maréchal Foch; *White*—Okanagan Riesling, Seyval Blanc

Blue Grouse Vineyards

4365 Blue Grouse Road   Telephone: (604) 743-3834
RR #7
Duncan, B.C.
V9L 4W4

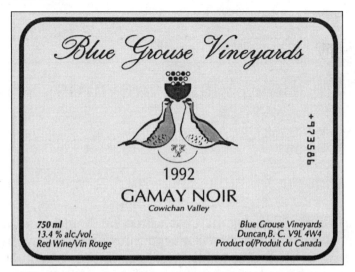

Berlin-born Hans Kiltz, a veterinarian who spent twenty years ministering to large animals in Africa, came to Canada in 1988 with his wife Evangeline. They settled on a thirty-one-acre farm in the heart of Vancouver Island's Cowichan Valley. On the property was an experimental vineyard which had fallen into neglect. As a hobby, Hans, who has a doctorate in microbiology, decided to revive it. The hobby turned into a business when the couple opened Blue Grouse Vineyards in 1993. Their bowl-shaped vineyard is recognized as one of the best microclimates on the island. The winery, on the ground floor of the house, sits on top of a hill. The emphasis here is on white wines, although Gamay and Pinot Noir are grown.

Winemaker: Dr. Hans Kiltz

Acreage: 8

Soil: Sandy loam, the warmest spot in the Cowichan Valley, protected by evergreen mountains, with a refreshing breeze from the ocean.

Grape varieties: Ortega, Müller-Thurgau, Bacchus, Pinot Gris, Siegerrebe, Gamay Noir, Pinot Noir

Average tonnage crushed: 12

Winemaking philosophy: "Vancouver Island is the most recent viticultural region. It is important to us that we produce distinctive wines which clearly reflect the unique growing conditions on the island and our continuous search for quality."

Wines: **Own store**: *White*—Ortega, Müller-Thurgau, Bacchus, Pinot Gris
Red—Gamay Noir, Pinot Noir
Tours: Yes (up to 12 people)
Public tastings: Wednesday, Friday, Saturday, Sunday, 11 am-5 pm

Blue Mountain Vineyard & Cellars

RR #1, S3, C4	Telephone: (604) 497-8244
Okanagan Falls, B.C.	Fax: (604) 497-6160
VOH 1R0	

Ian Mavety spent twenty-one years growing grapes on his Okanagan property before deciding to produce wine. He and his wife Jane made their first wines in 1991 — a barrel-fermented Pinot Blanc and a blended barrel-and-tank fermented Pinot Gris. With their first effort they also produced one of the best Pinot Noirs that B.C. consumers had ever enjoyed. And as if this wasn't enough, they went on to make a series of *methode champenoise* sparklers of distinction with help from oenologist Raphael Brisbois, who worked at Iron Horse in Sonoma. Then the Mavetys turned their attention to barrel-fermented Chardonnay. Taking their cue from Burgundy, whose climate resembles their own, they decided to concentrate on Chardonnay and Pinot Noir rather than the Valley's ubiquitous Riesling.

Situated in the hills south of Okanagan Falls, Blue Mountain is one of the region's most picturesque sites and well as being one of its best producers.

Winemaker: Ian Mavety
Acreage: 54

Soil: Light, sandy

Grape varieties: Pinot Blanc, Pinot Gris, Chardonnay, Pinot Noir, Gamay

Production: 5,500 cases (ultimately 12,000 planned)

Winemaking philosophy: "The quality of the wines reflect the quality of the grapes, and winemaking at Blue Mountain begins in the vineyard where restricted yields concentrate the grape flavours. In the cellars, our winemaking is traditional. French oak barrels are used extensively to soften and add complexity to the wines."

Wines: **Own store only:** *White*—Pinot Gris**, Pinot Blanc*, Chardonnay

Red—Pinot Noir, Gamay Noir

Sparkling—Vintage Brut*, Reserve Brut, Rosé

Tours: By appointment

Public tastings: By appointment

Brights Wines (B.C.) Ltd.

(See under Vincor International, page 164)

Burrowing Owl Vineyards

Suite 200
620 West 8th Avenue
Vancouver, B.C.
V5Z 1CS

Telephone: (604) 874-8228
Fax: (604) 874-0273

In late 1993 and early 1994, Vancouver businessman Jim Wyse acquired approximately 220 acres in the southern Okanagan to the south of the Inkameep Vineyard. He bought the property from Albert LeComte to whom he now supplies grapes. The acquisition and re-planting costs will reach $3.3 million, and in full production the L-shaped vineyard will produce 1,100 tons of *vinifera* grapes. In addition to the original twenty-acre block of Pinot Blanc planted in 1985, there will be Chardonnay, Pinot Noir, Merlot and Cabernet Franc. There are plans to construct a winery in 1996, "set into the hillside in the centre of the vineyard, with a fabulous view of the valley, the mountains to the west and Osoyoos Lake to the south."

Calona Wines

1125 Richter Street   Telephone: (604) 762-3332
Kelowna, B.C.   1-800-663-5086
V1Y 2K6   Fax: (604) 762-2999

In 1932, when the original company was formed, apples were the raw material for their products. Later, other fruits were introduced under the Jack line (Cherry Jack is still in Calona's portfolio). Since its founding during the Depression, the winery has been associated with the Capozzi family who make no bones about the fact that they modelled their products and sales strategies on those of Ernest & Julio Gallo, the world's largest winery. In fact, in 1969 there was talk about an amalgamation of the two wineries. Calona's continuing prosperity has historically been based on its blended products, including such popular labels as Schloss Laderheim, Sommet Blanc and Sommet Rouge. The winery also bottles Almaden, Inglenook and Buena Vista wines from California and Hogue Cellars under the Washington Vineyards label.

The wines generally have a sweetness of flavour due to backblending of 20 percent or more of fresh juice after fermentation.

Over the past few years, Calona has made a commitment to VQA wines. Their red and white varietal wines have been wining medals in competitions. Their prestige VQA wines are bottled under the Dunfield Soon Artists Series label. Their best Okanagan fruit comes from the Sun Rise Vineyard and Burrowing Owl.

Winemaker: Howard Soon assisted by Richard Weberg
Production: 8,000,000 cases
Annual tonnage purchased: 400

Grape varieties: Johannisberg Riesling, Chardonnay, Rougeon, Chelois, Souvereign Opal

Winemaking philosophy: "Everything we do has a marketing emphasis. We find out what people like, what they're looking for. We look worldwide to see what's happening."

Wines: **LDB**: *White*—Mountain Sauterne, Premium Select White, Royal White, Sauvignon Blanc, Schloss Laderheim (also Light and Dry versions), Sommet Blanc, White Dry

VQA—Dunfield Soon Chardonnay, Bacchus/Chardonnay, Bacchus, Chardonnay, Gewürztraminer*, Johannisberg Riesling, Pinot Blanc Dry, Pinot Blanc, Semillon, Sovereign Opal

Red—Cabernet Sauvignon, Merlot, Premium Select Red, Red Dry, Royal Red, Beaupré Royal Red, San Pietro, Sommet Rouge, Superieur, Rougeon

VQA—Chancellor, Reserve Chancellor, De Chaunac/Merlot, Dunfield Soon Merelot/Pinot Noir, Rougeon

Own store: Pinot Noir**

Sparkling—La Scala Spumante, Pastel Peach

Fortified—Cream Sherry, Cocktail, Royal French Vermouth white and red, Okanagan Valley Port, (own store) LBV Port

Store hours: Summer: 9 am-6 pm; Winter: 10 am-5 pm

Tours: 10 am-4 pm, on the hour

Public tastings: During store hours

Carriage House Wines

RR #1, S46, C19   Telephone: (604) 498-8818
Oliver, B.C.
V0H 1T0

Dave and Karen Wagner made their first crush in 1994. They used the Kerner they grew on their 8.5-acre vineyard located at the north end of Black Sage vineyards, on the east side bench between Oliver and Osoyoos. In 1995, they added Pinot Noir, Merlot and Cabernet Sauvignon to their white varieties. They use French and American oak.

Winemaker: David Wagner

Acreage: 8.5

Soil: Rich sandy clay, southwest exposure

Grape varieties: Kerner, Pinot Blanc, Chardonnay, Pinot Noir, Merlot, Cabernet Sauvignon

Average tonnage crushed: 40

Annual tonnage purchased: 3 - 5

Production: 4,000 cases (at full production)

Winemaking philosophy: "Small quantities, high quality with the customer's satisfaction in mind."

Wines: Own store: Kerner (Dry and Semi-sweet); 1996—Chardonnay, Kerner and Pinot Blanc; 1998—Merlot, Pinot Noir, Cabernet Sauvignon

Store hours: 9 am-9 pm

Tours: Yes

Public tastings: Yes

Cartier Wines & Beverages

(See under Vincor International, page 164)

CedarCreek Estate Winery

5445 Lakeshore Road	Telephone: (604) 764-886
Kelowna, B.C.	Fax: (604) 764-2603
V1Y 7R3	

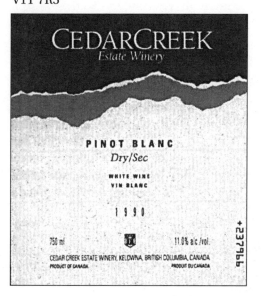

In 1986, David Ross Fitzpatrick of Kelowna bought Uniacke winery and vineyards (founded by grower David Mitchell in 1980). The contemporary

Mediterranean-style winery built above the cellar was designed by a Uniacke partner, David Newman-Bennett. The winemaker then was the youthful Weinsberg-trained oenologist Tilman Hainle who went on to create his own winery with his grape grower father, Walter, in 1985.

CedarCreek is situated twelve km south of Kelowna near Okanagan Mission at an elevation of 300 metres. Fitzpatrick originally hired winemaker Vienna-born Helmut Dotti, who had worked at Ste. Michelle facilities across the country and for Mission Hill. Ann Sperling took over the winemaking duties and now consults. Extensive use of French oak in barrel fermenting and aging. Chardonnay is a combination of barrel fermentation, barrel aging and stainless steel. CedarCreek's first Icewine was produced from Riesling grapes in 1991.

Winemaker: Ann Sperling (consultant), Ross Mirko (resident winemaker)

Acreage: 35 (CedarCreek), 35 (Greata Ranch)

Soil: Well-drained sandy loam that ranges from light to heavy from top to bottom of the steep southwest facing slope. Moderately saline and calcareous.

Grape varieties: Auxerrois, Riesling, Chardonnay, Gewürztraminer, Pinot Noir, Merlot, (Greata Ranch—to be planted: Pinot Blanc, Chardonnay, Pinot Noir, Merlot)

Production: 24,000 cases

Average tonnage crushed: 360

Annual tonnage purchased: 50 percent

Winemaking philosophy: "As an estate winery, we use only grapes grown in British Columbia and must by definition keep our production limited, emphasizing quality above all. We devote the time and care necessary to produce world-class wines with a distinctive Pacific Northwest flavour. Our tradition continues — one that guarantees excellence with each glass of wine produced under the CedarCreek label."

Wines: LDB: *White*—Proprietors' White* (Auxerrois, Kerner, Gewürztraminer)

Own winery store: *White*—Riesling, Pinot Blanc*, Dry Riesling, Chardonnay*, Johannisberg Riesling*, Gewürztraminer, Ehrenfelser*, Select Late Harvest Optima**, Riesling Icewine**

Red—Proprietors' Red* (Maréchal Foch, Chancellor, Baco Noir), Chancellor*, Merlot**, Pinot Noir*

Store hours: *November to March*: 9:30 am-5 pm; *April to October*: 9:30 am-5:30 pm

Tours: May to October

Tastings: During store hours

Chateau Ste. Claire

5031 Trepanier Bench Road   Telephone: (604) 767-3113
Peachland, B.C.
V0H 1X0

The oldest estate winery in the Okanagan, Chateau Ste. Claire, has a history dating back to 1972 when Marion Jonn planted the vineyard and called the winery he opened five years later Chateau Jonn de Trepanier. In 1979, he sold the winery to Bob Claremont, who named the property after himself. Claremont was forced to sell in 1986 to Goldie Smitlener, a Croatian who grew up within sight of vineyards in Zagreb. She renamed the winery after an order of nuns. Bill Finley made the first wines, but now Goldie's son, Boris is the winemaker. Like Karl Kaiser at Inniskillin, he was destined for the priesthood but has chosen to serve humanity in a different garb. There are eight acres of Auxerrois and Chardonnay in the vineyard and the style of wines is unremittingly off-dry to sweet.

Chateau Wolff

2354 Maxey Road   Telephone: (604) 753-9669
RR #3
Nanaimo, B.C.
V9R 5K3

Harry von Wolff, a native of Riga in Latvia, discovered his love of wine while at hotel school in Lucerne, Switzerland. After a stint in the hotel business in B.C., he became a shoemaker whose business in Nanaimo on Vancouver

Island flourished and grew into the Island Boot and Saddle Shop. An amateur vineyardist who grew vines around his house, he indulged his hobby by buying an eight-acre farm with its two-storey farmhouse in 1987. He cut down the trees to subsidize the creation of a commercial vineyard and planted it with Pinot Noir and Chardonnay in the upper portion and Müller-Thurgau, Bacchus and Siegerrebe in the lower belt. He also has some Viognier in the 4.5-acre vineyard.

His goal is to create cellars tunnelled into the hillside and remain small, producing around 1,000 cases a year. In 1994, 1,000 litres of Pinot Noir and 500 litres of Müller-Thurgau were crushed.

Cherry Point Vineyard

840 Cherry Point Road   Telephone: (604) 743-1272
RR# 3   Fax: (604) 743-1059
Cobble Hill, B.C.
V0R 1L0

Wayne Ulrich's farming background, interrupted by a stint with Agriculture Canada, gave him the necessary background to open his own winery in 1993 with his wife Helena. The introduction of B.C.'s farmgate winery legislation in 1989 was the only spur they needed to start looking for a farm in the Cowichan Valley. They settled on a former mink ranch and moved there in January 1990, raising sheep while they waited for their vines to mature. The Ulrichs have planted an experimental plot with thirty-two varieties to augment in future the six already in the ground.

Winemaker: Wayne Ulrich

Acreage: 12

Soil: Glacial moraine in a small microclimate of the Cowichan Valley, "meaning a warm land compared to the best of the Alsace and Chablis locations."

Grape varieties: Pinot Blanc, Pinot Noir, Gewürztraminer, Ortega, Auxerrois, Müller-Thurgau

Production: 2,000 cases (increasing yearly)

Average tonnage crushed: 30

Winemaking philosophy: "To make wine in a way that respects and develops the advantages given us by Nature. Our flock of one hundred sheep helps provide environmental sustainability."

Wines: **Own store**: *White*—Pinot Blanc, Gewürztraminer, Auxerrois, Helena (blend)

Red—Pinot Noir

Store hours: 11:30 am-6 pm daily

Tours: By appointment

Public tastings: During store hours

Crowsnest Vineyards

Box 501
Keremeos, B.C.
V0X 1N0

Telephone: (604) 499-5192

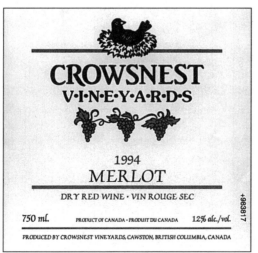

A course in food processing at B.C.'s Institute of Technology set Andrea McDonald in pursuit of the grape. As a lab technician at Okanagan Vineyards (and subsequently at Brights), she married fruit farmer Hugh McDonald and together they planted their first two acres of Pinot Auxerrois

in 1990 on the family property overlooking the Similkameen River on an eastern slope. Their first crush was in 1994.

Winemaker: Andrea McDonald

Acreage: 12

Soil: Well-drained sandy loam soils. High heat units.

Production: 500 cases

Average tonnage crushed: 7 (will increase yearly)

Winemaking philosophy: "K.I.S.S. We want the flavours that have developed in the vineyard to come through."

Wines: **Own store**: *White*—Auxerrois, Riesling, Chardonnay, Kerner

Red—Merlot, Pinot Noir

Tours: Yes

Public tastings: Yes (hours to be determined)

Divino Estate Winery

Road 8, Box 866   Telephone: (604) 498 2784
Oliver, B.C.   Fax: (604) 498 6518
V0H 1T0

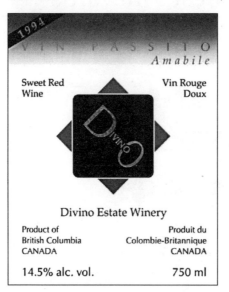

Joseph Busnardo is something of a maverick in the B.C. wine industry, choosing not to be part of the B.C. Wine Institute. He has been growing grapes for twenty-seven years, experimenting with over 100 varieties, most of which came from his native Veneto. Currently he is making wine from the eight most successful *vinifera* varietals in his Oliver vineyard. His winery was founded in 1982 and is now the largest of the B.C. estate wineries. His winemaking technique is defiantly Italian and Veneto in particular. He favours whole berry fermentation *à la maceration carbonique*. He uses only stainless steel for his Chardonnay and his state-of-the-art bottling line is his pride and joy. Joe has a bistro facility at the winery.

Winemaker: Joseph Busnardo

Acres: 70.8

Soil: Rocky, gravelly, high pH factor. ("However, it is probably the best soil in the Okanagan Valley for *Vitis vinifera*.")

Grape varieties: Merlot, Cabernet Franc, Chardonnay, Trebbiano, Tocai, Pinot Bianco, Pinot Grigio, Malvasia, Perle of Csaba, Pinot Nero

Production: 20,000 cases

Average tonnage crushed: 250 - 300

Winemaking philosophy: "My style of winemaking could be classed as *primitivo* and 'earthy.' I am attempting to produce wines indicative of the Okanagan Valley. In order to have a good wine, you must have good grapes. My philosophy is that 'if the wine is good enough for me, then it is good enough for the general public!'"

Wines: **LDB**: *White*—Chardonnay, Malvasia*, Pinot Bianco*, Pinot Chardonnay*, Pinot de Pinot, Trebbiano*, Soave

Red—Merlot/Cabernet

Own stores: Bacaro, Bianco di Giuseppe, Chardonnay Classico, Tesoro

Dry rosé—Pinot Grigio

Red—Bacaro, Cabernet, Merlot*, Rosso di Giuseppe, Pinot Nero

Sparkling—Il Segreto Brut (Charmat process)

Dessert wines—Perle of Csaba, Tocai Late Harvest*, Passito Amabile Rosso*, Passioto Amabile Bianco

Stores:
Vancouver: Corks 'n Candles, 1610 Robson St.
West Vancouver: Sacaldferri's Deli, 2409 Marine Dr.
New Westminster: Divino's Quayside Cellar, 810 Quayside

Domaine Combret

P.O. Box 1170   Telephone: (604) 498-8878
Oliver, B.C.   Fax: (604) 498-8879
V0H 1T0

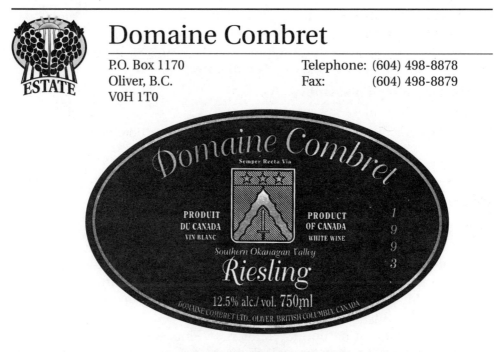

Robert Combret, his wife Maité and Montpellier-trained winemaker son Olivier had a triumph before they even had an on-site store to sell their first wines (Chardonnay and Riesling 1993) to visitors. Their '93 Alsace-style Riesling won a silver medal at the Challenge International du Vin at Blaye-Bourg in Bordeaux in 1994. In March 1995, they had an even bigger success: Domaine Combret Chardonnay 1993 was judged among the best "Chardonnay of the World" at the annual international Chardonnay challenge in Burgundy.

Robert, who emigrated from Provence to Canada with his family in 1992, comes from a long line of winemakers stretching back ten generations to 1638, and was himself president of the AOC Coteaux d'Aix-en-Provence and owner of Château Petit Sonnailler (cattle bell). The spanking new 7,700-sq.-ft. gravity-feed winery with wooden catwalks and arched wooden doors is a model of efficiency and state-of-the-art technology with its computer-controlled double-jacketed tanks, below-ground barrel-aging cellar and selection of barrels from puncheons (Seguin Moreau) and *foudres* to a 7,500-litre oak tank. The facility enjoys a panoramic view of Osoyoos Lake and the town of Oliver.

The Chardonnay is barrel fermented and aged. Wines are exported to Europe and Asia.

Winemaker: Olivier Combret

Acreage: 30

Soil: Granitic gravelly soil with a southeastern exposure, low percentage of relative humidity.

Grape varieties: Chardonnay, Riesling, Cabernet Franc, Gamay Beaujolais

Production: 5,000 cases

Average tonnage crushed: 60

Winemaking philosophy: "Traditional French winemaking, grapes 100 percent grown, matured and processed on site."

Wines: **Own store**: Chardonnay*, Riesling*

Tours: By appointment

Public tastings: By appointment

Domaine de Chaberton

1064 - 216th Street   Telephone: (604) 530-1736
Langley, B.C.   530-5398
V3A 7R2   Fax: (604) 533-9687

In July 1991, Claude Violet opened his winery named after the farm he owned in southern France. A Parisian by birth, Claude comes from a French Catalan family that can trace itself back through nine generations of winemakers over a period of 350 years to Manaut Violet, cooper and grape grower. When Claude came to Canada in 1981, he brought his winegrowing experience that encompassed dealings in France, Switzerland and Spain. Instead of choosing the Okanagan, he bought a fifty-five-acre farm in South Langley and converted it into vineyards, becoming the first commercial grape grower in the Fraser Valley. His winery is the most southerly on the B.C. mainland.

Winemakers: Elias Phiniotis and Claude Violet

Acreage: 27

Soil: "Top quality soil. Much less rain than Vancouver."

Grape varieties: Bacchus, Madeleine Angevine, Madeleine Sylvaner, Ortega, Chardonnay, Chasselas Doré

Average tonnage crushed: 52

Winemaking philosophy: "In winemaking there must be love. I grew up in the atmosphere of wine so it is so natural, so normal. For me, it's quality before quantity."

Wines: **Own store**: *White*—Madeleine Angevine, Madeleine Sylvaner, Bacchus, Ortega*, Chardonnay

Red—Pinot Noir

Store hours: Monday to Saturday, 10 am-6 pm; Sunday, noon - 5 pm

Tours: Yes

Public tastings: During store hours

Dosman Vineyards

1751 Stamps Road
RR #1
Duncan, B.C.
V9L 1M3

Roger Dosman and his wife Nancy sold up his Vancouver auto body shop in 1988 to live an outdoor life. They purchased the ten-acre farm in the Cowichan Valley on Vancouver Island in 1992 and two years later planted Bacchus, Siegerrebe, Kerner, Schonburger and Auxerrois. Roger also put in the early ripening German red variety, Dornfelder. The first crush in 1993 was made from grapes brought in from neighbouring growers. The winery will be in a converted barn on the property and the Dosmans aim to make 2,000 cases a year. The couple also runs a bed-and-breakfast inn.

Gehringer Brothers Estate Winery

RR #1, S23, C4   Telephone: (604) 498-3537
Oliver, B.C.   Fax: (604) 498-3510
VOH 1T0

Walter and Gordon Gehringer made their first wine 1985, but not before both had acquired sound experience in oenology and viticulture at Germany's famed schools Geisenheim and Weinsberg, respectively. During their summer vacations, the brothers brought back winemaking equipment as well as techniques they had learned to apply to the grapes grown by their father Helmut and his brother Karl. Slowly, they evolved the style which has become the benchmark for the company's white wines: fermentation to dryness and then backblending with 10 percent fresh juice just before bottling.

In 1981, the Gehringers selected their vineyard site eight km north of Osoyoos, which lies north of Mount Kobau, and one year later Gordon returned to manage it. All white varieties were planted. In 1984, Walter, who spent five years as winemaker for Andrés both in Ontario and B.C., joined the enterprise. The following year they began construction of the winery. In 1995, the brothers bought their neighbour's land, augmenting their property to sixty acres.

No oak is used in the winemaking process. In 1991, the brothers produced their first Icewine. A consistent gold medal winner.

Winemakers: Walter and Gordon Gehringer

Acreage: 30 (45 plantable)

Soil: Located on a narrow upper bench of the valley above the frost zone at the southern end of the Okanagan. South-facing slope offers good exposure and air drainage.

Grape varieties: Johannisberg Riesling, Verdelet, Pinot Auxerrois, Ehrenfelser, Schonburger

Production: 15,000 cases

Average tonnage crushed: 220

Annual tonnage purchased: 40 percent

Winemaking philosophy: "In the fall, the grapes are pressed and a portion of the juice is stored fresh and unfermented. Before bottling in the spring, we blend the unfermented juice, which has retained its rich flavour, back into the dry wine. This results in the varietal fruit flavour components being combined with the developed wine, yielding a complex, full-bodied wine. All our wines have a pleasant, harmonious taste, bringing out the subtle, yet distinctive flavours of each grape variety."

Wines: *LDB*: *White*—Ehrenfelser**, Ehrenfelser Dry, Johannisberg Riesling Dry (vintage** and non-vintage), Johannisberg Riesling**, Müller-Thurgau*, Pinot Auxerrois**, Select Pinot Auxerrois**, Verdelet*, Riesling Ice Wine*

Red—Cuvée Noire (Baco Noir, Rougeon, Rosette, Chancellor)

Own store: Schonburger*, Pinot Gris*, Desert Sun (Pinot Auxerrois/Riesling)

Store hours: *July to September*: Daily, 10 am-5 pm. *October to June*: Monday to Friday, 10 am-5 pm; Saturday, 10 am-1 pm

Tours: By appointment ($2 per person)

Public tastings: During store hours

Gersighel Wineberg

RR #1, S40, C20   Telephone: (604) 495-3319
Oliver, B.C.
V0H 1T0

Dirk De Gussem and Gerda Tork founded their winery in 1995. They are located the furthest south on Highway 97, across the valley from some of

the large vineyard plantings on the east bench between Oliver and Osoyoos. Their tasting room is "at home," and at the time of writing they offer one wine — a 1994 Pinot Blanc. By 1997 they hope to have a full product line reflecting all the varieties they have in the ground. The winery's unusual name is drawn from the names of Dirk's three children — Gerd, Sigrid and Helgi — and Wineberg because it "sounds better than Wine Mountain," derived from the ski hill Mount Baldy, visible on the eastern horizon. This concept inspired the label featuring the head of a bald eagle. He hopes to reach 4,000 cases by 1997.

Winemaker: Dirk De Gussem

Acreage: 7.5

Soil: Loam and sand, fertile top soil; southeastern slope backed by a heat-retaining mountain.

Grape varieties: Pinot Blanc, Chardonnay, Tokay, Perle of Csaba, Viognier, Pinot Noir, Merlot

Production: 1,000 cases (1995)

Winemaking philosophy: "It will take more than one generation to determine which variety a vintner will plant in his vineyard and where. Only time can tell but being farmers for generations and travelling all over Europe, living in France for three years, and visiting the wine regions of South Africa, I am convinced that the Okanagan will produce Grand Cru wines — but as everywhere else in the world, not too many. I looked for the microclimate of an open hill and the structure of the soil; that's the first step in making great wines."

Public tastings: By appointment

Gray Monk Cellars

P.O. Box 63   Telephone: (604) 766-3168
Okanagan Centre, B.C.   1-800-663-4205
V0H 1P0   Fax: (604) 766-3390

The vineyards sweep down the eastern slope from the winery which commands a spectacular view of Okanagan Lake. It used to be the most northerly estate winery on the continent until Bella Vista opened its doors. George Heiss, born and raised in Vienna, started building his classically simple farmhouse-style winery in January 1982, ten years after he had torn out acres of aged orchard and planted his first European vines. The winery name is a translation of what the Austrians call the Pinot Gris grape — Gray Monk.

George, his wife Trudy and German-trained son, George Jr., make some of the best white wines in B.C. as evidenced by the number of medals the winery has won in provincial, national and international competitions. The style, as you would expect, is Germanic but remarkably delicate. All of the wines are made in stainless steel. Some are exported to Japan.

Winemaker: George Heiss, Jr.

Acreage: 25

Grape varieties: Auxerrois, Pinot Gris, Ehrenfelser, Bacchus, Kerner, Kerner, Rotberger, Seigerrebe, Gewürztraminer

Production: 15,000 - 18,000 cases

Average tonnage crushed: 240

Annual tonnage purchased: 100

Winemaking philosophy: "We take pride in producing 100 percent varietals and showing the marketplace what can be done in the Okanagan."

***Wines*: LDB**: *White*—Bacchus*, Ehrenfelser (Auslese*, Spätlese**), Gewürztraminer Kabinett, Gewürztraminer Reserve, Johannisberg

Riesling**, Kerner (Auslese**, Spätlese*, Dry), Müller-Thurgau, Pinot Auxerrois**, Pinot Blanc**, Pinot Chardonnay**, Pinot Gris*, Siegerrebe**

Red—Pinot Noir*, Rotberger Rosé**, Merlot

Own store: Latitude Fifty

Store hours: *May 1 to October 31*: 10 am-5 pm every day. *November 1 to April 30*: Tuesday to Friday, 1 pm-5 pm; Saturday, 11 am-5 pm; Sunday, 12 am-4 pm until Christmas

Tours: Yes (large groups by appointment)

Public tastings: During store hours

Hainle Vineyards

5355 Trepanier Bench Road   Telephone: (604) 767-2525
RR #2, S27A, C6   Fax: (604) 767-2543
Peachland, B.C.
V0H 1X0

The Hainle family has been making wine in the Okanagan for over twenty-two years, and before that for ten generations in Germany. Father Walter made Canada's first Icewine from Okanagan Riesling in 1973 for the benefit of family and friends. Sadly, Walter died in a hiking accident on the property on January 1, 1995.

His son Tilman had become winemaker at Uniacke Cellars at the tender age of twenty-one. He left when the winery was sold (to become CedarCreek) and joined his father across the lake near Peachland to create Hainle Vineyards in 1985.

Father and son built up an inventory of wines until they had sufficient to receive an estate winery licence in 1987. The winery is a 3,000-sq.-ft.

block-construction building which will eventually allow for the 40,000-gallon annual production limit for estate wineries.

In 1991, Tilman began making champagne method sparkling wine (60 percent Pinot noir, 30 percent Chardonnay, 10 percent Pinot Meunier). He adds sulphur dioxide only after fermentation to preserve the wine, believing that some oxidation of the fresh juice helps to clarify the wine so that little or no fining and filtering — which can rob the wine of varietal character — is necessary.

A second floor addition to the winery was completed in May, 1993, affording an additional 3,000 sq. ft., including a tasting room, catering kitchen, lab and office space.

Hainle, the first Canadian winery to produce Icewine, holds a library of products going back to 1979. Tilman has made an experimental batch of port from Baco Noir and has two sparklers, on a traditional cuvée, the other from Riesling. Starting with the 1995 vintage, all Estate Bottled wines are made from organically grown grapes.

Winemaker: Tilman Hainle

Acreage: 18.5 (fully certified as organic — no insecticides or herbicides used. Yields are kept low to make plants more resistant to disease and pests.)

Soil: Very light sandy soils, pH 6.5 - 6.8. High gravel content; glacio-fluvial slopes with south to south southeast exposure. Very good air circulation.

Grape varieties: Riesling, Traminer, Chardonnay, Chasselas, Pinot Noir and small plantings of Merlot, Pinot Meunier, Perle of Csaba

Production: 5,500 cases

Average tonnage crushed: 60

Annual tonnage purchased: 20 - 25 (Inkameep Vineyards, Hans Fischer, Southview Vineyards, Elisabeth Harbeck)

Winemaking philosophy: "We specialize in fully fermented, completely dry wines which are ideal for matching with food. We strive for as natural a product as possible, starting with organic grape growing, and continuing with minimal intervention in the cellar. Sulphite levels are kept as low as possible. The wines age well in the bottle for an average of five to seven years."

Wines: **LDB**: *White*—Kerner Fischer Vineyard*, Riesling Estate Bottled*, Pinot Blanc Elisabeth's Vineyard*

Winery store: *White*—Chardonnay Estate Bottled**, Pinot Gris Fischer Vineyard*, Traminer Estate Bottled, Dry Muscat Estate Bottled, Riesling Icewine**

Red—Baco Noir Inkameep Vineyards*, Merlot, Pinot Noir* (Estate Bottled and Elisabeth's Vineyard), Lemberger

Winery store hours: *November to April:* 1 pm-5 pm. *May to October:* Tuesday to Sunday, 10 am-5 pm

Tours: By appointment

Public tastings: During shop hours

Hillside Cellars

1350 Naramata Road   Telephone/Fax: (604) 493-4424
Penticton, B.C.
V2A 6J6

Vera and Bohumir Klokocka came to Canada in 1968 when Soviet tanks rolled into Czechoslovakia. They settled in Kelowna and eventually bought a house and orchard in Naramata in the mid-1970s and began growing grapes. Vera taught herself winemaking and in 1990 she applied for a farm-gate winery licence. She uses stainless-steel tanks and in 1991 made her first twenty-five cases of Cabernet Sauvignon (with 25 percent Merlot). Among their wines Vera also has Pinot Noir and Cabernet Sauvignon in appreciable (for a farm winery) amounts.

Winemaker: Vera Klokocka

Acreage: 5.6

Soil: Mostly stony, sloping vineyard overlooking Naramata Road and Lake Okanagan.

Grape varieties: Johannisberg Riesling, Pinot Auxerrois, Muscat d'Ottonel, Gamay Beaujolais, some Cabernet Sauvignon and Pinot Noir

Production: 1,000 - 1,200 cases

Average tonnage crushed: 10 - 15

Annual tonnage purchased: 25 percent

Winemaking philosophy: "We produce the varietal wines dry fermented, 100 percent grape juice, no additives except sulphides. We try to stay as close to Nature as we can."

Wines: Johannisberg Riesling (no sweet reserve added), Pinot Auxerrois, Muscat, Gamay, Pinot Noir, Cabernet Sauvignon

Winery store hours: *April 1 to October 31*: 10 am-6 pm. *November 1 to March 31*: Tuesday to Sunday, 1 pm-5 pm

Tours: On request

Tastings: During store hours

House of Rose Vineyards

2270 Garner Road   Telephone/fax: (604) 765-0802
Kelowna, B.C.
V1X 4K4

Vern Rose, a former Alberta school teacher, bought his farm that sits high above the lake on the old Belgo Bench in 1982. He began making wine for himself from the established vineyard. He took a course in winemaking at UC Davis and attended a symposium on cool climate viticulture in New Zealand before establishing his winery in 1992. His vineyard favours hybrids and his northerly location and distance from the lake make it possible for him to grow Icewine.

Winemaker: Vern Rose

Acreage: 10

Soil: Alluvial bench soil, good gravel sub-soil; semi-arid valley conditions require irrigation

Grape varieties: Chardonnay, Verdelet, Perle of Zala, Semillon, Okanagan Riesling, Maréchal Foch, Pinot Noir

Production: 2,000 cases

Average tonnage crushed: 35 ("increasing")

Annual tonnage purchased: 6

Winemaking philosophy: "Grow top-quality grapes to produce the best possible wine. Keeping as close as possible in harmony with nature, avoiding the use of additives to wine wherever possible.

Wines: **Own store**: *White*—Chardonnay, Verdelet Dry, Verdelet (2), Johannisberg Riesling, Perle of Zala, Semillon, Vintner's Choice Dry (Verdelet, Chardonnay, Okanagan Riesling, Perle of Zala), Vintner's Choice (2), Okanagan Trocken

Red—Proprietors' Reserve (Pinot Noir, Maréchal Foch, Merlot, De Chaunac), Maréchal Foch

Rosé—Rose Rosé

Store hours: 10 am-5:30 pm

Tours: Yes, during store hours

Public tastings: During store hours

Kettle Valley Winery

2988 Hayman Road	Telephone: (604) 496-5118
Naramata, B.C.	Fax: (604) 496-5298
V0H 1N0	

In a Vancouver apartment, geologist Tim Watts and his chartered accountant and brother-in-law Bob Ferguson made wine as amateurs as early as 1980, using only Okanagan fruit. When Tim moved to the Naramata in 1985, he planted Chardonnay and Pinot Noir on the east side of Okanagan Lake, a hundred feet above the water. Seven years later, Bob joined him to create Kettle Valley Winery, named for the railroad that once ran on the east side of the valley.

They have concentrated on the noble French varieties, protecting them from the scavenging birds with netting to ensure maximum ripeness. The first two vintages were made in Bob's garage while the winery was being designed and built.

French and American oak are used to age the wines.

Winemakers: Bob Ferguson and Tim Watts

Acreage: 6

Soil: A mix of clay, sand and gravel, south and west facing slopes.

Grape varieties: Chardonnay, Pinot Noir, Cabernet Sauvignon, Cabernet Franc, Merlot

Production: 1,000 cases (1994)

Average tonnage crushed: 20 - 25

Winemaking philosophy: "We operate a small farm winery. Our goal is to produce quality barrel-aged wines. We produce three wines only: a Chardonnay, a Pinot Noir and a blend of Cabernet and Merlot. Our focus is French style, quality wines."

Wines: **Own store**: Chardonnay, Pinot Noir, Bordeaux blend

Store hours: To be set

Lakebreeze Vineyards

P.O. Box 9   Telephone/fax: (604) 496-5894
Naramata, B.C.
V0H 1N0

Paul and Verena Moser emigrated from Switzerland to South Africa where they lived for twenty-five years. Part of their business involved supplying stainless-steel tanks and winemaking equipment to the industry there. In the spring of 1995, they bought a twelve-acre vineyard near Naramata from Barry and Sue Irvine. The vineyard has Pinot Blanc, Pinot Noir, Semillon, Gewürztraminer and Ehrenfelser. A winery is planned for their first crush, and Paul will continue with his business as a wine industry supplier.

Lang Vineyards

RR #1, S11, C55   Telephone: (604) 496-5987
2493 Gammon Road   Fax: (604) 496-5706
Naramata, B.C.
VOH 1N0

Lang Vineyards has the distinction of being the first farm winery in Canada. In 1980, Guenther and Kristina Lang moved from Nuertingen, Germany, and settled in the Okanagan Valley. They bought the existing old vineyard in Naramata on the sunny east side of the Okanagan Lake. First they built their house and then they started to replant the vineyard with new grape varieties.

What started as a hobby for the Langs turned into a business. In 1985, Guenther approached the B.C. government and asked if he could sell the wines he made. After some years of lobbying, a proffered bottle to then-premier Bill Van der Zalm seemed to oil the wheels of government because in 1990 the legislation was passed to set up farm wineries. In 1993, the Langs built a 4,000-sq.-ft. winery with an on-site wine store.

Winemakers: Guenther and Kristina Lang

Acres: 9

Soil: West-facing slope, sandy-stone/clay soil.

Grape varieties: Riesling, Gewürztraminer, Chardonnay, Pinot Noir, Pinot Meunier, Maréchal Foch, Merlot

Production: 3,000 cases plus

Average tonnage crushed: 35 plus

Annual tonnage purchased: 7 (local)

Winemaking philosophy: "We strive for the highest quality grapes possible by controlling every step of viticulture, especially thinning to have a lighter crop. We harvest as late as possible to have a high degree of ripeness. We only make wine from healthy, truly ripe grapes using only *Vitis vinifera* varietals (apart from Maréchal Foch)."

Wines: **Own store only**: *White*—Riesling Dry, Riesling Farm Winery Reserve**, Riesling Late Harvest Dry*, Medium Dry** and Select, Riesling Icewine*, Gewürztraminer**, Chardonnay

Red—Maréchal Foch Medium**, Pinot Noir Dry**, Pinot Meunier Dry**, Merlot Dry, Cabernet Sauvignon Dry

Store hours: *May 1 to October 15*: 11 am-6 pm daily. *October 16 to April 30*: By appointment

Tours: By arrangement

Public tastings: During store hours

LeComte Estate Winery

Box 480 Green Lake Road
Okanagan Falls, B.C.
V0H 1R0

Telephone: (604) 497-8267
Fax: (604) 497-8073

Albert LeComte bought the old twenty-one-acre Green Lake vineyard in 1983, expanded it to over fifty acres and opened his winery in 1986. It's located on a western hillside overlooking Skaha Lake, three miles southwest

of Okanagan Falls. Bordering the property is Green Lake which teems with goldfish. The LeComte's historic family home (where you can taste the wines) is an old stone homestead of settlers from the beginning of the century. The winery tour includes the old wine cellar and a dog cemetery where the original owner of the property buried his pets.

Winemakers: Albert LeComte and Eric von Krosigk

Soil: Light sandy loam, hillside slopes

Acreage: 52

Grape varieties: Gewürztraminer, Bacchus, Seyval Blanc, Müller-Thurgau, Ehrenfelser, Chardonnay, Pinot Blanc, Chelois, Maréchal Foch, Muscat Ottonel, Pinot Noir, Riesling, Gamay Beaujolais

Production: 5,000 cases

Average tonnage crushed: 100

Annual tonnage purchased: 40

Winemaking philosophy: "To produce quality wines. People are more interested in wine and this in turn has made wine producers more interested in creating quality wines."

Wines: BLC: *White*—Bacchus*, Chardonnay, Chenin Blanc, Gewürztraminer*, Gewürztraminer Late Harvest**, Johannisberg Riesling, Müller-Thurgau, Okanagan Riesling*, Pinot Blanc*, Pinot Gris

Red—Chelois, Chelois Private Reserve**, Maréchal Foch, Pinot Noir

Own store: Blanc de Noir, Spice Wine, Kerner, Pinot Meunier, Gewürztraminer Icewine

Store hours: *May and June*: 10:30 am-5 pm (Wednesday through Sunday). *July to April:* 10:30 am-5 pm daily

Tours: *July to October*: 12 pm, 2 pm, 4 pm daily. (Off season, call ahead)

Public tastings: During store hours

Madrona Valley Vineyard

171 Chu An Drive
Saltspring Island, B.C.
V8K 1H9

Telephone: (604) 537-1989

Jim Hamilton has planted half an acre of vines on his farm near Vesuvius on Saltspring Island and intends to plant more annually so that he will have sufficient Müller-Thurgau, Pinot Gris, Chardonnay, Pinot Noir and Ortega to start production. Next year he plans to begin construction of the winery to complement his Victorian-style bed-and-breakfast inn.

Mission Hill Winery

1730 Mission Hill Road   Telephone: (604) 768-7611
Westbank, B.C.   Fax: (604) 768-2044
V4T 2E4

MISSION HILL
Private Reserve

PINOT BLANC

11.5% alc./vol.   750 mL
PRODUCT OF CANADA   WHITE WINE · VIN BLANC   PRODUIT DU CANADA
PRODUCED & BOTTLED BY MISSION HILL WINERY, WESTBANK, OKANAGAN VALLEY, BC V4T 2E4

Mission Hill, one of B.C.'s most beautifully sited wineries, no longer owns vineyards but buys in its grape needs from over 200 contracted growers. This is a large enterprise that thinks like a sophisticated California estate winery and consistently produces award-winning wines. It takes its style from its flamboyant owner, Anthony von Mandl, president of The Mark Anthony Group, a wine, beer, spirit and cider conglomerate which also owns beverage alcohol stores.

Founded in 1966 by a consortium of Okanagan businessmen under chemist R.P. "Tiny" Walrod, Mission Hill has undergone several changes of ownership and name. It was taken over by Ben Ginter in 1970 who called it Uncle Ben's Gourmet Wines and then Golden Valley Wines. His larger-than-life activities in the brewing industry brought the winery close to bankruptcy. Ultimately, he was forced to sell to von Mandl who began to create a new image of quality for the winery, pumping in an investment of $2 million. The original winemaker was Daniel Lagnaz, who studied oenology in his native Switzerland. John Simes, a New Zealander, was lured away from a Montana winery to B.C. in 1992 and is now producing some of B.C.'s finest whites, including the Grand Reserve Chardonnay 1992 that won the Avery Trophy as the best Chardonnay at the International Wine & Spirit competition in London in 1994.

Currently, Mission Hill has 400 French and American Oak barrels with 200 more coming. In 1992, it released its first champagne method sparkling wines — Cuvée Chardonnay and Cuvée Chenin Blanc.

Mission Hill bottles under four labels — Grand Reserve (VQA wines and non-VQA wines), Private Reserve, Vintner's Selection — and has 1,000 oak barrels, mainly American.

Winemaker: John Simes

Production: Over 205,000 cases

Average tonnage crushed: 1,100 - 1,200

Annual tonnage imported: 300 - 400 (mainly Washington fruit)

Winemaking philosophy: "At Mission Hill, we have been inspired by the vision Robert Mondavi brought to the Napa Valley. In this spirit, our focus has been on quality and innovation. As the Okanagan Valley is a relatively young wine producing district, we felt it was important to experiment with a wide variety of *vinifera* varietals, allowing us over time to focus on those wines we believe have the greatest potential. Our focus is principally on dry wines, both white and red, and where we see exceptional potential to produce strictly limited quantities of specialty wines. Our primary objective is to produce wines that show true varietal character and have excellent aging potential."

Wines: **LDB**: *VQA wines white*—Mission Hill Grand Reserve Bacchus Icewine**, Grand Reserve Optima Late Harvest**, Grand Reserve Pinot Blanc*, Grand Reserve White; Private Reserve Chenin Blanc Bin 66*, Private Reserve Late Harvest Riesling**, Private Reserve Pinot Blanc*, Private Reserve Riesling*, Private Reserve Sauvignon Blanc*, Private Reserve Semillon Bin 1*, Private Reserve Chardonnay**, Private Reserve Verdelet/Riesling (organic), Private Reserve Gewürztraminer*; Mission Hill 49 North*

VQA wines red—Mission Hill Grand Reserve Red, Mission Hill Vin Nouveau; Private Reserve Maréchal Foch (organic)

Non-VQA wines white—Mission Hill Private Reserve Chardonnay, Vintners Chablis, Vintners Chenin Blanc, Proprietors' Select White, Vintners Harvest Riesling, Vintners Riesling, Vintners Semillon/Sauvignon, Vintners Traminer/Riesling, Winemakers Reserve White, Mission Ridge Light White, Mission Ridge Premium Dry White

Non-VQA wines red—Mission Hill Private Reserve Cabernet Sauvignon*, Private Reserve Cabernet Sauvignon/Merlot*, Private Reserve Merlot; Mission Hill Vintners Burgundy, Proprietors' Select Red, Vintners Kuhlmann Cabernet; Mission Ridge Premium Dry Red

Rosé—Mission Hill Winemakers Reserve Blush

Own stores: *White*—Grand Reserve Chardonnay**, Grand Reserve Riesling*, Grand Reserve Gewürztraminer*, Grand Reserve Riesling Icewine**; Private Reserve Muscat of Alexandria

Fortified—Private Reserve Dry Sherry, Mark Anthony Aperitif

Stores: (in addition to winery boutique)

Burnaby: Charlie's Wine Cellar, 1120C-4700 Kingsway, Eaton Centre

Coquitlam: Charlie's Wine Cellar, #940 Sunwood Square, 3025 Lougheed Highway

Saanich: Mark Anthony's Winemart, 2560-A Sinclair Rd.

Vancouver: Broadway International Wine Shop, 2752 West Broadway

Granville Island Brewing Company, 1441 Cartwright Street, Granville Island

Marquis Wine Cellars, 1034 Davie St.

North Shore Wine Cellars, Lonsdale Quay Market, 159-123 Carrie Cates Court

White Rock: Mark Anthony's Winemart, Royal Centre, 15220 North Bluff Rd.

Winery store hours: 7 days a week. *May long weekend through June*: 10 am-6 pm. *July and August*: 10 am-8 pm. *September to Thanksgiving*: 10 am-6 pm. *Thanksgiving to May long weekend*: 10 am-4 pm

Tours: May long weekend through June: hourly from 10 am until one hour before closing time. *September to Thanksgiving*: 11 am, 1 pm, 3 pm, 5 pm. *Thanksgiving to May long weekend*: Call for schedule.

Public tastings: During store hours

Newton Croft Vineyards

1595 Newton Heights Road   Telephone: (604) 652-9294
Saanichton, B.C.
V0S 1M0

In 1996, Peter and Wendy Loncroft plan to open their farm winery in Saanichton, which will be British Columbia's most southerly winery. For their 1995 crush they had a half acre of Ortega. Currently in the ground and ready for the '96 crush are half an acre each of Pinot Noir, Pinot Blanc and Pinot Gris.

Nichol Vineyard & Farm Winery

1285 Smethurst Road   Telephone: (604) 496-5962
Naramata, B.C.
V0H 1N0

1992

NICHOL VINEYARD

Cabernet Franc
Okanagan Valley

750 ml   12.3% alc./vol.
Red Wine   Vin Rouge

PRODUCT OF/PRODUIT DU: BRITISH COLUMBIA, CANADA
NICHOL VINEYARD FARM WINERY, NARAMATA, BRITISH COLUMBIA, CANADA V0H 1N0

Alex Nichol, a former symphony double bassist, has long been the conscience of the Okanagan. As a writer he has documented its history in *Wines and Vines of British Columbia* and has worked tirelessly to improve its wines. In 1989, he began to practice what he preached when he acquired his own vineyard with his wife Kathleen, under a granite cliff across the water from the Summerland Research Station. The sun's reflection off the 300-foot rock face and the heat that it holds allows Alex to ripen such warm-climate grape varieties as Syrah (B.C.'s first barrel-aged Syrah). He now makes some of the most powerful, flavourful and majestic wines of the region. His split canopy "Open Lyre" trellising system is unique in the valley. The wines are aged in "reworked" French *barriques*.

Winemaker: Alex Nichol

Acreage: 4.5

Soil: Clay-rich yet stony soil of glacial till.

Grape varieties: Pinot Gris, Pinot Noir, Syrah, Cabernet Franc, Ehrenfelser, St. Laurent

Production: 800 cases

Average tonnage crushed: 16

Winemaking philosophy: "We are dedicated to the production of premium barrel-aged red wines and barrel-fermented and/or *sur lie* white wines. The wines are made as natural as possible. Red wines from the barrel are unfiltered."

Wines: **Own store**: *White*—Pinot Gris, Ehrenfelser, Ehrenfelser Late Harvest
Red—Pinot Noir, Syrah, Cabernet Franc, Clairet (Cabernet Franc, Syrah,
    Pinot Gris), Maréchal Foch-Michurinetz
Specialty wine—Ehrenfelser Select Late Harvest*
Store hours: Seasonal—hours vary
Tours: By appointment only
Public tastings: During store hours

Okanagan Vineyards/Oliver Cellars

RR #1, S24, C5   Telephone: (604) 498-6663
No. 11 Road West   Fax: (604) 498-4566
Oliver, B.C.
V0H 1T0

Mike Daley runs this winery founded in 1984 with its Spanish-style building. The investment comes from a U.K. company, Bimbadex Ltd. The first
vintage of Cabernet Sauvignon, Merlot and Chardonnay will be in 1993.
VQA wines are bottled under the Okanagan Vineyards label. Imported
California and Washington State wines are sold under the Ocean Crest label.

Winemaker: Sandor Mayer

Acreage: 22

Soil: Partially stony soil with light loam, sloping gradually with southern exposure. The vineyard is located a few kilometres from Canada's only desert.

Grape varieties: Cabernet Sauvignon, Merlot, Chardonnay, Johannisberg Riesling, Pinot Noir, Gewürztraminer

Production: 22,000 cases

Average tonnage crushed: 100

Annual tonnage purchased: 100

Winemaking philosophy: "To develop distinct personality for the winery and provide style continuity through the production of high-quality wines."

Wines: **LDB**: *White*—(Okanagan Vineyards) Bacchus, Müller-Thurgau*, Perle of Csaba*

Red—Premium Red (Oliver Cellars) Cabernet Foch Hidden Valley, Maréchal Foch

Winery store: Johannisberg Riesling, Late Harvest Riesling, Verdelet; Cabernet Sauvignon, Merlot, Pinot Noir

Non-VQA—Private Reserve White, Dry Riesling, Oliver Cellars Premium Select, Hidden Valley Mountain Chablis, Johannisberg Riesling, Chardonnay, (4L) Classic Chablis, Medium White, Dry White, Chablis, Premium White, Blanc de Blanc, Ocean Crest, French Colombard, Chardonnay Colombard

Store hours: 10 am-4 pm daily (seasonal)

Tours: May to October

Public tastings: During store hours

Poplar Grove Farm Winery

1060 Poplar Grove Road   Telephone: (604) 492-2352
RR #1
Penticton, B.C.
V2A 6J6

Ian Sutherland's love of claret led him to fly in the face of tradition and plant two and a half acres of Merlot and Cabernet Franc — instead of white varieties — on the eight-acre property he and his wife Gitta bought outside Penticton in 1992. Inspired by his winery-owning neighbours, Bohumir and Vera Klokocka of Hillside Cellars, Ian pulled out apple trees to make way for his red grapes and planted in clay loam soil not unlike that of St. Emilion where the Merlot grape flourishes. His next variety is expected to be Syrah, having witnessed the success that Alex Nichol has had in growing this Northern Rhône variety. Currently planted are Merlot and Cabernet Franc. The winery is projected to be open to the public in the fall of 1997.

Prpich Vineyards

RR #1, S30, C8   Telephone: (604) 497-8246
Okanagan Falls, B.C.
V0H 1R0

Dan Prpich (pronounced Pur-pitch) began his winemaking as an amateur in Hamilton, Ontario, in 1959 using *labrusca* grapes. When he and his family moved to the Okanagan in 1973 he bought his sixty-acre farm and pulled out some of the orchards to plant Okanagan Riesling and Maréchal Foch as well as some Chardonnay and Cabernet Sauvignon from Washington State, and then some Verdelet. He ripped out twenty acres of the hybrids during the pull-out program and then replanted, concentrating on varietals such as Chasselas, Pinot Noir, Merlot as well as preferred hybrids such as Vidal and Seyval Blanc. Further replanting will include Cabernets, Ehrenfelser and Lemberger.

    A new three-storey, gravity-feed winery is planned to open in 1996.

Quails' Gate Vineyards Estate Winery

3303 Boucherie Road   Telephone: (604) 769-4451
RR #1, Site 14   1-800 420-WINE
Kelowna, B.C.   Fax: (604) 769-3451
V1Z 2H3

Quails' Gate is sited on one the region's oldest settlements. The Stewart family first planted the seventy-acre vineyard in 1961 on a site on the west side of Lake Okanagan first chosen by the original pioneers, John and Susan

Allison, in 1873. Their original log cabin homestead has been restored for use as the company's wine shop. When Ben and Ruth Stewart decided to make the leap from grape growers to a farm winery, they hired oenologist Elias Phiniotis as their winemaker. Hungarian-trained Elias, who made wine in his native Cyprus before coming to Canada in 1976, worked for many years at Casabello.

In 1994, the Stewarts hired Jeff Martin as winemaker. Jeff spent fourteen years with McWilliams Wines in New South Wales and became head red winemaker for that company's Barwang winery in 1989. Quails' Gate has undergone extensive construction since 1994. A large, underground cellar stocked with French and American oak has been built and the heritage wine shop has been enlarged using old timber to remain true to the 1873 idiom.

Winemaker: Jeff Martin

Acreage: 70 (total estate 115 acres)

Soil: South sloping exposure with soils varying from clay to sand.

Grape varieties: Riesling, Chasselas, Chardonnay, Pinot Noir, Optima, Chenin Blanc, Gewürztraminer

Production: 11,000 cases

Average tonnage crushed: 150

Annual tonnage purchased: 15

Winemaking philosophy: "To pursue excellence through quality control from grapes to bottle. To provide the means and take the time to offer the market above average to excellent quality wines, packaged in their own personality labels and appearance. To combine wine with heritage and contemporary life style."

Wines: **LDB**: Riesling, Riesling Dry*, Chasselas, De Chaunac-Rougeon*

Own store: Chardonnay*, Pinot Noir, Botrytis Optima

Winery store hours: Monday through Sunday, 10 am-5 pm

Tours: Yes

Public tastings: During store hours

St. Hubertus Vineyard

5225 Lakeshore Road	Telephone: (604) 764-7888
Kelowna, B.C.	1-800-989-WINE
V1Y 7R3	Fax: (604) 764-0499

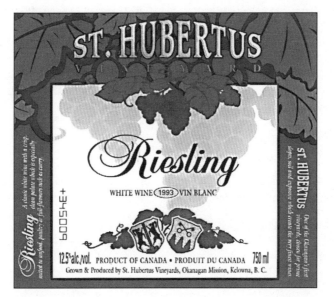

St. Hubertus is named after Leo Gebert's family lodge in Switzerland. The vineyard is located forty metres from the shores of the lake, opposite a public park with a kilometre of beach. Established in 1948 (one of the oldest in the Okanagan, known as the Beau Séjour vineyard), Leo purchased it in 1984. His winery licence was issued in 1992 as St. Hubertus Farm Winery (Hubertus is the Swiss patron saint of hunters). Three years later it changed its status to an estate winery. With his wife Barbara, Leo brings to the Okanagan years of experience in grape-growing from his native country and insists on organic viticulture. The wines produced are very much in Swiss style — clean, dry and crisp. In 1993, Leo made his first Icewine from Bacchus and in 1994 experimented with a red Icewine! Picnic tables for customers are set in the vineyard.

Winemaker: Leo Gebert

Acreage: 32 planted (20 vacant)

Soil: Sandy, close to Lake Okanagan

Grape varieties: Riesling, Bacchus, Pinot Blanc, Verdelet, Gamay Noir, Pinot Meunier, Chasselas, Pinot Meunier, Maréchal Foch

Production: 2,500 cases

Average tonnage crushed: 58 ("25 tons for our own use")

Annual tonnage purchased: 5

Winemaking philosophy: "The Okanagan has an excellent and unique microclimate for growing grapes. We don't have to compete with other wine regions; we simply have to promote our own distinct taste. Since we operate a small cottage winery we know and understand the needs of our customer and are able to give them the wine which matches the wine lover's taste."

Wines: Own store: *White*—Riesling*, Verdelet, Bacchus*, Pinot Blanc*
Red—Gamay Noir, Maréchal Foch**
Specialty wines—Bacchus Icewine, Riesling Icewine

Store hours: *May long weekend to October 15*: 10 am-5:30 pm daily. *October 15 to December 31*: Tuesday to Saturday, noon-5 pm. *January 1 - May long weekend*: Hours vary (call ahead)

Tours: Daily, June to October

Public tastings: During store hours

St. Laszlo Vineyards

RR #1, S95, L8   Telephone: (604) 499-6663
Keremeos, B.C.
V0X 1N0

Joe Ritlop and his family made the first crush at St. Laszlo in 1978 (Joe named the winery after his birthplace in Yugoslavia). They had already planted vineyards in the early 1970s, south of Keremeos on slopes above the Similkameen River, experimenting with a range of hybrid and *vinifera* vines. Joe is considered something of a maverick in the B.C. industry and has followed an independent path from the beginning. He makes his wine organically, using no chemicals in the vineyard and no sulphides, sorbates or preservatives in the cellar. The grapes are fermented on their own yeasts. The St. Laszlo style is full-bodied. Joe's late harvest wines such as Tokay Aszu and Golden Nectar are well worth trying, though costly. He has made Icewine since 1982.

Winemaker: Joe Ritlop

Grape varieties: Tokay, Riesling, Perle of Csaba, Pinot Auxerrois, Chardonnay, Semillon, Sovereign Royal, Verdelet; Maréchal Foch, Rougeon, De Chaunac, Cabernet Franc

Winemaking philosophy: "I will create my wine in my own fashion. I cannot do anything else. We can make as good or better white wines here than any of the European countries."

Scherzinger Vineyards

7311 Fiske Street
Summerland, B.C.
V0H 1Z0

Telephone/fax: (604) 494-8815

Edgar Scherzinger's first love is wood carving, a passion he inherited from his father in the Black Forest. Evidence of his talent can be seen all around the winery's tasting room. In 1974, he and his wife Elizabeth bought a cherry orchard overlooking Summerland. Cherries were a losing proposition, so they planted *labrusca* grapes which produced wines Edgar hesitated to sell to the public. He understood that only *vinifera* would work and took a gamble by planting Gewürztraminer in 1978, at a time when the accepted wisdom was that noble European varieties could not live long in the Okanagan. He sold the fruit to Sumac Ridge and eventually added Chardonnay and Pinot Noir to the vineyard. In 1994 to decided to make the leap from grower to winemaker.

Winemaker: Edgar Scherzinger

Acreage: 6.6 (no pesticides or herbicides, minimal sulphur)

Soil: Coarse sandy soils

Varieties: Gewürztraminer, Chardonnay, Pinot Noir

Production: 460 cases (1995), 900 cases (1996)

Average tonnage crushed: 30

Winemaking philosophy: "Quality in wines."

***Wines*: Own store**: *White*—Gewürztraminer, Gewürztraminer Caroline (sweet), Chardonnay

Red—Pinot Noir
Store hours: 10 am-6 pm
Public tastings: 10 am-6 pm
Tours: Yes

Sumac Ridge Estate Winery

17403 Highway 97, P.O. Box 307	Telephone:	(604) 494-0451
Summerland, B.C.	Fax:	(604) 494-3456
V0H 1Z0		

Harry McWatters has run Sumac Ridge since it foundation in 1980. Originally, grower Lloyd Schmidt was a partner (his son Allan made wine there before moving east to Vineland Estates). Now Bob Wareham has joined the operation. The ample and bearded Harry, who was instrumental in getting Ontario's VQA regulations accepted in B.C., is a leading force in B.C.'s wine industry. Sumac Ridge has a nine-hole public gold course on the property and an in-house restaurant. Players can sample the wines in the clubhouse restaurant as well as wines of competitors.

The winery uses French oak tanks of Limousin and Nevers and is the largest B.C. producer of barrel-fermented Chardonnay. Sumac Ridge was the first B.C. producer to make a *methode classic* sparkling wine. The Pinot Noir goes into the sparkling wines, and Cabernet Franc and Merlot have also been planted. Sumac Ridge is part owner of the Black Sage Vineyards between Oliver and Osayoos.

Winemakers: Mark Wendenberg and Harold Bates
Acreage: 132 (105 producing)

Grape varieties: Chardonnay, Pinot Blanc, Sauvignon Blanc, Gewürztraminer, Riesling, Merlot, Pinot Noir, Cabernet Sauvignon, Cabernet Franc

Average tonnage crushed: 275

Production: 40,000 cases

Winemaking philosophy: "We have attempted to be leaders and innovators with 1) such grapes as Chancellor; 2) new products such as our *methode classic*. We are dedicated to the marriage of food and wine. We produce distinctive wines to complement distinctive food flavours."

Wines: **LDB**: *White*—Chardonnay*, Dry Riesling**, Gewurtzling Po Toe, Gewürztraminer Private Reserve**, Gewürztraminer Dry**, Riesling**, Okanagan Blanc, Perle of Csaba*, Pinot Blanc**, Verdelet**

Red—Chancellor*

Rosé—Okanagan Blush**

Own store: *White*—Chardonnay Private Reserve*, Pinot Blanc Private Reserve*, Elegance (sweet Muscat)

Sparkling—Stellar's Jay Cuvée, Blanc de Blancs*, Blanc de Noirs*

Fortified—Pipe (Chancellor "port")

Store hours: *Winter*: Monday to Friday, 9 am-5 pm; weekends, 11 am-5 pm. *Summer*: Daily, 9 am-7 pm

Tours: *Summer*: Daily, 10 am, noon, 2 pm, 4 pm. *Winter*: On request

Public tastings: During store hours

Summerhill Estate Winery

RR #4, S1, C22   Telephone: (604) 764-8000
4870 Chute Lake Road   1-800-667-3538
Kelowna, B.C.   Fax: (604) 764-2598
V1Y 7R3

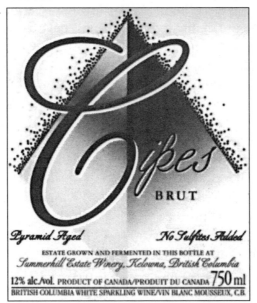

When New Yorker Steve Cipes founded his sparkling wine operation in 1991 at Summerhill Vineyards, south of Kelowna in Okanagan Mission he originally called it Pyramid Cellars after the thirty-foot-high pyramid he had built hard by the vineyard. (His belief is that the perfect shape of the structure adds a dynamic component to the ageing process.) Steve, an indefatigable promoter, chose as his first winemaker a native of the Okanagan, Eric von Krosigk, who had made still and sparkling wines at the German grape research station at Geilweilerhof in the Rheinpfalz and at estates in the Rheingau and Mosel. (Eric's father owns the Okanagan Springs Brewery.) Eric is now the winemaker at LeComte. The new winemaker, Alan Marks, came from the Hermannhof Winery in Missouri.

In its first year of operation Summerhill made 15,000 gallons of base wine from Pinot Noir, Chardonnay and Riesling for their sparkling wines. Small lots of 1,200 to 2,500 gallons are fermented and aged as reserves for the final blends. Apart from award-winning sparkling wine, Summerhill also makes a limited amount of table wine and Icewine from Riesling and Pinot Noir(!). Over 85 percent of its production is champagne-method sparkling wine.

Winemaker: Alan Marks
Acreage: 60 (36 planted)

Soil: A cross-section, sandy loam and chalk. "We use rock dust (glacial) and organic fertilizers."

Grape varieties: Riesling, Ehrenfelser, Chardonnay, Verdelet, Pinot Meunier, Pinot Noir, Gewürztraminer

Production: 20,000 cases

Average tonnage crushed: 225

Annual tonnage purchased: 50 percent

Winemaking philosophy: "Our wines are made from 100 percent B.C. grown grapes without pesticides, herbicides or chemical fertilizers. We use a 1964 Wilmes bladder press at 2 Bar pressure —a gentle press of only the first 65 percent to 70 percent of the juice, assuring no harshness in the wines and bubbles. Our vineyard is certified organic. We age the bubblies in a replica of the Cheops pyramid for thirty to ninety days' "marriage period" after dosage. Daily pyramid taste tests prove noticeable difference in flavour after pyramid aging versus 'square' warehouse ageing."

***Wines*: LDB**: *White*—Nordique Blanc Ehrenfelser, Nordique Riesling*

Sparkling—Cipes Brut**

Own store: *White*—Pinot Blanc*, Gewürztraminer Dry, Chardonnay Reserve*, Riesling**, Late Harvest Riesling**, Ehrenfelser**, Riesling Eis Wein**, Pinot Noir Eis Wein, Pinot Noir Blush**, Gewürztraminer

Red—Pinot Noir**

Sparkling—Summerhill Brut, Cipes Pinot Noir Brut, Cipes Brut de Brut, Cipes Brut Gold Reserve

Store hours: 10 am-6 pm, daily

Tours: Yes, "champagne" making and Pyramid tours

Public tastings: During store hours, every day year round

Sunset Vineyards

c/o International Bag Manufacturers Ltd.
#104-1650 Broadway   Telephone: (604) 941-4666
Port Coquitlam, B.C.
V3C 2M8

Rob Milne, an accountant and co-owner of a company that manufactures plastic wrapping for industry, purchased ninety-two acres south of Oliver — a former terraced vineyard then planted to alfalfa. In 1994, he planted twenty acres of Cabernet Sauvignon, Pinot Noir, Merlot and Chardonnay. The winery is expected to be operational in 1996.

The Vineyard at Bowen Island

P.O. Box 135   Telephone: (604) 947-2398
Bowen Island, B.C.   Fax: (604) 947-0693
N0N 1G0

Larry and Elena Wildman have an acre and a half vineyard on Bowen Island off Horseshoe Bay planted to the three Pinots. Other plots totalling four and a half acres include Gewürztraminer, more Pinot Noir, Ortega and Siegerrebe. The plan for the Waldmans and their neighbours is have twenty acres by the turn of the century. A winery that is currently under construction (with six guest rooms) is expected to open in 1997.

Tinhorn Creek Vineyards

RR #1, S58, C10   Telephone: (604) 498-3743
Oliver, B.C.   Fax: (604) 498-3228
V0H 1T0

Calgary oilman Robert Shaunessy took a businessman's approach to wine and hit the ground running when he bought vast tracts of established vineyard land in 1993, at a time local growers were still smarting from the pullout program of 1988. Inspired by the Napa and Sonoma Valley experience he and his wife Barbara envision the same success for the Okanagan.

With partners Ken and Elizabeth Oldfield, the Shaunessys created one of the largest and most impressive estate wineries in the region. Ken, an Ontario-born chemical engineer who is currently taking his masters in viticulture at UC Davis, looks after the vineyard and the winery. The intention is to grow 60 percent red and 40 percent white *vinifera* varieties and crop at four tons per acre to get intense flavours. All the wines, apart from Gewürz, will spend time in

American oak. The plan is to produce 40,000 cases by the turn of the century. Construction of an 8,500-sq.-ft. winery and tasting room is under way and should be completed by 1997. A restaurant is planned for 1998.

Winemaker: Sandra Cashman (UC Davis-trained)

Acreage: 170 (currently 23 acres producing)

Soil: Fifty acres are within "the Golden Mile," South Okanagan West, side bench lands on rocky slopes; 120 acres on South East Bench, predominantly sand.

Grape varieties: Pinot Gris, Chardonnay, Merlot, Pinot Noir, Kerner, Gewürztraminer, Cabernet Franc, (1996) Pinot Blanc

Production: 1,500 cases (1994); 40,000 cases (2000)

Winemaking philosophy: "To produce only premium vinifera-based red and white table wines by focusing on tightly controlled, low cropping, viticultural practices; and by vinting in an "American" style."

Wines: (1995) *White*—Pinot Gris, Chardonny, Kerner Icewine, (1996) Gewürztraminer

Red—Merlot, Pinot Noir, (1996) Cabernet Franc

Store hours: 10 am-5:30 pm

Tours: Yes

Public tastings: During store hours

Venturi-Schulze Vineyards

4235 Trans Canada Highway   Telephone/Fax: (604) 743-5630
Cobble Hill, B.C.
V0R 1L0

Giordano Venturi, a former electronics instructor from Italy and his wife Marilyn Schulze, an Australian-born microbiologist and French teacher, decided to moved to the tranquility of Vancouver Island in 1988. They purchased a 100-year-old farm near Cowichan Bay and immediately planted a test block of twenty-five grape varieties which they have now narrowed down to twelve. A system of netting and electrified wires protect the small, organically farmed acreage against marauding wildlife. They got their licence in 1993 and began producing wines that are truly hand-crafted, beginning with careful attention to the vineyard. Some French and Slovenian oak are used.

Apart from home-winemaking Giordano has been producing balsamic vinegar for twenty-five years, a nod towards his heritage (he grew up near Modena) and his production is kept well away from the winery in a separate facility. In addition to wine and aged balsamic vinegar bottle-fermented sparkling wine is also produced. Giordano designed and built the riddling machine.

Every V-S bottle carries a tiny pamphlet describing how the wine was made and a profile of the operation. The couple also write an engaging newsletter and offer "special food and wine functions for small groups."

Winemakers: Giordano Venturi and Marilyn Schulze

Acreage: 4.5 planted (3 acres producing in 1995)

Soil: Clay, heavy in part, over deep sand and gravel. South-facing slope cooled by the ocean influence.

Grape varieties: Pinot Noir, Pinot Auxerrois, Pinot Gris, Schönburger, Müller-Thurgau, Madeleine Sylvaner, Siegerrebe, Ortega, small plantings of Kerner, Chasselas, Gewüztraminer, Madeleine Angevine

Production: Over 500 cases

Average tonnage crushed: 9

Winemaking philosophy: "We grow the grapes that we use in our wines without the use of pesticides and herbicides. We take great pride in being personally accountable for every aspect of our operation. The winery philosophy is simple—ensure that the quality of the grapes is reflected in the purity of the wine. We aim for intensity of flavour and cautiously use oak on occasion for added dimension, but not as a condiment. Our techniques vary depending on our focus for each wine; some varieties benefit from extended lees contact, others do not. In our whites, we generally avoid skin contact and press very lightly. Our reds are destemmed manually to avoid incorporating green stem tannins into the wine."

Wines: **Own store**: *White*—Madeleine Sylvaner, Schönburger, Kerner, Siegerrebe, Millefiori (Madeleine Angevine/Siegerrebe), Pignoletto Aromatico (Schönburger, Ortega, Gewürztraminer)

Red—Pinot Noir (expected release 1997)

Sparkling—Brut Naturel Black Label (Pinot Auxerrois, Chasselas, Pinot Gris), Brut Naturel White Label (100% Müller-Thurgau), Brut Naturel Old Cuvée (Black Label blend)

Store hours: By appointment only

Tours and tastings: "Welcomed for individuals and small groups when product is available, but strictly by appointment."

Vigneti Zanatta

5039 Marshall Road
RR #3
Duncan, B.C.
V9L 2X1

Telephone: (604) 748-2338
Fax: (604) 746-5684

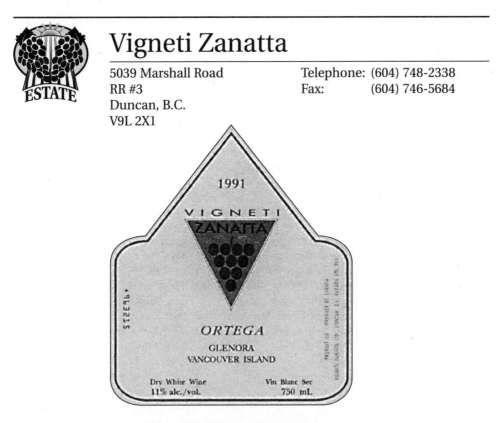

Dennis Zanatta, a native of Treviso in northern Italy, and his wife Claudia bought a dairy farm in the Cowichan Valley on Vancouver Island in 1959 and began planting experimental vines. In 1983, he took part in a government-sponsored trial program to see what varieties were sustainable on the island. Among the grapes planted were five acres of Ortega and Cayuga which flourished. Now the Zanatta family operates a twenty-five-acre vineyard and winery (the oldest on the island) which is under the guiding hand of daughter Loretta, who studied oenology in Italy. The historic family home, built in 1903, houses the wine shop.

Winemaker: Loretta Zanatta

Acreage: 25

Soil: Sandy loam, south facing rolling slope

Grape varieties: Ortega, Cayuga, Pinot Noir, Pinot Auxerrois, Siegerrebé, Pinot Gris, Castel, Leon Millot

Winemaking philosophy: "Our goal is to produce quality wines with exceptional regional character. We achieve this by using only Vancouver Island grapes and unrushed winemaking techniques which allow for complete expression of the wines."

Wines: **Own store:** Ortega

Sparkling—Glenora Fantasia

Public tastings and tours: By appointment

Vincor International

Box 1650   Telephone: (604) 498-4981
Oliver, B.C.   Fax: (604) 498-6505
V0H 1T0

(For details on Vincor, see Ontario section, page 90)

Brights Wines (B.C.) Ltd.

Box 1650   Telephone: (604) 498-4981
Oliver, B.C.   Fax: (604) 498-6505
V0H 1T0

Brights' contemporary-rustic 45,000-sq.-ft. building stands in splendid soli-tude in a wilderness of pine-clad granite mountains and arid plains in southern B.C. On the wall by the entrance hangs a framed photograph showing the chief of the Osoyoos Indian Band, Sam Baptiste, shaking hands with the then managing director of Brights, Ed Arnold. It is dated May 14, 1982, the official opening date of the winery (although the company had 1981 wines on the market, produced at the winery before the roof was on.)

The Indian Band farms the Inkameep vineyard adjacent to the winery. This vineyard is the largest in the Okanagan, 200 acres of which are con-tracted to Brights. Lynn Bremmer, B.C.'s first female winemaker, presided over the winemaking for eleven years until 1992, when Frank Supernak became head winemaker.

As in Ontario, Brights has been in the forefront of experimentation and grape research, the fruits of which appear as limited-edition wines under the Brights label. A small amount of Vidal Icewine is made.

Brights' B.C. plant is also the largest cider producer in Canada and is used by Inniskillin for their B.C. wine production.

Winemaker: Frank Supernak

Acreage: 200 acres contracted

Soil: Ranges from sandy to clay

Production: 492,000 cases

Average tonnage crushed: 900

Annual tonnage purchased: 2,000 — from California and Washington

Winemaking philosophy: "The Okanagan Valley in the south central B.C. area of Canada has unique geographical and climatological variations, making it well suited to the production of premium grape vines. To produce a great wine, vines must be grown near the northern limit of their cultural adaptability. Vincor realizes that they are in a global market. We purchase wines from around the world for our marketplace — unique to Canada in that we bring in the raw material to Canada and process it here to keep jobs here."

Wines: *LDB*: *White*—Cuvée du Berceau, Entre Lacs, Entre-Lacs Classic Chardonnay, Entre-Lacs Classic Sauvignon Blanc, Entre-Lacs Classic Chablis, Dry House White, Liebesheim, Classic Light, Manor St. David Medium Dry, Toscano Bianco, Toscano Light,

Sawmill Creek label: Chardonnay

Red—Entre Lacs, Entre-Lacs Classic Burgundy, Classic Cabernet Sauvignon, Toscano Rosso

Sawmill Creek label: Merlot

Sparkling: Vaseaux Cellars Okanagan Champagne, Blackcomb Private Reserve Vaseaux Cellars

Fortified: Pale Dry Select, '67 Sherry, '74 Sherry, '74 Port

Winery store: Optima, Ste. Michelle Bacchus, California House Red & White

Vaseaux Cellars label—Kerner*, Ehrenfelser, Rkatsiteli, Matsvani, Perle of Csaba, Bacchus, Gewürztraminer, Müller-Thurgau, Schonburger, Sereksia Chornaya

Ste. Michelle label: Monta Rosa Chablis, Monta Rosa Burgundy, Ste. Michelle Johannisberg Riesling**, Le Villageois, Spumante, B.S. Rich Red, Toscano Bianco, Toscano Rosso

Store hours: *September to April*: Monday to Friday, 8 am-4 pm; *May to August*: Monday through Sunday, 8 am-5 pm

Tours: Summer months only (May to August)

Public tastings: *May to September*, 9 am-5 pm daily

Cartier Wines & Beverages

P.O. Box 1650
Highway #97 North
Oliver, B.C.
V0H 1T0

Telephone: (604) 498-49810621
Fax: (604) 492-6990

In 1966, a new company called Southern Okanagan Wines crushed its first grapes in Penticton. One year later, the winery changed its name to Casabello. Located on the town's Main Street, it became a major tourist attraction. Purchased by Labatts in 1973, the winery became the B.C. arm of Ridout Wines, which included Ontario's Château-Gai operation. In 1989, the winery was bought by the management team who ran both wineries (see Cartier Wines & Beverages in Ontario), and in 1993 it was merged with Brights under the Vincor International umbrella.

The company produces a wide range of bulk-blended wines, but is concentrating on some good VQA products under the Jackson-Triggs label. The range of varietals includes Riesling, Pinot Blanc, Chardonnay, Late Harvest Gewürztraminer, Late Harvest Ehrenfelser, Merlot and a Blanc de Noir blend of Bacchus and Soreksia Chomoya. International blends are also made under the Jackson-Triggs label (Chardonnay, Cabernet Sauvignon and Merlot), so the company is going to make it a little easier on the consumer by offering a three-tier Jackson-Triggs labelling system: a VQA label, a super-premium VQA label, and a label for off-shore varietal blends.

Winemaker: Bruce Nicholson

Production: 500,000 cases

Average tonnage crushed: 300 tons of B.C. grapes (American fruit bought in as required)

Winemaking philosophy: "Quality wines require commitment and involvement. Our grape growers, processing and bottling employees work together to achieve the highest standards possible."

***Wines*: LDB**: *White*—Adagio, Alpenweiss, Capistro, Capistro Dry, Capistro

Light, Chenin Blanc, Gala Dry, Gala Medium, Gewürztraminer*, L'Ambiance, White Riesling*

Casabello label: Chablis Blanc, Gala Dry, Gala Medium, L'Escapade, Osoyoos Select Dry, San Gabriel, Summerland Riesling

Red—Okanagan Reserve Chancellor**, Gala Medium Dry, L'Ambiance

Casabello label: Burgon Rouge, Gala Italian, Gala (Dry, Medium, Rich), Osoyoos Select Dry, Regal

Jackson Triggs label: *White*—Reserve Chardonnay*, Dry Riesling, Pinot Blanc*, Chenin Blanc, Gewürztraminer, Late Harvest Gewürztraminer, Late Harvest Ehrenfelser, Johannisberg Riesling Icewine*

Red—Merlot**, Reserve Cabernet Sauvignon

Fortified: Bounty, Private Stock Sherry*, Hallmark Cream Sherry

Imported wines: (French) Chantonné white and red; Cuvée Sélectionée white and red; (Germany) Weinkeller; (California) San Gabriel California Chablis

Store hours: Monday to Friday, 8 am-2 pm (off-season); 8 am-5 pm (summer months)

Tours: Yes

Public tastings: During store hours

Wild Goose Vineyards

RR #1, S3, Cll   Telephone: (604) 497-8919
Okanagan Falls, B.C.   Fax: (604) 497-6853
V0H 1R0

Along with Guenther Lang and the Klokockas, Adolf Kruger was one of the pioneers of the farm winery concept in B.C. A consulting engineer and talented

amateur winemaker formerly from Kehrberg in East Germany, Adolf was forced to make his hobby a profession when a downturn in the economy left him without work in electrical engineering. With his sons Roland and Hagen, he opened Wild Goose Vineyards in June 1990, days after Lang Vineyards started up as the first farm winery in Canada. Adolf had realized his dream of turning his vineyard (planted in 1984) into a winery to take advantage of free trade possibilities. He represents the farm wineries on the B.C. Wine Institute board.

The winery has twelve French oak barrels.

Winemaker: Adolf Kruger

Acreage: 10

Soil: Riesling has a southern exposure on rocky soil which absorbs a lot of heat during the day and releases it in the evening. Gewürztraminer is planted in clay-like soil with scattered stones. Very hot summers.

Grape varieties: Riesling, Gewürztraminer

Production: 1,100 cases

Average tonnage crushed: 15

Annual tonnage purchased: 3

Winemaking philosophy: "As a small family winery, we take much pride in the wines we vint. Minimal filtration is used and all production is done by the family unit. Trying to produce the best wines possible, no wine will be bottled or sold before it passes our strict tasting standards. People visiting our winery are given personal treatment and always are met by one of the smiling family members."

Wines: **Own store:** Johannisberg Riesling Dry and Semi-Dry, Gewürztraminer, Pinot Blanc, Maréchal Foch

Store hours: 10 am-5 pm

Tours: By appointment

Public tastings: During store hours

BULK WINE PRODUCER

Wolf Creek Cellars

1093 Laburnum Avenue   Telephone: (604) 941-2252
Port Coquitlam, B.C.   Fax: (604) 941-WINE
V3B 1K2

Paul Warwick, a wine educator, teamed up with one of his students, Brent Nelson, to create a bulk wine operation housed in a 5,000-sq.-ft. facility in Burnaby. The finished wines — destined to be sold in large format to restaurants, bars and wine stores — will be imported from California, South Africa and South America and blended with B.C. wines. A vineyard in the southern Okanagan is planned where Paul wants to grow Pinot Noir, Chardonnay, Ehrenfelser, Riesling and Gewürztraminer (from which he intends to make a sparkling wine) for a line of VQA products.

QUEBEC

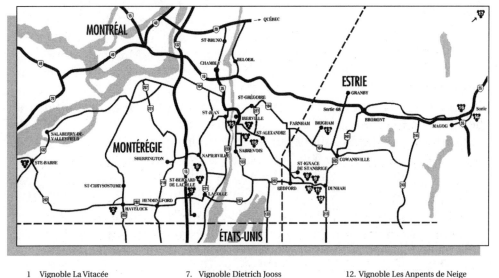

1 Vignoble La Vitacée	7. Vignoble Dietrich Jooss	12. Vignoble Les Anpents de Neige
2. Vignoble du Marathonien	8. Vignoble de l'Orpailleur	13. Vignoble La Bauge
3. Vignoble Angell	9. Vignoble Les Blancs Coteaux	14. Vignoble Le Cep D'Argent
4. Vignoble Morou	10. Vignoble Domaine des Côtes	15. Vignoble St-Alexandre
5. Vignoble Le Royer St-Pierre	d'Ardoise	16. Vignoble Sous les Charmilles
6. Vignoble des Pins	11. Vignoble Les Trois Clochers	17. Le Vignoble Angile

WINE REGIONS OF QUEBEC

When you think of Canadian wine, images of Ontario's Niagara Peninsula or B.C.'s Okanagan Valley spring readily to mind. With a little imagination, perhaps you might conjure up Nova Scotia's Annapolis Valley or the Northumberland Strait.

But wine made from grapes in Dunham, Quebec?

The idea that they actually grow wine in the Eastern Townships eighty km southeast of Montreal is not only a revelation to most Canadians, but an ongoing source of amazement to virtually all the 3,108 inhabitants of this old Loyalist village.

Dunham is to Quebec what Bordeaux is to France — in microcosm: the epicentre of the province's wine industry, accounting for nearly half of all bottles bearing Quebec labels. Since 1985, a number of licensed cottage wineries have mushroomed along the Vermont-New York State border from Ste-Barbe to Sherbrooke.

Although some wineries have just opened, some closed, and others have merely changed hands, the number of enterprises seems to have momentarily stabilized at seventeen, of which fifteen are members of l'Association des Vignerons du Québec. The association, which brings the vignerons together to share knowledge on growing vines and making wine in Quebec's "special" climate, also makes volume equipment purchases to save money for its members. As well, the association publishes a pamphlet outlining Quebec's wine route, on which most of the wineries figure.

A few more wineries were expected to have come on line by now, but viticultural problems have slowed things up. For example: one winery that had — rather naively — planted the tender Muscadet/Melon de Bourgogne *vinifera* as their sole grape variety, lost over 75 percent of the young plantation to the horrible winter of 1993-94.

It's stories like these — of which there are many — that remind us that these men and women are heroic pioneers. These are the people with the vision that turned this rolling landscape of farms and orchards into vineyards, produce some 250,000 bottles a year, roughly the annual output of Château Mouton-Rothschild in the Médoc. But Quebec makes 90 percent white wine, mostly from the hybrid Seyval Blanc grape, and its vignerons accomplish the feat against horrendous odds, not the least of which is the bureaucratic indifference of the provincial liquor board — but more of that later.

The winemakers themselves speak lovingly yet defensively about their magnificent obsession — an obsession that the *Montreal Gazette*'s wine columnist, Malcolm Anderson, affectionately calls "a fine madness." The terms "artisanal" and "marginal" are often used when they refer to the wines and the *terroir* that provides them, because there is something Quixotic about the compulsion to make wine in Quebec, a place of snow and polar temperatures where winter's only harvest used to be maple syrup. But soon the winter harvest may be Icewine if the dreams of Jacques Breault and his highly motivated colleagues are realized. Icewine could be the saviour of the Quebec wine industry which currently exists from vintage to vintage on its novelty value rather than the quality and price of its products. Nine dollars or more for a fresh, young wine similar in style to a Muscadet is a hefty charge for a domestic Seyval, especially when a Sauvignon Blanc or Chardonnay from Chile, Southern France or South Africa can be had for a similar amount. But Montrealers are showing the flag by taking the bridge south for a day in the country and bringing back a few bottles as souvenirs.

Winemaking in Quebec is not a twentieth-century phenomenon. In 1535, when Jacques Cartier sailed down the St. Lawrence on his second voyage to New France, he anchored off "a great island" where he found wild *labrusca* grape vines growing up the trees.

Various attempts at establishing a wine industry in Lower Canada were tried during the eighteenth and nineteenth centuries, but these were abandoned because of the severity of the climate. Ice can split the trunk of a vine stock and even the hardiest *labrusca* plants are susceptible to winter kill. A vine will only grow in temperatures of ten degrees Celsius or higher and it requires a certain number of sunshine hours during the growing season to ripen the fruit. The average Quebec sunshine hours during this season are approximately 930, but in Dunham and Magog the figure rises to 1150 (in Bordeaux the average sunshine hours are 2069). Dunham's secret, along with the other growing regions in Quebec, is microclimate — highly localised topographical features that create warm spots and allow a vine to thrive. These features could be a body of water near a vineyard that stores up heat during the summer and acts like a hot water bottle during the winter as well as reflecting the sun's rays onto the vines, or it could be a warm wind that blows down the valley from Montreal, or a well-protected south-facing slope.

But the problem of winter and frozen vines remains. The most radical measure to safeguard the plants is burial — to cut them back after the harvest and cover them with earth until the Spring. The operation is called "hilling"; that is, banking earth over the roots by back-ploughing between the rows of vines, an exercise that costs the grower at least four cents a plant to cover and another four cents to uncover.

The concept of hilling was brought to Quebec by an oenologist from the South of France, Hervé Durand, who had learned of it in Russia and China. In 1980, he purchased a farm in Dunham and two years later planted a vineyard. His neighbour Frank Furtado was so intrigued that he bought into the dream and with winemaker Charles-Henri de Coussergues (and later Pierre Rodrigue) founded what has become Quebec's most successful winery. The enterprise owes it name to the province's renowned singer-poet, Gilles Vigneault, who told Durand, "To make wine in Quebec is like panning for gold."

L'orpailleur is the French term for those who search for gold by panning (literally, "gold washer"), an apt metaphor for the time, patience and skill it takes to extract wine from the soil of *la belle province*.

Literally next door, Pierre Genesse and his wife Marie-Claude own Les Blancs Coteaux, a *bijou* winery with a production of 6,000 bottles. Twenty-four-year-old Pierre, another Ste-Hyacinthe graduate, learned his wine-making in Burgundy while picking grapes in the Mâconnais. All his products are hand labelled, including the vinegar, jams and jellies, dried flowers and herbs he and his wife sell from their beautiful old farmhouse. In addition, they offer picnic tables for those guests who want to spend a pleasant moment outdoors with a glass of wine and some gourmet products from their *boutique champêtre*.

Further east on Route 202 towards the town of Dunham is Domaines de Côtes d'Ardoise, a name that speaks to the slaty soil in the eight-hectare vineyard shaped like an amphitheatre. This unique landscape configuration, Dr. Jacques Papillon will assure you, permits an extra two weeks of growing season over his competitors.

The vineyard was originally planted by Papillon and Christian Barthomeuf, a self-taught winemaker from Arles in southern France, whose former career was as a film producer. He came to Quebec on sabbatical in 1974 and stayed. He planted the Domaine in 1977, remaining with Papillon as winemaker until the early 1990s.

Incidentally, Barthomeuf, after his split with the Domaine de Côtes d'Ardoise, tried working with a couple of apple producers (Dunham is a region carpeted with orchards) and has settled in at La Pommelière which is, ironically, just a kilometre down the road from Les Côtes d'Ardoise. There he makes what may just be the world's first "ice wine" made from apples. Although reviewing all of Quebec's mead, fruit wine and cider producers is beyond the scope of this book, it should be noted that Barthomeuf's apple "ice wine," selling at $9.90 for a Niagara look-alike half-bottle, is a delicious, rich, glycerine-laden nectar, with a warm, spiced butter and cream finish.

Another kilometre east and you can stop into Dunham's newest vineyard, Les Trois Clochers, a name which refers to the bell towers of the three churches of Dunham. Here, Claude Rhéaume and Réal Normandeau offer a crisp Seyval, as well as a fragrant, yeasty strawberry wine.

Once in the town of Dunham, head up the hill to the Vignoble Les Arpents de Neige, a name that resonates with French history ("a few acres of snow" were not worth fighting for, according to French King Louis XIV's advisors.) Originally planted by Jacques Breault, who once worked for l'Orpailleur, Les Arpents de Neige went into bankruptcy and was bought in 1992 by Gilles Séguin, a restaurateur who, with the help of his French winemaker, Jean Paul Martin, made a very good Seyval in 1994. As well, Séguin offers — naturally — meals for groups who book ahead.

Just north of Dunham you can visit Vignoble La Bauge, where wine is a passionate sideline for Alcide and Ghislaine Naud, whose main occupation is raising *sanglier* (wild boar), as well as llamas, highland cattle and many other exotic farm animals, including a chicken with fur!

The most northerly vineyard in the Eastern Townships (Cantons de l'Est) is the Cep d'Argent in the Magog/Sherbrooke vicinity, where French (Champagne) know-how combines with Quebecer ingenuity to make a solid range of wines.

The Montérégie

The Montérégie is emerging as a separate wine region in its own right; it already has eight vineyards to the Townships' eight! The Montérégie are a series of extinct volcanos (Mont-Royal, which forms the Island of Montreal, is the best known) that jut suddenly and impressively out of the vast, flat plains that run from Montreal south to the U.S. border. Essentially a region of market "salad bowl" gardens and grain farmers (unlike the dairy country of the Eastern Townships), Le Montérégie is hardly somewhere you drive through on the way to "cottage country," yet thousands of Montrealers are nevertheless slowly discovering the vinous riches of the region.

Although the soil is made up largely of black earth and heavy clay, hardly ideal for winemaking, if the viticultural property is well chosen, there are soils that include deposits of sand and small stones in their makeup, debris left behind by the receding waters of Lake Champlain and the St. Lawrence River, both of which entirely covered the Montérégie some 60,000 years ago.

Now, while it is an established fact that almost every vigneron will tell you that they have *the* warmest microclimate in Quebec, it is becoming clear — even at this early stage in the young wineries' history — that the Montérégie is marginally warmer than the Dunham region. What remains unclear is whether this is due to the more southerly location, or to the fact that air currents are warmed as they pass over Montreal.

This does not necessarily mean that the wines produced here are better than those in Dunham, but only that some different characteristics are beginning to emerge in the wines. The Montérégie's Seyvals, for instance, seem to be somewhat rounder and fuller, while those of Dunham have more intense, mineral and white pepper bouquets. Another of the distinguishing features of the Montérégie is that grapes such as Cayuga and Vidal — as well as two Geisenheim clones from Germany — are beginning to be grown here while they are virtually ignored in Dunham.

One of the Montérégie's best wineries is Vignoble Dietrich-Jooss. Victor and Christiane hail from Ingersheim, in Alsace, where they learned the family business — making wine. Their Quebec wines are typically Alsatian, with just a kiss of residual sugar to balance perfectly the naturally high acidity of the grapes. In their beautiful France-meets-North-America-styled winery, just a kilometre or two from the wide Richelieu River, they make six elegant wines that set the standard for their neighbours. The Cuvée Stephanie, named after their winemaker-to-be daughter, is a light but luscious Vendange Tardive wine that falls somewhere between a late-harvest wine and an Icewine in style.

Nearby neighbour, the Piedmont-born Domenic Agarla, runs Vignoble St. Alexandre, which specializes in red wine from the hybrid De Chaunac grape. A few kilometres away, Gilles Benoit runs Vignoble des Pins, where he makes some fine Seyval and Méthode Champenoise Sec sparkler on his small, but extremely well-cared-for, property.

Further south, across the Richelieu River, Vignobles Le Royer-St. Pierre are turning out a lovely, scented wine from the Cayuga grape, while Étienne Héroux at Vignoble Morou is making whites with finesse and elegance rare in Quebec, as well as some light but sensuous reds.

Even further south, near Lacolle (the "Glue"), a town that is practically soldered to the U.S. border, hard-working Jean-Guy Angell and his son Guy are also turning some good wines.

At Le Marathonien (the Marathon-runner), smack in the middle of apple country near Havelock and Hemmingford, Jean and Line Joly are making nice wines that rival the quality of those of their mentor, Victor Dietrich-Jooss. Réjean Gagnon has taken over La Vitacée, which remains Quebec's only vineyard dedicated to finding grape varieties that do not need to be "hilled." With the help of Luc Rolland, who also vinifies at Le Bauge, he turns out Quebec's deepest-coloured red, the Rhône-style(!) Barbe-Rouge.

A Note on Hybrids

Quebec's difficulty in bringing grapes to full maturity (i.e., without the need to chaptalise; that is, to add sugar during fermentation to bring up the alcohol level) is proving something of a boon; vignerons are noticing that wines from varieties such as the American-bred Cayuga are not showing any musky, foxy, *labrusca* characteristics that appear when they are fully ripe or overripe, as they would be in Niagara, Ont., British Columbia, or even the New York Finger Lakes regions. Maréchal Foch, De Chaunac, Seyval and other hybrids also show pure fruit flavours in Quebec.

The SAQ, Taxes and the Future

What makes the wineries of Dunham and their confrères in other parts of Quebec "marginal" are the regulations under which they are forced to operate. While most sell all the wines they can produce, they have to rely on the passing tourist traffic and the sale of sweatshirts and other souvenirs (Vignoble de la Bauge in Brigham offers homemade wild boar pâté!) to stay in business. But the only place they can sell what they produce is at the winery, which means their customers have to come to them. The provincial liquor board is not interested in carrying the products, and restaurants are frightened off by the monstrously high handling charge the SAQ insists upon to supply the local wines to the hospitality industry. Yet for all the difficulties presented by God and man, the winemakers of Quebec are buoyant about their future. Quebec's wine regions may never be the Napa Valley or even Niagara-on-the-Lake — unless global warming accelerates to a point where the region of L'Estrie enjoys as many sunshine hours as Bordeaux — but it will continue to provide a cottage industry of growing confidence and quality. The wines are fresh and well made and they speak to the soil and the climate in which they are produced.

However, in all fairness, it must be said, for the SAQ's part, that letting the wineries sell at the farm gate (at a very low tax rate) is a form of protectionism that allows Quebec vineyards to price their wine competitively, despite their horrendously high costs of burying and unearthing their vines each year. Some vignerons are happy with this status quo; others rally for change, including the right to deliver their wines to customers.

Most will privately acknowledge that the real opposition to their plans is not coming solely from the SAQ, but from the *transformeurs* — the long-established bigger wineries that own no vines in Quebec yet "make" and blend "Quebec" wines sold in the province's corner-stores from concentrate, must and bulk wine imported from California, Chile and God knows where else.

The viticultural scene in Quebec is undeniably thriving; medals from Intervin and the Atlanta Wine Summit bear testimony to that fact. Add that to the recent *jumellage* (twinning) of the region with Graves in Bordeaux (where the high quality of the Sauvignon-like Seyval shocked many a Bordeaux vigneron with lower expectations of Quebec wines) and the future looks bright.

With most vignerons still selling out the lion's share of each vintage before the next vintage comes along — all at the winery door — the vineyards are slowly becoming financially viable. As the vines age and the vignerons become more confident vinifying under Quebec's unique set of circumstances, the wines just keep getting better.

Quebec Wineries

Don't miss the opportunity to visit the wineries of Quebec — even if you don't speak French. All Quebec winemakers and their colleagues enjoy receiving English-speaking visitors whether their command of the language varies from the tentative to the flawlessly fluent. The language of wine, after all, is universal.

LEGEND

** Gold Medal Winning wine in competition
* Silver or Bronze Medal winning wine in competition

The type and/or winery is indicated by the symbol accompanying the winery's profile.

Domaines des Côtes d'Ardoise

879, Route 202   Telephone: (514) 295-2020
C.P. 189   Fax: (514) 845-6307
Dunham, Quebec
J0E 1M0

Ardoise means slate, which speaks to the soil of Dr. Jacques Papillon's horseshoe-shaped vineyard behind the weathered old barn that acts as winery and tasting room. Christian Bartomeuf, a film producer from Arles, came to Quebec in 1974 on sabbatical and stayed. He bought the farm in 1977 with Jacques Papillon, a Montreal plastic surgeon, and planted the vineyard two years later.

Hybrids were first planted, but Jacques is convinced that his particular microclimate can support the noble European varieties, so in 1983 he put in Riesling, Chardonnay, Gamay and Pinot Noir.

The winery offers an unusually large number of products for a Quebec enterprise of this nature. The winemaker, Patrick Barrelet, was trained in Dijon and worked in Puligny-Montrachet. He took over from Bartomeuf in 1991 and looks after the vineyards, the winery and the commercial aspects. His red wines are aged in Limousin oak.

Winemaker: Patrick Barrelet

Acreage: 20

Soil: Slatey, north-facing slope in a natural amphitheatre

Grape varieties: Aurore, Seyval Blanc, De Chaunac, Maréchal Foch, Riesling, Gamay, Vidal

Average tonnage crushed: 25

Production: Approximately 1,600 cases

Winemaking philosophy: In the vineyard is a printed sign: "*The only thing on earth that I know is serious is the culture of the vine.* (Voltaire)"

Wines: *White*—La Maredoise (Aurore with Seyval, Gamay or Riesling), Carte d'Or Seyval (oak-aged)**, Riesling

Red—Haute Combe (Maréchal Foch/De Chaunac), Côte d'Ardoise (Maréchal Foch/Gamay oak-aged), Estafette (fortified vin doux naturel from five varieties)

Specialty wines—Vidal Icewine

Store: Yes (restaurant open June to September)

Tours: Group reservations (four or more) from May 15 to October 15. Wine and cheese visits, tours with meals etc. by reservation.

Public tastings: Yes

La Vitacée

816 Chemin de l'Eglise   Telephone: (514) 373-8429
Sainte-Barbe, Quebec
VOS 1P0

Two biochemists from the Université de Montréal, Robert Cedergren and the late Roger Morazain, created this bijou operation in 1979 when they planted their original vineyard. In spite of the size of their winery, they have done much to increase the knowledge of what varieties will thrive in Quebec's difficult growing conditions with their experimental plantings of esoteric hybrids. Réjean Gagnon — a former customer of the winery — and Alain Loiselle are the new owners. Réjean has continued Roger's work of experimentation in the vineyard, growing hybrids high on a trellis without hilling in winter (unheard of in Quebec!). The buds are kept from freezing by the heat of a string of sixty-watt bulbs suspended from the top wire. He has plans to enlarge the vineyard to four times its current size as well as providing visitors with a self-guided tour and shaded picnic spots for hot summer days.

The red wines are aged in Missouri oak.

Winemakers: Réjean Gagnon and Alain Loiselle (with oenologist Luc Rolland)

Acreage: 10

Microclimate: Situated near Lac Saint-François in the warmest region of Quebec; gravelly soil with some clay. Lightly sloped Montérégie vineyard.

Grape varieties: De Chaunac, St. Croix, Kay Gray, Saint-Pépin, Lacrosse

Production: 2,500 bottles

Winemaking philosophy: "Since its foundation, our principal activity has been to concentrate on evaluating new hybrid varieties that don't need winter protection and have the potential to produce good wines. While continuing to evaluate these new varieties, we have begun planting larger quantities of those grapes we have kept and production ought to increase in the coming years."

Wines: Barbe-Rouge, Barbe-Blanc, Barbe-Rosé

Winery store hours: *April to December,* Tuesday to Sunday, 12 am-5 pm

Tours: Yes

Public tastings: During store hours

Le Vignoble Angile

267, 2e. Rang Ouest (Route 218)   Telephone/fax: (418) 884-2583
Saint-Michel-de-Bellechasse, Quebec
G0R 3S0

Since 1985, André Lefevbre has made fruit wines from his twenty acres of strawberries and raspberries as well as blended table wines from three eso-teric hybrids, including two Russian varieties — the *riparia* Eona and Michurinetz — which Roger Dial introduced to the Grand Pré vineyard in Nova Scotia's Annapolis Valley back in the late 1970s. The winery is a thirty-five-minute drive east of Quebec City.

All the wines are made in stainless steel.

Winemaker: André Lefevbre

Acreage: 5.5 (vines); 20 (soft fruit)

Soil: gravelly; south facing slope

Grape varieties: Eona, Minnesota, Michurinetz

Production: 500 cases

Average tonnage crushed: 3

Winemaking philosophy: "My objective is to produce 15,000 bottles a year."

Wines: **Own store**: Cuvée d'Angile Blanc (Sec), Cuvée d'Angile Rouge (Sec)

Fruit wines—Picoline (14% alcohol, strawberry), Ambrosia (14% alcohol, strawberry and raspberry with maple syrup), Grand Frisson (14% alcohol, raspberry)

Store hours: Saturday and Sunday, 9 am to 6 pm (open seven days a week from June to August)

Tours: By reservation, $5 per person

Public tastings: During store hours

Vignoble Angell

134 Rang St-Georges   Telephone (Montreal):
St-Bernard de Lacolle, Quebec   (514) 522-1012
J0J 1V0   (Vineyard): (514) 246-4219

Jean-Guy Angell is one of the original Quebec vignerons. He planted 200 vines in 1978 and opened his doors in 1985 with the requisite 5,000 vines. He now has 32,000 in the ground with 15,000 more currently being planted. This is the largest family-owned vineyard in Quebec. Jean Guy's son, Guy, is poised to take over the winemaking duties from his father, who still oversees and plans the running of the estate. Jean-Guy swears that their New York-border vineyard in Montérégie gives them a three-week advantage over Dunham, and certainly their 1992 white won a signal honour: it was chosen to be served in the Quebec legislature. In 1995, the ever-industrious Jean-Guy (who also owns a string of karate schools across Canada) has expanded the barrel-aging room in the rock-floored cellar of his traditional Québecois stone house, as well as adding a banquet room where he serves Méchoui (spit-roasted marinated lamb.)

Winemakers: Jean-Guy and Guy Angell

Acreage: 18 (9 in production)

Soil: A mixture of sand, black earth and clay. Typically flat Montérégie vineyard.

Grape varieties: Seyval Blanc, Vidal, Chardonnay, De Chaunac, Merlot, Pinot Noir (currently on trial)

Production: 20,000 - 25,000 bottles

Wines: **Own store**: Vignoble Angell Blanc, Vignoble Angell Rouge

Tours: Yes; picnic facilities, wine and cheese tasting

Vignoble de l'Orpailleur

1086 Route 202   Telephone: (514) 295-2763
Dunham, Quebec   Fax: (514) 295-3112
J0E 1M0

Hervé Durand, a winemaker from Avignon who studied in Dijon and taught oenology in Argentina, bought the Dunham farm in 1980 and planted his vineyard two years later. His neighbour, Frank Furtado, an impressario who puts on firework displays, was so intrigued by the notion that he became a

partner. Later publisher Pierre Rodrigue bought in, and with French wine-maker Charles-Henri de Coussergues the winery has become the commercial leader in the province. Gilles Vigneault inadvertently named the enterprise when he told Hervé, "making wine in Quebec is like panning for gold." L'Orpailleur is a man who does just that.

A white woodframe farmhouse stands in front of a modern cedar-built winery with a magnificent terrace where you can dine on summer days. The store sells sweatshirts and other winery memorabilia. French and American oak barrels are used.

Winemaker: Charles-Henri de Coussergues

Acreage: 24

Soil: Sand and gravel. The soil is very dry and warm, gentle slopes.

Grape variety: Seyval Blanc

Production: 6,500 cases

Average tonnage crushed: 85

Winemaking philosophy: "Our wine is made exclusively from grapes grown in Quebec. We will continue to do research to discover the best varieties to plant in our soil."

Wines: **Own store**: L'Orpailleur Vin Blanc*, L'Orpailleur élevé en fût de chêne*, Apérid'Or, Vin Nouveau, La Mousse d'Or (*méthode champenoise* sparkling wine)

Store hours: *April 15 to November 15*: daily 9 am-6 pm. *November 15 to April 15*: Saturday and Sunday, 10 am-12 noon and 1 pm-5 pm (the rest of the week by appointment)

Tours: During store hours

Public tastings: During store hours

Restaurant: First weekend of June to October 22 (group reservations required)

Vignoble des Pins

136 Grand Sabrevois   Telephone: (514) 347-1073
Sabrevois, Quebec
J0J 2G0

Vignoble des Pins

Vin Rosé   Rosé Wine

Alpenrose

Gilles Benoit, Propriétaire récoltant
136 Grand Sabrevois, Sabrevois, Québec

750 ml   11% alc./vol.

PRODUIT DU QUÉBEC • PRODUCT OF QUÉBEC

If you've ever dreamed of making wine, Gilles Benoit is the man you should visit. He has realized his dream: to plant a manageable five-acre vineyard, stay small and make wines the way he wants to make them. Being small, he can take the time to experiment, like laying straw on top of his hilled-up tender *vinifera* during winter months to lovingly making a *methode champenoise* sparkler by hand. Gilles' Vignoble des Pins opened in May 1990.

Situated in the plains, he named his winery after the stands of red and white pine around the property. His soil has more clay than the hillier region around Dunham, which gives more body to his red wines. The vineyard was first planted in 1986 with French hybrids and some *vinifera*. Production is two-thirds white.

There are picnic and tasting facilities for fifty people.

Winemaker: Gilles Benoit

Acreage: 5

Soil: Clay-loam

Grape varieties: Seyval, Cayuga, Geisenheim 318 & 322, Bacchus, Vidal, Maréchal Foch, Gamay, Cabernet Franc

Average tonnage crushed: 8 - 10

Production: 800 cases

Winemaking philosophy: "We are aiming for a light fruity style in our wines, although our red Maréchal can be fairly concentrated due to bleeding of the tank (20%) to produce our Alpenrose. We also produce a blanc de blancs sparkler using Seyval grapes and the *méthode champenoise.*"

Wines: Own store: *White*—Pin Blanc* (85% Seyval, 10% Aurore, 5% Vidal), Edelweiss (Bacchus/Cayuga blend)

Red—Maréchal* (Maréchal Foch), Alpenrose (Maréchal Foch rosé)

Sparkling—Mousse des Pins* (75% Seyval, 25% Auore)

Store hours: 9 am-6 pm year round

Tours: Yes

Public tastings: Yes ($3 per person charge for tour and tasting for bus tours)

Vignoble Dietrich-Jooss

407 Grande-Ligne   Telephone: (514) 347-6857
Iberville, Quebec
J2X 4J2

Husband and wife Victor Dietrich and Christiane Jooss come from the Alsace village of Ingersheim where their respective families had been immersed in viticulture and winemaking for generations. The couple founded their company in 1986 and the following year planted the vineyard in the Richelieu Valley, east of Iberville. In order to find the best varieties for their microclimate, they have some thirty-six different plants in the ground, primarily white. An experimental plot includes vines from South Africa, Australia, the United States, South America and the noble varieties of Europe, including several Geisenheim clones which, says Victor, appear promising. These grapes go into his wines neck-labelled Cuvée Spéciale.

Their label bears a replica of the coat of arms that appeared on the bottles Victor made in his native Alsace. He believes that Chasselas, Gamay and certain Pinot varieties could do well in Quebec. Much of the equipment comes from Alsace. American oak is used. The winery is located in a large wood barn and the enthusiastic reception of visitors won the couple two Quebec tourism awards.

Victor is currently president of the Association des Vignerons, a man whose expertise and experience have inspired many young Québecois who have come into the profession. His daughter Stephanie (for whom the late harvest cuvée is named) is studying oenology in Bordeaux.

Winemaker: Victor Dietrich

Acreage: 11

Soil: Silty-sand, lightly pebbled; benefits from the proximity of two bodies of water, the Richelieu River and Lac Champlain.

Grape varieties: French hybrids, including Seyval, Cayuga, Vidal and Vineland 50201, several Geisenheim clones. Reds include Maréchal Foch, De Chaunac, Chancellor and Villard Noir. Some *vinifera* is planted, including Chardonnay and Riesling.

Production: 1,400 cases (350 cases red and rosé)

Winemaking philosophy: "As a winemaker from Alsace in Quebec, I want to use traditional Alsatian winemaking techniques to create that particular style in the wines we make here. My experiments in the vineyard are aimed at finding wines that resemble Riesling in character."

Wines: **Own store:** Vin Blanc*, Vin Rosé*, Vin Rouge*, Vin Blanc Cuvée Spéciale*, Storikengold* (a wine made for fish and sea food)

Specialty wine—Cuvée Stephanie (Late Harvest/Icewine)

Store hours: 9 am-7 pm, every day year-round

Tours: Yes; guided tours for groups are $4 per person

Public tastings: Yes (group reservations necessary)

Vignoble du Marathonien

318 route 202
Havelock, Quebec
J0S 2C0

Telephone: (vineyard)
(514) 826-0522
Telephone/fax in Montreal:
(514) 321-9347

VIN ROUGE

Vignoble du marathonien

Produit du Québec ~ Product of Québec
Mis en bouteille à la propriété
Line et Jean Joly, vignerons
Vignoble du marathonien, 318 route 202, Havelock (Québec) J0S 1E0
11% alc./vol.   750 ml

If you drive along the orchard-studded route 202 between Hemmingford and Havelock, you'll be parallel to the U.S. border which lies a few kilometres to the south. Just east of Havelock, turn left into what is perhaps the quaintest vineyard in the province — and certainly one of the best for tourists. A pretty, well kept, red-roofed white house and surrounding converted barn that sits at the end of a long gravel driveway surrounded by vineyards and an apple orchard. Line and Jean Joly own and work the vineyard but it is Jean, a full-time engineer, whose determination and love of winemaking drives the place. Whether their endurance comes from running marathons or from parenting four children is another question, but there is no doubt that this picturesque young vineyard is making some really nice white wines.

Winemaker: Jean Joly

Acreage: 3

Soil: Small rocks and gravel, black earth, little clay. Flat vineyard.

Grape varieties: Seyval, Cayuga, Vidal, SV 23512, Geisenheim 318; Maréchal Foch, Pinot Noir, Cabernet Franc, a little Merlot

Production: 5,000 bottles

Average tonnage crushed: 7

Winemaking philosophy: "In winemaking, we must never stop learning; and a good wine must begin with the careful pruning of the vine."

Wines: **Own store**: *White*—Vin Blanc, Cuvée Spéciale (Seyval, Cayuga, SV 23512), Vidal Vendange Tardive

Red—Vin Rouge

Tours: Self-guided; guided tours for busloads: small charge

Public tastings: *June to August*: Daily; *March to May and September to October*: Weekends. At other times by appointment.

Vignoble La Bauge

155 des Erables   Telephone: (514) 263-2149
Brigham, Quebec
J0E 1J0

The boar eating grapes on the label of Alcide Naud and Ghyslaine Poulin-Naud's *vin blanc* gives the game away. La Bauge actually means a "boar's den." Alcide had been a dairy farmer for forty years in Brigham before he bought a herd of wild boar, deer, wild sheep and stags. He began growing wine in 1987 and now rears his game menagerie for terrine, and for the sport hunters who pay $120 each to bring their bow and arrow and hunt their own "Sanglier" in the woods. Most wine lovers will, perhaps, prefer looking at the boar from the other side of the fence and settle for taking away a jar of the Wild Boar terrine with a bottle of Alcide's wine.

Besides Sanglier, they also raise deer, faun, Picari (dwarf boar) and many types of wild pheasant and other exotic fowl, including a chicken with fur! Incidentally, their barrel-aged "Solitaire" is named after the lone male who heads a pack of several females: a "solitaire" because he permits no other male in his presence.

Picnic tables are available.

Winemaker: Alcide Naud helped by their oenologist, Luc Rolland, who also consults/makes the wine for La Vitacée

Acreage: 7

Soil: Gravelly

Grape varieties: Seyval Blanc, Chancellor (some Pinot Noir is planned)

Average tonnage crushed: 8

Production: 500 cases

Winemaking philosophy: "I hope that one of my five sons will follow in my footsteps, because it's a fascinating pursuit."

Wines: Seyval Blanc, Bête Rousse, Solitaire (Seyval oak-aged)

Store hours: Daily, 9 am-6 pm

Tours: Vineyard and animal reserve tour by car—$6 per person ($3 for children aged 5 to 12)

Public tastings: Yes

Vignoble le Cep d'Argent

1257 Chemin de la Rivière
Magog, Quebec
J1X 3W5

Telephone: (819) 864-4441
Fax: (819) 864-7534

Le Cep d'Argent is Estrie's most easterly winery, situated between Magog and Sherbrooke. From eight grape varieties, winemaker François Scieur makes four different products to attract consumers to this small facility

across the railway tracks from the banks of Petit Lac Magog. Here, perhaps more than anywhere else in Quebec, the majestically sloping fields with their pine-topped hills and plots with vine rows set at varying angles to each other are vineyards reminiscent of the Grand Crus of France and Italy.

François and his brother Jean Paul are originally from the Champagne region which accounts for the presence of champagne method sparkling wine, kir and ratafia on their product list. In fact, they were the first to produce sparkling wine from grapes grown in the province. The winery was founded in 1985 after research to find the right site for the vineyard was undertaken by Jacques Daniel and his son Marc. The other partner in the enterprise is Denis Drouin. The champagne cellar with its A-frames set up for riddling is well worth seeing.

The reception hall resembles a medieval armoury and accommodates 150 people, while upstairs the windowed, prettily designed dining room has the swank and elegance — as well as the sunset view across the water — to carry off a wedding reception or other special event.

Winemaker: François Scieur

Acreage: 30

Soil: Silty sandy-clay; south-south-east slope

Grape varieties: Seyval, Maréchal Foch, De Chaunac, Geisenheim and "Wiley White" from Niagara

Production: 4,500 cases

Average tonnage crushed: 65

Winemaking philosophy: "Our philosophy is to ignore the ideas of people who say that the vine can't produce wines of quality in Quebec."

Wines: Le Cep D'Argent Vin Blanc (Seyval Blanc), Le Réserve du Chevalier (barrel-aged), Fleuret (Pineau des Charentes-style aperitif), Mistral* (Ratafia-style aperitif), L'Archer (digestif made from red wine, cognac and maple syrup), Sélection des Mousquetaires* (*méthode champenoise blanc de blancs*), Sélection des Mousquetaires Rosé

Winery store hours: Daily, 9 am-5 pm

Tours: Hour-long bilingual tours with tasting $3.75 per person (children 12 and under free). Restaurant facilities by reservation.

Vignoble Le Royer St-Pierre

182 route 221   Telephone/fax: (514) 245-0208
St-Cyprien de Napierville, Quebec
J0J 1L0

Robert Le Royer and Lucie St-Pierre founded their winery in 1990 and were determined to grow Chardonnay. They are currently studying different root-stocks for the sixteen varieties they have planted. They are also experimenting in the vineyard with different trellising systems — all on the same vine. Vignoble Le Royer St. Pierre, a kilometre away from Morou, is a testimony to Robert's passion for the grape and his quest for their Holy Grail — the "right" variety for Quebec. The wines themselves have intriguing names that involve local history, geography or geology.

The property is distinguished by a very solid-looking white silo that could, with a little imagination, become the subject of another quaint label.

The couple have four American oak barrels for ageing. They receive visitors enthusiastically, seven days a week, and offer buffet meals "or lamb roast on request."

Winemaker: Robert Le Royer

Acreage: 42 (not all planted)

Grape varieties: Cayuga white, Maréchal Foch, De Chaunac, Seyval Blanc, Aurore, Geisenheim 318 and 322, Léon Millot. In production shortly: Vedelet, Baco Noir, Dornfelder, Chardonnay, Gamay, Cabernet Franc, Schonberger.

Soil: Sandy with a little clay and clay with gravel. Lake Champlain provides a warm microclimate on the valley region.

Production: 675 cases

Average tonnage crushed: 9 - 10

Winemaking philosophy: "In our procedures the most inventive techniques are used. Also, in the vineyard due to the harsh climate all the vines are buried under twenty inches of earth in the fall. Our pruning system is *gobelet* mixed with double Guyot and a little double Geneva curtain, all on the same vine."

Wines: **Own store**: *White*—Les trois sols, La Dauversière

Red—Terre de St-Cyprien, Les trois sols Rosé Reserve

Specialty wine—Cayuga white/Geisenheim Icewine (trial basis, not available commercially yet)

Store hours: 10 am-8 pm, seven days a week

Tours: Yes ("anytime")

Public tastings: Yes ("anytime")

Vignoble Les Arpents de Neige

4042 rue Principale   Telephone: (514) 295-3383
Dunham, Quebec
J0E 1M0

Just a stone's throw or three up the hill south from the town of Dunham, you'll find the vineyard of Les Arpents de Neige, a name that resonates with French history. "A few acres of snow" were not worth fighting for, according to French King Louis XIV's advisors. Originally planted by Jacques Breault, who once worked for l'Orpailleur, Les Arpents de Neige went into bankruptcy and was bought in 1992 by Gilles Séguin, a restaurateur who, with the help of his French winemaker, Jean-Paul Martin, made a very good Seyval in 1994. In addition, as one would expect, Gilles Séguin offers meals for groups who book ahead.

Winemaker: Jean-Paul Martin

Acreage: 12

Soil: Deep, gravelly

Grape varieties: Seyval, Vidal, Vineland 50201, Pollux, Ortega, Cayuga, Chancellor

Wines: Seyval Blanc, Cuvée Sélectionnée, Cuvée 1er Neige

Store hours: Daily, 9 am-9 pm

Tours: Yes

Public tastings: Yes

Vignoble Les Blancs Coteaux

1046 Route 202   Telephone: (514) 295-3503
Dunham, Quebec
J0E 1M0

The youthful Pierre Genesse and his wife Marie-Claude founded their tiny winery in 1989. Pierre learned his winemaking in Burgundy while picking grapes in the Mâconnais. He also studied physical geography in Sherbrooke. The beautiful old wood farmhouse which doubles as the cellar and the couple's home also has a shop where you can buy homemade vinegars, jams, jellies, dried flowers and herbs. Bottling and labelling are done by hand, and the crush is done nearby at a colleague's facility.

Pierre removes leaves to expose the grape clusters to the sun. He vinifies in stainless steel to maintain the perfume of the fruit although he does have ten French and American oak *barriques* and is currently experimenting with Bacchus. He also makes ciders, fortified cider and dry apple wine.

Winemaker: Pierre Genesse

Acreage: 5

Soil: Rocky loam on slate above clay. Warm air currents off Lake Champlain avoid spring and early fall frost. Situated at the foot of a hill; good drying wind and heat during the day.

Grape variety: Seyval Blanc

Production: 1,250 cases

Average tonnage crushed: 5

Winemaking philosophy: "To maintain very high-quality standards without becoming a large commercial producer. Small is beautiful."

Wines: **Own store**: Seyval Blanc La Taste, Vendange Sélectionée

Specialty item: Empire** (cider and Calvados)

Store hours: Thursday to Sunday, 9 am-5 pm (small restaurant during the summer)

Public tastings: During store hours

Vignoble Les Trois Clochers

314 Route 202　　　　　　　　　Telephone: (514) 295-2034
Dunham, Quebec
J0E 1M0

Vignoble Les Trois Clochers is just two km or so north east of Les Côtes d'Ardoise on the road into Dunham. The very friendly Claude Rhéaume and Réal Normandeau are working hard to make their new winery a force to be reckoned with.

Besides the obligatory Seyval Blanc and a very nice Strawberry wine, the team also sells many homemade fine food products. A boutique above the winery that is becoming more attractively decorated all the time. The vineyard was first planted in 1986.

Winemaker: Claude Rhéaume

Acreage: 7.5

Soil: Gravelly

Grape varieties: Seyval in production, Chancellor and Maréchal to come. Iona will be planted this year (1995).

Production: 5,000 bottles

Wines: Vin Blanc, Vin de Fraises (a red to come)
Store hours: Daily, 10 am-5 pm (January and February by appointment)
Tours: Yes
Public tastings: Yes

Vignoble Morou

238 Route 221
Napierville, Quebec
J0J 1L0

Telephone/fax: (514) 245-7569

Monique Morin and Etienne Héroux, a chemical engineer, founded Vignoble Morou in 1987 close to the head of Lake Champlain. They planted a range of hybrids to see what was best for their particular microclimate. They use American oak barrels to age their best reds as well as their elegant white, Clos Napierois.

In the sports world, a "Most Improved Player" award is often bestowed. If such an accolade were bestowed on winemakers, it would go to Etienne and Monique for sheer industry and commitment. Etienne rolls all his vats outside for up to a week in -5 degree Celsius weather to precipitate as much tartaric acid as possible (the small growers in Meursault open their doors to their white wine cellar to achieve the same effect). This is the true mark of a vigneron — not wanting to adulterate his wines with chemical de-acidification.

Winemaker: Etienne Héroux
Acreage: 4.5
Soil: Sandy-loam, flattish vineyard with a slight slope.
Grape varieties: Seyval, Vidal, Seibel V502201, Geisenheim clones;
   Maréchal Foch, Gamay, Chancellor and some Cabernet Sauvignon

Production: 7,500 bottles (1994)

Winemaking philosophy: "Small family vineyard, wines of superior quality and a warm welcome for visitors."

Wines: Own store: White—Morou Blanc Reserve*, Clos Napierois* (barrel-aged Geisenheim clones), Cuvée Spéciale (Cayuga)

Red—Morou Cuvée Spéciale (Gamay), Morou Rouge Reserve*, Morou Rosé Reserve*

Store hours: *May to October*: Wednesday to Sunday, 10 am-6 pm. (For the rest of the year, call the house for product availability.)

Tours: Yes (reservations for groups of 10 or more; group packages for wine and cheese and cold meals)

Public tastings: Yes ($1 per variety)

Vignoble St-Alexandre

364, Grande-Ligne   Telephone: (514) 347-2794
St-Alexandre d'Iberville, Quebec
J0J 1S0

If you happen to be out visiting Vignoble Dietrich-Jooss, take a drive two km further east down the highway to Vignoble St-Alexandre where you'll meet Domenic Agarla, an opinionated, forceful man who definitely marches to his own drummer.

Not only does he refuse to be a part of the Association de Vignerons, he is also the only vigneron in Quebec making a living from selling red wine only! A native of Piemonte, Italy (Barolo region), he makes wine the way he learned in Italy — in vast cement vats. In the vineyard, things are organic and traditional as well, with the vines being pole-trained — a separate pole for each vine.

After trying a multitude of vines, Domenic has ripped them all out and stayed with De Chaunac, the variety he believes makes the most agreeable reds in Quebec. He is fiercely committed to being "a real vigneron" and will not de-acidify his wines chemically, as many others do. As well, he rarely chaptalizes, and —very unusual for Quebec, and very commendable — only releases his reds when they are ready to drink. His 1992 is on the market now, and he will simply not be releasing his 1993 because he was not happy with the year.

He is proud to be making "honest wine" and of selling it at a bargain price. Domenic believes that wine should be natural, that each vintage should have its own character, and the winemaker shouldn't alter that character. He is an *organic* winemaker; he uses no pesticides except copper sulphate and no fertilizers except his own compost.

Winemaker: Domenic Agarla

Acreage: 3 hectares

Soil: Pebbly-clay, semi-light for the flat Montérégie plain

Grape variety: De Chaunac

Production: "No *real* vigneron would ever tell you how much he makes."

Winemaking philosophy: "Man does what he can, but it's *le Bon Dieu* and
    the weather that make the vintage."

Wines: Domar Red

Store hours: Open all year

Tours: Yes

Vignoble Sous les Charmilles

3747, chemin Dunant   Telephone: (819) 346-7189
Rock Forest, Quebec
J1N 3B7

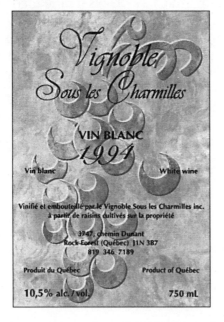

In 1986, consulting winemaker Alain Bélanger's (Les Arpents de Neiges, Les Blancs Coteaux, La Bauge, Les Trois Clochers) father planted a few vines near Sherbrooke *pour s'amuser*. What was a hobby has become a passion, and Quebec's newest winery opened its doors in late summer 1995.

Alain Bélanger, who incidentally has a day job as a wine agent (and who has also worked as a sommelier), first caught the winemaking bug in Beaujolais in 1984 when he helped vinify in a few *caves* near Villefranche after picking grapes. A two-month stint in a cellar in Alsace in 1987 honed his winemaking skills and a stay at the winemaking school in Mâcon-Davayé in 1989 brought his laboratory techniques up to par.

Although his winery, based in the Eastern Townships hills near Sherbrooke, may take more time to bring Seyval Blanc to maturity than his *confrères* in the Montérégie region, Alain feels that the well-drained, gravelly soil brings a complexity to the wines not found in flatter vineyards with richer soils.

Alain's wine philosophy includes minimal settling of the grape must (to keep as much of the richness in the fruit as possible), minimal handling and careful pumping of the wine, and bottling in the month of March (and not before Christmas, as many stock-strapped Quebec vignerons are forced to do), which he has found, through experience, to be the ideal "bottling window" to preserve the fruit and character of Quebec's Seyvals.

Although most Quebec vignerons use earth to bury their vines in winter, Alain has found a revolutionary new material — leaves! He has Sherbrooke's wine enthusiasts saving him their lawn rakings all autumn long, and after the winter passes he takes off the leaves, composts them, and uses them for natural fertilizer!

Winemaker: Alain Bélanger

Acreage: 3

Soil: Rocky, sandy, gravelly

Grape varieties: Seyval Blanc; experimental: Bacchus, Ortega, Maréchal Foch

Production: 5,000 - 8,000 bottles when all vines are in production

Wines: Vignoble sous les Charmilles Vin Blanc

Store: Opening summer 1995

Tours: Yes

Public tastings: Yes

NOVA SCOTIA

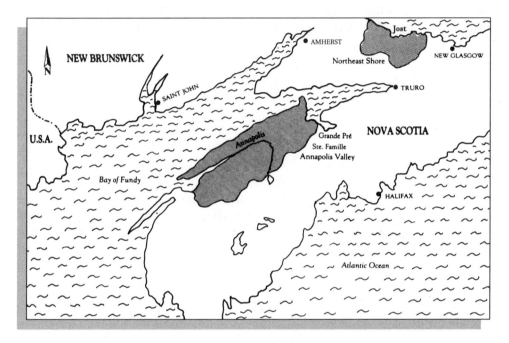

WINE REGIONS OF NOVA SCOTIA

*L*ief Ericsson may have discovered wild grapes in Newfoundland at the beginning of this millennium, but there is harder evidence to support Nova Scotia's claim to be a wine-growing province at least as far back as the beginning of the seventeenth century. In 1611, Louis Hébert, Samuel Champlain's apothecary, loaded his canoe with vines he brought with him from France and paddled up the Bear River between Annapolis and Digby counties to plant a vineyard.

Serious attempts to turn the province into a wine-growing region had to wait until this century. As early as 1913, the Agriculture Canada research station at Kentville had been planting experimental plots to see what varieties might flourish in the province's short, cool growing season (to date they have evaluated over 200 cultivars). After several decades of trial and error, in 1971 the researchers suggested in a departmental publication that only table varieties seemed viable (even the hardy Concord did not ripen sufficiently). But a decade later, they would be proved mistaken.

Nova Scotia is situated midway between the Equator and the North Pole, and the time between the last spring frost and the first fall frost is much shorter than in Ontario or British Columbia. The average daily temperature during the growing season is also lower than the other two grape-growing provinces.

But happily there are always those healthy sceptics who challenge accepted wisdom and more often than not are proved correct. Roger Dial, a Californian born in 1942, can justifiably claim to be the father of the Nova Scotia wine industry. Although Andrés had a bottling plant in Truro, there were no wine grapes grown on a commercial scale in the province until the late 1970s. Andrés opened its winery in Truro's industrial park in 1965 and purchased Chipman Wines in 1983, an enterprise founded in 1941 that produced fruit wines from apples, cherries, elderberries, blueberries and cranberries.

A political scientist by training, Roger Dial came to lecture at Dalhousie in 1969. During his university days in California, he had worked his way through school as a wine sales representative and had been a partner in the small Davis Bynum winery in Healdsburg. At Dalhousie he met an economist, Norman Morse, who had planted some table grapes on his property at Grand Pré. Roger convinced him to plant wine grapes that he had purchased for his own home winemaking production. In 1978, the two men put in a further three acres of vines — no *vinifera*, since they had been advised against these tender plants, but two hardy Russian varieties from the Amur Valley on the Chinese border, Michurinetz and Severnyi. (This has a certain resonance for Roger Dial since his Ph.D. was in Chinese politics.) The vines had been imported to Canada as a result of a barter deal with the Soviets — Nova Scotian raspberries for Russian vines. The stocks had originally been propagated at the Summerland research station in British Columbia and another barter deal landed them in Kentville. This time the commodity was Nova Scotia blueberries. (The planting of vines must have a domesticating effect because, in 1981, Roger purchased the vineyard and his colleague's house — a splendid 1819 Georgian woodframe building — with the intention of creating a cottage winery.)

Emboldened by the success of the Russian varieties in his basement winemaking activities, Roger Dial convinced Morse to plant more vines and to extend to *vinifera* varieties as well. In 1979, Chardonnay and Gewürztraminer were put into the ground — the first in eastern Canada — but the weather during the following year was so bad that it nearly killed the entire vineyard. Yet 1980 was not without its triumphs. That vintage of Cuvée d'Amur, a Michurinetz-based wine, won a gold medal in New York at the International Wine and Spirit Competition and a silver in Bristol, England. Subsequent harvests proved that wine grapes could flourish in Nova Scotia if they were placed in suitable microclimates. In 1982, Cuvée d'Amur was voted by wine writers as the best Canadian red at a Department of External Affairs tasting to select wines for Canadian embassies and High Commissions around the world. It just may have been coincidence, but that was the year when the Wine Growers' Association of Nova Scotia was founded with Roger Dial as chairman and Hans Jost as vice-chairman, a grape farmer in Malagash, Cumberland County, who would start Nova Scotia's second cottage winery two years later.

In 1983, Roger Dial had planted a twenty-two-acre vineyard fifteen miles from his winery at Lakeville and was busy contracting the produce of other local growers to satisfy the demand for his wines at provincial liquor stores. It was not until 1986 that the Nova Scotia government passed the Farm Winery Act enabling him to sell wines at the winery directly to licensees and the visiting public. By 1988, he had 200 acres of vineyards that were either owned outright, bought as joint ventures or contracted in, and had annual sales of $1.2 million. Grand Pré had a healthy 6 percent of the provincial wine market. Unfortunately, the combined pressures of the October 1987 stock market crash and the Free Trade Agreement eventually took their toll and forced Roger Dial's winery into receivership. After a couple of years of restructuring, Jim Landry and Karen Avery took over the operation, bringing in the late Bob Claremont as consulting winemaker and wine buyer. But this new effort too was doomed to failure and the partners sold the business in 1994 to Swiss interests.

The Farm Winery Act, though long in coming, helped to consolidate Nova Scotia's nascent wine industry. Under its provisions a winery could sell 350 cases of wine at the farm gate for every acre under vine (minimum ten), even if those newly planted vines had yet to produce a crop. Nor did the wines sold have to be from grapes grown in the province. In order to give incentive to farm wineries to plant grapes, the government allowed them to bottle imported wines, either blended into locally grown grapes or as 100 percent imports. These are usually sold through the Nova Scotia Liquor Commission (NSLC) and the estate-bottled wines are available at the wineries.

At this time, there are three estate farm wineries in Nova Scotia (Grand Pré is currently inactive) whose grapes are augmented by thirty-eight growers managing 130 acres of vines in seven counties. Production varies from 140 to nearly 200 tons. Suitable grape varieties for winemaking in Nova Scotia are more limited than Ontario and British Columbia. The most widely planted varieties are reds — Michurinetz, Maréchal Foch; whites — Seyval Blanc, New York Muscat, L'Acadie Blanc and a Geisenheim clone, GM.

More early-ripening *vinifera* varieties are now being planted in Nova Scotia. These more sensitive plants are being protected against the cold winters by "hilling" (covering the trunk with earth in the late fall, a technique practised in Quebec) or by the use of straw. The vines are grown closer to the ground to benefit from heat retained in the soil. Trellising systems used in Europe with certain modifications have improved production and the survival rate of the vines.

Nova Scotia Wineries

Grand Pré Estate Winery

P.O. Box 18
Kings County, Nova Scotia
B0P 1M0

Grand Pré, the winery founded by the visionary Roger Dial in 1980, went into receivership in 1988. The estate was taken over by Jim Landry and Karen Avery with the late Bob Claremont as consulting winemaker. This new enterprise also failed and the winery was purchased in 1994 by a Swiss company. The new owners are currently replanted the seventeen-acre vineyard and do not expect the winery to be in production for four or five years.

A number of Swiss varieties are being planted. Under consideration are Charmont, Granoir, Müller-Thurgau, Chasselas and Pinot Noir. The son of one of the owners is currently apprenticed to a winery in Switzerland and will ultimately take over the winemaking responsibilities.

Jost Vineyards

Malagash, Nova Scotia	Telephone: (902) 257-2636
B0K 1E0	Fax: (902) 257-2248

Hans Christian Jost took over the winemaking and management duties of the family business when his father, Hans, died in 1988. The older Jost, who had owned a winery in the Rhine Valley before emigrating to Canada in 1970, was a grape farmer who started Nova Scotia's second cottage winery in 1984. His son went to study winemaking at Geisenheim.

Jost Vineyards, located on the Northumberland Strait along what is called the "Sunshine Coast of Nova Scotia," is one of three such enterprises in the province. The winery was located in the basement of a small log cabin crammed with stainless-steel tanks, but an expansion in the spring of 1993 augmented the cellar by 540 square metres and created a large, open sales and tasting facility.

Hans buys in grapes from Ontario and Washington State to augment his needs. He still holds the record for Canada's most expensive wine — St. Nicholas Icewine 1985 from Riesling, Kerner and Bacchus grapes. It sold for $60.25 a half bottle.

Winemaker: Hans Christian Jost

Acreage: 21

Soil: Clay loam-loam clay with a reddish hue due to iron content.

Grape varieties: Maréchal Foch, De Chaunac, Seyval Blanc and Geisenheim clone 6493-4

Production: 30,000 cases

Average tonnage crushed: 300

Annual tonnage purchased: 200

Winemaking philosophy: "Our goal is to produce crisp, clean wines. The flavour of the wine should come from the fermentation of clean grapes and juice. Minimal movements of the juice and wine in the cellar maintain the full flavours of the wine. The wine is actually made in the vineyard with the cellar work purely assisting in bringing to the fore-front the flavours that have been created in the vineyard."

Wines: **NSLC**: *White*—Riesling/Vidal, Riesling Gold Label, Sonnenhof Vidal, Christiane Gewürztraminer, Habitant Blanc*, Beaver Creek Geisenheim, Chablis, Christinenhof Cabinett, Comtessa, Kellermeister

Red—Comtessa Red, Maréchal Foch*

Rosé—Jost Blush

Winery store: Dry White House, Rhine House, Cuvée Blanc, Eagle Tree Muscat, Seyval Blanc*, Avondale Blanc*, Habitant Chardonnay

Specialty wines—Matina Ice Wine*, Glow Wine (mulled red wine)

Winery store hours: *Summer*: Daily, 7 days a week, 10 am-6 pm. *Winter*: 10 am-6 pm, closed Sunday

Tours: Summer at noon and 3 pm

Public tastings: During store hours

Sainte Famille Wines

Dyke Road (Exit 7 off Highway 101)   Telephone: (902) 798-8311
Falmouth, Nova Scotia   1-800-565-0993
B0P 1L0   Fax: (902) 798-9418

In 1989, Suzanne and Doug Corkum opened their tiny winery next to their vineyard (planted in 1979) on an old Acadian village site known as "la Paroisse Sainte Famille de Pisquit," a community settled in the 1680s. Today it's known as Falmouth — the gateway to the Annapolis Valley. The square wood building that acts as a winery and gift shop has a California feel to it. The shop promotes local products such as cheese, jams, crafts, etc.

Nevers, Limousin and Allier oak are used in the winemaking. An expansion is planned for 1995 that will include a barrel-ageing cellar, additional cellar space, café and deck.

Winemaker: Suzanne Corkum

Acreage: 24 (a further 6 to be planted in 1996)

Microclimate: South-facing slope protected by the Avon River from extremes of temperature during the winter months.

Grape varieties: Chardonnay, Riesling, Seyval Blanc, Ortega, Auxerrois, German hybrids, Michurinetz, Maréchal Foch

Production: 3,000 cases (aiming at 6,000 maximum)

Average tonnage crushed: 66

Winemaking philosophy: "I prefer my whites to be clean and crisp with a good balance of fruit. My reds are barrel aged using Nevers, Limousin and Allier oak. In 1994, we experimented using partial carbonic maceration on the Maréchal Foch which has given us a completely different style of wine for Foch. In future, once our expansion is complete, I plan to start to barrel-ferment some of our whites."

Wines: NSLC Ports of Wine store: *White*—Chardonnay

Own store: *White*—Dry Riesling, Johannisberg Riesling, Estate Seyval, Vidal Blanc, Chardonnay, Premium Chablis, Gold Bell (blended, semi-sweet), Fleur de Blanc (L'Acadie Blanc, Vidal)

Red—La Paroisse Rouge (a bland of Maréchal Foch and Michurinetz)

Specialty wine—Acadianna Reserve barrel-aged port-style (Maréchal Foch)

Store hours: *January to March*: Monday to Saturday, 9 am-5 pm. *April to May*: Monday to Saturday, 9 am-5 pm; Sunday, noon - 5 pm. *June to December*: Monday to Saturday, 9 am-6 pm; Sunday, noon - 5 pm

Tours: *May to October*: Daily, 11 am and 2 pm (large groups are requested to book in advance)

Public tastings: During store hours

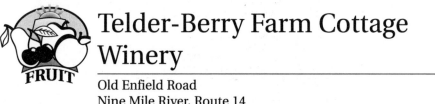

Telder-Berry Farm Cottage Winery

Old Enfield Road
Nine Mile River, Route 14
Hants County, Nova Scotia

Bob Telder and his son Brian began making fruit wines from raspberries, blueberries and strawberries grown in their twenty-acre U-pick farm. The "wines" are fermented in a newly constructed 2,200-sq.-ft. facility, which opened on July 1, 1993. The product are made without additives in dry, off-dry and sweet styles. Visitors can see the operation from behind glass windows, in deference to Department of Health regulations.

Rodrigues Markland Cottage Winery

Markland, Newfoundland   Telephone: (709) 759-3005
A0B 3K0

Dr. Rodrigues took over a decommissioned cottage hospital on the Avalon Peninsula, fifty miles west of St. John's, to open his fruit winery in 1994. The main product is a dessert-style Blueberry Wine at 8 percent alcohol. Experiments to make wine from Partridge berries, a tart berry that grows profusely in Newfoundland, are under way, and coming soon is Cloudberry liqueur. The winery has the capacity to produce 2,000 gallons of fruit wine every three weeks — which must be the envy of grape wineries. The back label of the Blueberry Wine reads: "...This rich ruby wine is a young feisty wine from a young winery with an old Newfoundland recipe. Serve slightly chilled."

*I*CEWINE

*C*anada is becoming recognized as one of the world's best producers of Icewine. Ontario is the most prolific source of this gift of winter to the wine lover; currently, twenty-five wineries in the province produce the honeyed nectar on an annual basis.

Inniskillin gave this fact global recognition at Vinexpo 1991 in Bordeaux when it won the Grand Prix de l'Honneur for its Vidal Icewine 1989 — one of only nineteen such medals out of 4,100 entries. The message was further driven home when Stonechurch won a Grand Gold Award at Vinitaly, Verona, in 1994 for its 1991 Vidal Icewine, and Reif in 1995 for its Vidal Icewine 1993. Since then, Ontario Icewine has regularly won gold at international competitions.

Canada is, in fact, the world's largest producer of this vinous rarity. Ontario alone produces 15,000 to 20,000 cases. (Small amounts are made in British Columbia, Quebec and Nova Scotia.)

Icewine, or *Eiswein* as the Germans call it, is the product of frozen grapes. A small portion of the vineyard is left unpicked during the September-October harvest and the bunches are allowed to hang on the vine until the mercury drops to at least -7 seven degrees Celsius. At this frigid temperature the sugar-rich juice begins to freeze. If the grapes are picked in their frozen state and pressed while they are as hard as marbles, the small amount of juice recovered will be intensely sweet and high in acidity. The wine made from this juice will be an ambrosia fit for Dionysus himself.

Like most gastronomic breakthroughs, the discovery of Icewine was accidental. Producers in Franconia in 1794 made virtue of necessity by pressing juice from frozen grapes. They were amazed by the abnormally high concentration of sugars and acids which hitherto they had achieved only by allowing the grapes to desiccate on straw mats before pressing or by the effects of Botrytis Cinerea. (This disease is known as "noble rot"; it afflicts grapes in autumn usually in regions where there is early morning fog and humid, sunny afternoons. A mushroom-like fungus attaches itself to the berries, puncturing their skins and allowing the juice to evaporate.

The world's great dessert wines such as Sauternes, Riesling Trockenbeerenauslese and Tokay Aszu Essence are made from grapes afflicted by this benign disease.)

It was not until the middle of the last century in the Rheingau that German winegrowers made conscious efforts to produce Icewine on a consistent basis. However, they found they could not make it every year since the sub-zero cold spell has to last for several days to ensure that the berries remain frozen solid during picking and the lengthy pressing process which can take up to three days or longer. Grapes are 80 percent water, and when this water is frozen and driven off under pressure as shards of ice, the resulting juice will be miraculously sweet. A sudden thaw causes the ice to melt, diluting the sugar in each berry.

This means that temperatures for Icewine are critical. In Germany, the pickers must be out well before dawn to harvest the grapes before the sun comes up. Some German producers even go so far as to rig an outdoor thermostat to their alarm clocks so as not to miss a really cold morning. But in Ontario there is no need for such dramatics. The winemakers can get a good night's sleep secure in the knowledge that sometime between November and February our climate will afford them a stretch of polar temperatures. As a result, Ontario Icewine is an annual event and as predictable as the turning maples. Sometimes the cold comes early, as it did in 1991. On October 29, in British Columbia, Hainle Vineyards, CedarCreek and Gehringer Brothers were able to pick frozen grapes for Icewine when temperatures plunged to -13 degrees Celsius.

Not all grapes can make Icewine. Only the thick-skinned, late-maturing varieties such as Riesling and Vidal can hang in there for the duration against such predators as gray rot, powdery mildew, unseasonal warmth, wind, rain, sugar-crazed starlings — and the occasional Ontario bureaucrat. The very first attempts at producing Icewine in Canada on a commercial basis were sabotaged by bird and man. In 1983, Inniskillin lost its entire crop to the birds the day before picking was scheduled. Walter Strehn at Pelee Island Vineyards had taken the precaution of netting his vines to protect them from the feathered frenzy. Some persistent blue jays, however, managed to break through his nets and were trapped in the mesh. A passing bird-fancier reported this to the Ministry of Natural Resources whose officials descended upon the vineyard and tore off the netting. Strehn not only lost $25,000 worth of Riesling grapes to the rapacious flock but, to add insult to injury, he was charged with trapping birds out of season — using dried grapes as bait! Happily, the case was dropped, and with the grapes that were left Strehn managed to make fifty cases of Riesling Icewine 1983.

Since those days, more and more Ontario wineries have jumped on the Icewine bandwagon. Their wines literally sell out the moment they reach the stores. To avoid disappointment, customers have been encouraged to reserve their bottles while the grapes are still hanging on the vine. In Japan, these wines sell for up to $200 the half bottle (the price in Canada ranges from $29.95 to $50.) Note: Many Ontario wineries are making a second pressing of their Icewine grapes to produce a more affordable and less concentrated dessert wine they call Select Harvest or Winter Wine.

But whenever you leave grapes on the vine once they have ripened, you are taking an enormous gamble. If birds and animals don't get them, mildew and rot or a sudden storm might. So growers reserve only a small portion of their Vidal or Riesling grapes for Icewine — a couple of acres at most.

A vineyard left for Icewine is really a very sorry sight. The mesh-covered vines are completely denuded of leaves and the grapes are brown and shrivelled, hanging like so many bats from the frozen canes. The wrinkled berries are ugly but taste wonderfully sweet — like frozen raisins.

The stems that attach the bunches to the vine are dried out and brittle, so a strong wind or an ice storm could easily knock them to the ground. A twist of the wrist is all that is needed to pick them.

Usually there is snow and a high wind which makes picking an experience similar to Scott's trek to Antarctica. When the wind howls through the vineyard, driving the snow before it, the wind-chill factor can make a temperature of -10 degrees Celsius seem like -40 degrees. Harvesting Icewine grapes is a torturous business. Pickers, fortified with tea and brandy, brave the elements for two hours at a time before rushing back to the winery to warm up.

And when the tractor delivers the precious boxes of grapes to the winery, the hard work begins. Since the berries must remain frozen, the pressing is done *al fresco* or the winery doors are left open. The presses have to be worked slowly, otherwise the bunches will turn to a solid block of ice yielding nothing. Some producers throw rice husks into the press which pierce the skins of the berries and create channels for the juice to flow through the mass of ice. Sometimes it takes two or three hours before the first drop of juice appears. These drops will be the sweetest since grape sugars have a lower freezing point than water.

Roughly speaking, one kilogram of grapes will produce sufficient juice to ferment into one bottle of wine. The juice from a kilogram of Icewine grapes will produce one-fifth of that amount and less, depending on the degree of dehydration caused by wind and winter sunshine. The longer the grapes hang on the vine, the less juice there will be. So a cold snap in December will yield more Icewine than having to wait for a harvest date in January when there will be a crop weight loss of 60 percent or more over normal harvest weights.

The oily juice, once extracted from the marble-hard berries, is allowed to settle for three or four days and then it is clarified of dust and debris by racking from one tank to another. The colourless liquid is cold and will not permit fermenting to start, and a special yeast has to be added to activate that process in stainless steel tanks. Because of the very high sugars, the fermentation is very slow and can take months. But when the amber wine is finally in bottle, it has the capacity to age for a decade or more.

While Germany may be recognized by the world as the home of Icewine, ironically the Germans cannot make it every year. Canadian winemakers can. Klaus Reif, the winemaker at Reif Winery, has produced Icewine in both countries. While studying oenology at the Geisenheim Institute in Germany, he worked at a government winery in Neustadt in the Pfalz. In 1983, he made his first Icewine there from Riesling grapes. Four years later he made Icewine from Vidal grapes grown in his uncle's vineyard at Niagara-on-the-Lake. "The juice comes out like honey here," says Klaus. "In Germany it drops like ordinary wine."

Robert Mielzynski, formerly of Hillebrand Estates, who had also studied winemaking in Germany, agrees: "A lot of the Icewines I tried in Germany were less viscous and more acidic that ours. We get higher sugar levels."

Neustadt is around the 50th latitude; Niagara near the 43rd. Although our winters are more formidable than those of Germany, we enjoy a growing season with more sunshine hours, resembling that of Burgundy. Our continental climate in southern Ontario gives us high peaking temperatures in July, the vine's most active growing month. This means that grapes planted in the Niagara Peninsula can attain higher sugar readings than in Germany, especially late-picked varieties because of dramatic fluctuations of temperature in the Fall season. "From September on," says Karl Kaiser, winemaker and co-owner of Inniskillin, "the weather can turn cold and then suddenly warm up again. This warming-freezing effect makes the grapes dehydrate. Loss of water builds up the sugars. In January we have very windy weather that further desiccates the grapes so that when we harvest the Icewine we have very concentrated flavours."

So when the thermometer takes that first plunge of winter, think of the grape pickers down on the Niagara Peninsula, bundling up to harvest the grapes of frost. Bat-brown and shrivelled like the old men of the mountains, those bunches hanging precariously from the vine may look unappetizing but the lusciously sweet wine they produce is worth all the numb fingers and raw cheeks. At least the vintners have machines to press the juice from the frozen berries; they don't have go through the procedure in their bare feet!

The credit for the first Canadian Icewine must go to the late Walter Hainle in B.C. who began making it from Okanagan Riesling in 1973 for family and friends. Tilman Hainle confesses that the family has one bottle of the 1974 vintage left ("in a glamorous Lowenbräu bottle with matching cap and homemade label"). "We have made Icewine every year since then, except in 1977. It is possible to make Icewine every year in B.C., although the picking dates and quantities vary widely. Usually, we have to wait until November or December for the appropriate temperatures."

Up until 1983, the Hainles used Okanagan Riesling to make their Icewine, but since then they have used a number of varieties including Traminer, Pinot Noir and Riesling. "We felt that Riesling is the most successful variety for our Icewine," says Tilman. Over the years their sugar levels have varied from 33 Brix to 57.5 Brix. A range of 35 to 40 Brix is typical at a temperature of -9 degrees Celsius to -12 degrees Celsius.

The quantity of juice the Hainles got from their frozen grapes ranged from as little as twenty litres in 1990 to as much as 580 litres in 1987. "The maximum quantity for us is limited by our mechanical capability — one press will yield from 150 to 300 litres of juice, and we don't have the crop or the time to do more than one press." Tilman Hainle is also reluctant to produce large quantities of Icewine. The wine, he contends, is a curiosity which garners a lot of publicity, chiefly because of its rarity and because it is not sufficiently cost efficient to warrant making it a large part of their portfolio.

Ontario Icewines
(half bottles)

RATING SYSTEM

No stars	An unacceptable wine
☆	A poorly made wine, chemical taste or has no character at all
☆☆	An acceptable wine with not much to recommend it
☆☆☆	A good wine, clean and well made, true to its grape type
☆☆☆☆	A fine wine, the best that Canada has to offer

I have also given half stars (½) when a wine falls between two categories. When I consider that the wine will be better with at least a year of bottle aging, I have used the following device: ☆☆☆ (>☆☆☆☆).

☆☆☆☆ Cave Spring Riesling Icewine 1991 (10.5% alc)

Colour: Gold **Bouquet**: Creamy, toffee, orange
Taste: Perfumed, rich, honey and orange blossom. Lingering barley sugar taste. Beautifully balanced

---

☆☆☆☆ Cave Spring Riesling Icewine 1992 (10.5% alc)

Colour: Yellow straw **Bouquet**: Fresh, hint of petrol
Taste: Peach, citrus, not overly sweet, beautifully balanced, lively acidity, lingering citric flavours

---

☆☆☆½ Château des Charmes Riesling Icewine 1991 (10.5% alc)

Colour: Pale gold **Bouquet**: Dried apricot, honey
Taste: Ripe, orange and peach, soft, touch bitter on the finish

---

☆☆☆½ Château des Charmes Riesling Icewine 1992 (9.5% alc)

Colour: Yellow straw **Bouquet**: Peach and lemon
Taste: Intense peach, lively acidity, light on the palate. Lingering tangerine flavour.

☆☆	Colio Icewine 1992 (12% alc)
	Colour: Gold **Bouquet**: Mealy **Taste**: Licorice, heavy, alcoholic

☆☆☆	Culotta Vidal Icewine 1993 (11.8% alc)
	Colour: Old gold **Bouquet**: Barnyard **Taste**: Intensely sweet, barley sugar, burnt finish. Heavy on the palate. Lacks balancing acidity

☆☆☆½	D'Angelo Ice Wine 1992 (11% alc)
	Colour: Old gold **Bouquet**: Apricot, tangerine **Taste**: Sweet, toffee, soft yet intense peach and apricot flavours with lively acidity

☆☆☆	Henry of Pelham Riesling Icewine 1991 (11% alc)
	Colour: Pale gold **Bouquet**: Honey, stewed peaches, vanilla **Taste**: Sweet, lemon crystals and honey. Synthetic middle taste

☆☆☆☆	Henry of Pelham Riesling Icewine 1992 (10.5% alc)
	Colour: Yellow straw **Bouquet**: Fresh, peachy **Taste**: Lively peach and apricot. Great length, a keeper

☆☆☆½	Hillebrand Vidal Icewine 1991 (10% alc)
	Colour: Old gold **Bouquet**: Candy apple **Taste**: Toffee, apple, orange. Good length, butter and toffee finish

☆☆☆☆	Hillebrand (Vidal) Icewine 1992 (11.5% alc)
	Colour: Yellow straw **Bouquet**: Vanilla, apricot, peach **Taste**: Honey sweet, intense peach flavour, great length

☆☆☆☆	Inniskillin Vidal Icewine 1986 (10.3% alc)
	Colour: Deep copper-bronze **Bouquet**: Mature, Tokay-like, toffee, orange **Taste**: Orange, tea leaf, spicy. Lively acidity, great length. Toasty barley sugar finish

☆☆½	Inniskillin Vidal Icewine 1991
	Colour: Straw **Bouquet**: Lean, vegetal **Taste**: Light, acidic, lemon and orange. Falls short

☆☆☆☆

Inniskillin Vidal Icewine 1992 (11.4% alc)

Colour: Straw **Bouquet**: Intense peach
Taste: Lively peach and apricot, medium sweet, tangy acidity but good fruity finish

☆☆☆☆

Inniskillin Vidal Icewine 1993 (11.4% alc)

Colour: Light gold **Bouquet**: Fresh, peachy
Taste: Delicate, medium-bodied, well balanced, orange and apricot flavours. Lovely toffee and sweet grapefruit finish

☆☆☆
(>☆☆☆½)

Jackson-Triggs Vidal Ice Wine 1993 (11% alc)

Colour: Yellow gold **Bouquet**: Fresh, peachy
Taste: Peachy sweet with aggressive tangerine-like acidity. Medium-bodied, good length. Needs time

☆☆☆

Kittling Ridge Icewine 1991 (11% alc)

Colour: Pale gold **Bouquet**: Peach
Taste: Honeyed peach, soft in the mouth, tobacco leaf finish

☆☆☆

Kittling Ridge Ice Wine & Brandy (17% alc) (Non-VQA)

Colour: Light amber **Bouquet**: Caramel, peach, spiritous
Taste: Sweet, Pineau des Charentes style, grassy finish

☆☆☆

Kittling Ridge Icewine & Eau-de-Vie (17% alc) (Non-VQA)

Colour: Almost water white, hint of lemon
Bouquet: Kirsch-like
Taste: Sweet, spiritous, white chocolate and cherry finish

☆☆☆

Kittling Ridge Icewine & Eau-de-Vie (17% alc) (eau-de-vie component made from distilled Icewine)

Colour: Aged ivory, the colour of old piano keys
Bouquet: Spiritous, Mirabelle-like
Taste: Off-dry, chocolatey

☆☆☆½

Kittling Ridge Icewine & Brandy (17% alc) (seven-year-old Ontario brandy)

Colour: Old gold **Bouquet**: Spiritous, caramel, orange
Taste: Soft, round, sweetish, well balanced. Little Icewine character, but very pleasant

★★★½

Kittling Ridge Icewine Grappa 1991 (30% alc) (Non-VQA)

Colour: Water white **Bouquet:** Spiritous, eau-de-vie nose
Taste: Sweetish quite elegant spirit that lingers on the palate

★★★

Konzelmann Vidal Icewine 1991 (11% alc)

Colour: Old gold **Bouquet:** Sweet canned peaches, vanilla
Taste: Very sweet, unctuous, perfumed. Needs more balancing acidity

★★★½

Konzelmann Vidal Icewine 1992 (11.3% alc)

Colour: Yellow straw **Bouquet:** Honeyed, spicey, peach
Taste: Intensely sweet, vanilla and canned peaches

★★★½

Lakeview Cellars Vidal Icewine 1991 (12.4% alc)

Colour: Old gold **Bouquet:** Intense honey and apricot
Taste: Rich extract, high acidity, good length

★★★

Lakeview Cellars Vidal Icewine 1992

Colour: Copper-gold **Bouquet:** Honey, dried apricot
Taste: Unctuously sweet, heavy, lacks balancing acidity

★★★½

LeBlanc Estate Icewine 1992 (11% alc)

Colour: Straw **Bouquet:** Vanilla, peach
Taste: Honey, light, elegant, lingering with good length and an orangey finish

★★★½

London Winery Vidal Icewine 1992

Colour: Bronze **Bouquet:** Peach, apricot, tobacco leaf
Taste: Orange, lively acidity, appley taste. Fresh, cleansing, tea-like finish. Acidic finish

★★★½

Marynissen Riesling Icewine 1991 (10.8% alc)

Colour: White gold **Bouquet:** Ripe peach
Taste: Rich, full-bodied, unctuous, toffee and orange. Good length

★★★

Marynissen Riesling Icewine 1992 (10.8% alc)

Colour: Pale gold **Bouquet:** Discreet, peachy
Taste: Shy flavours of peach and toffee. Sweet on the palate, a little heavy

☆☆½
(>☆☆☆)

Marynissen Vidal Icewine 1993 (8.5% alc)

Colour: Deep yellow gold **Bouquet:** Celery
Taste: Unctuous, rather ponderous, peach and apricot flavours, heavy on the palate. Lacks structure

---

☆☆☆☆

Reif Vidal Icewine 1991 (11.5% alc)

Colour: Yellow straw **Bouquet:** Delicate, apricot
Taste: Well balanced, great length

☆☆☆☆

Reif Vidal Icewine 1992 (11.5% alc)

Colour: Yellow straw **Bouquet:** Honeyed peach
Taste: Ripe, peachy, full-bodied, honey-sweet

☆☆☆☆

Stoney Ridge Vidal Icewine 1991 (11% alc)

Colour: Copper gold **Bouquet:** Intense lychee, peach
Taste: Rich, exotic Turkish Delight, intense. Long lingering burnt toffee finish

---

☆☆☆☆

Stoney Ridge Traminer Icewine 1992 (11.5% alc)

Colour: Yellow straw **Bouquet:** Exotic, Turkish Delight
Taste: Sweet, cardomom, orange. Unctuous, good acidity

☆☆☆

Stoney Ridge Vidal Icewine 1992 (11% alc)

Colour: Copper-gold **Bouquet:** Mealy, peachy
Taste: Unctuous, peach jam. Acid kicks in late

☆☆☆☆

Thirty Bench Riesling Icewine 1994 (11% alc)

Colour: Straw **Bouquet:** Classic Icewine nose, grilled apricot
Taste: Unctuous, toffee and dried apricot. Intense, luscious sweetness and balancing acidity

---

☆☆☆

Thirty Bench Riesling Icewine 1992 (11% alc)

Colour: Deep golden **Bouquet:** Sweet apple
Taste: Thick, unctuous, toffee, orange and raisins. Heavy with a raisiny finish and little bitterness

---

☆☆☆½

Vineland Estates Vidal Icewine 1991 (10.4% alc)

Colour: Bronze **Bouquet:** Sweet, minty tangerine
Taste: Soft, toffee and orange. Good length, sweet. Could do with a touch more acid

☆☆☆ Vinoteca Vidal Ice Wine 1991 (11.5% alc)

Colour: Golden copper **Bouquet:** Spirity, slightly volatile, caramel
Taste: Heavy, sweet, burnt sugar, tends to cloy, lacking cleansing acidity

☆☆☆½ Vinoteca Ice Wine 1992 (11.5% alc)

Colour: Yellow gold **Bouquet:** Spirity, burnt orange peel, hint of volatility
Taste: Rich toffee and orange flavours. Good length in the mouth, barley sugar finish

☆☆☆½ Vinoteca Vidal Ice Wine 1991 (14% alc) 8-4-93

Colour: Golden **Bouquet:** Botrytis, hint of olive
Taste: Sweet, toffee, orange. Sweet but light on the palate. Good length, grows in the mouth

☆☆☆ Vinoteca Vidal Ice Wine 1993 (12% alc) ornamental bottle

Colour: Straw **Bouquet:** Herbaceous, peachy
Taste: Sweet grapefruit, but lacks intensity. More like a late harvest Vidal

☆☆☆☆ Willow Heights Riesling Ice Wine 1992 (10.5% alc)

Colour: Deep straw **Bouquet:** Aromatic, orange, peach
Taste: Light-bodied, peachy-tangerine flavours, good acidity, not too sweet, good finishing acidity. Great length

British Columbia Icewines
(half bottles)

☆☆☆½
(>☆☆☆☆)
🍷

Hainle Riesling Ice Wine 1990 (17.1% alc)
(121 half bottles produced)

Colour: Pale gold   **Bouquet**: Chocolate and toffee
Taste: White chocolate, powerful in the mouth with sweet grapefruit acidity that prolongs the taste. Well balanced in spite of the high alcohol

---

☆☆
🍷

Jackson-Triggs Johannisberg Riesling Ice Wine 1993 (10.5% alc)

Colour: Yellow straw   **Bouquet**: Musty
Taste: Sweet, intense sweetness, good acidity, spoiled by off-flavours

---

☆☆☆½
🍷

Mission Hill Grand Reserve Bacchus Icewine 1993 (11.5% alc)

Colour: Golden   **Bouquet**: Lucious, honey, raisins, orange
Taste: Thick and unctuous, raisiny fruit, lemon and passion fruit flavours, with a Muscat raisin finish. A little more acidity would have brought the wine more into balance

---

☆☆☆½
🍷

Mission Hill Grand Reserve Riesling Icewine 1992 (10.8% alc)

Colour: Straw   **Bouquet**: Sweet, Botrytis nose, dried peach
Taste: Unctuous, peachy flavour, medium sweet, good acidity

☆☆☆½
🍷

Peller Estates Trinity Icewine 1994 (11% alc) half bottle
(60% Riesling, 35% Vidal, 5% Ehrenfelser)

Colour: Delicate straw   **Bouquet**: Apricot, peach, orange
Taste: Rich layered fruit. Smooth, viscous nectar

☆☆½
🍷

Summerhill Pinot Noir Eiswein 1993 (7% alc)

Colour: Ruby-mahogany   **Bouquet**: Cooked nose
Taste: Intensely sweet, thick, syrupy, raspberry jam flavour. More like a liqueur. Overpowers the palate

---

*T*ASTING NOTES

*T*he following tasting notes are my personal assessments of the wines at the time I sampled them. I have evaluated them on their colour, bouquet and taste, and then I rated them using a zero to four-star system. My tasting notes for British Columbia and Quebec are augmented by those of my colleagues, Dave Gamble and Thomas Bachelder, respectively. They followed the same rating criteria as I did.

Since wines mature in the bottle, they may change their characteristics: with age a young red wine will lose the astringency as its tannins soften, and whites will develop more bouquet. But there is an underlying architecture to a fine wine that does not change. If a wine is well balanced — when its fruit, alcohol, acidity and tannins (and oak if barrel-aged or barrel-fermented) are all in harmony with no one element overpowering the rest — then its breeding will show at every stage of its development.

Unless otherwise noted, all wines were tasted from the standard 750 ml bottles at room temperature. Where I tasted a barrel sample — a wine that was still in the cask or tank and had not yet been bottled — I have noted the fact.

I did not, for instance, put all the Ontario Chardonnays or B.C. Rieslings together and taste them in competition with each other. I judged each product on its merits as it presented itself in the glass, keeping in mind how the winemaker described it on the label. I have also noted alcohol strength (when available), although this can vary by a degree.

Vintage-dated wines speak to the quality of the fruit that year, but the notes will give you an idea of the winemaker's individual style which will impress itself on the wine like a fingerprint. Where the information was available, I have given the constituents of the blends.

In some cases, I have given four stars to the least expensive wines when I deemed them to be well-made examples of what they are and have noted when I consider a wine to be of good value in terms of its price-quality ratio.

The tasting notes for Ontario and B.C. wines are based, for the most part, on VQA bottlings.

RATING SYSTEM

No stars	An unacceptable wine
☆	A poorly made wine, chemical taste or has no character at all
☆☆	An acceptable wine with not much to recommend it
☆☆☆	A good wine, clean and well made, true to its grape type
☆☆☆☆	A fine wine, the best that Canada has to offer

I have also given half stars (½) when a wine falls between two categories. When I consider that the wine will be better with at least a year of bottle aging, I have used the following device: ☆☆☆ (>☆☆☆☆).

DESCRIPTIVE TERMS

Trying to convey a sense of smell and taste in words is not easy. Wines can smell and taste of fruits, flowers, vegetables, nut, hay and grass, and more organic substances such as tobacco, earth, chalk, petrol, tea and chocolate. They can also smell of leather or rotting hay, like a barnyard or forest undergrowth (which is not necessarily unpleasant, as any lover of red Burgundy will tell you). I have used certain terms repeatedly almost as short-hand, which I would like to expand on here.

Colour: White wines I see as varying shades of straw colour ranging to lemon and gold. If I say straw-lime, to me it means a basic straw colour with hints of lime green. For reds, the range is cherry to purple-black with the majority falling in the ruby category. When reds begin to age, they can take on a tawny hue with hints of browning in the ruby.

Appearance: For sparkling wines, I have also assessed the quality of the bubbles (mousse) and have noted if it's made by the Champagne method (secondary fermentation in the bottle) or by the Charmat process (secondary fermentation in steel tanks).

Aromatic: Spicy, usually referring to the nose of Riesling, Muscat or Gewürztraminer.

Bouquet: When the wine offers little in the way of bouquet, I call it shy (others may say "dumb").

Austere: Very dry, lean fruit.

Citric: The fresh, acidic smell of citrus fruit.

Commercial: A wine that is made to appeal to a wide range of palates, usually with some residual sugar.

Complexity: A wine with more than one flavour; nuances in the bouquet and taste.

Extract: The flavour of the grape, more concentrated when fully ripe and yields are small.

Finish: The final taste; the taste that's left on the palate when you've swallowed the wine.

Flat: A wine that lacks acidity.

Flinty: The smell of struck flint.

Good Length: A lingering flavour carried along by the acidity.

Herbaceous: Grassy; leafy bouquet and flavour.

Herby: The smell of dried herbs.

Lactic: The smell of milk, from lactic acid. Usually after a malolactic fermentation.

Maderized: Aged white wines that tastes like sherry.

Off-dry: A touch of sweetness balanced by acidity.

Oxidized: Browning apple taste.

Residual sugar: A winemaker will stop the fermentation to leave some sugar in the wine or will add concentrated fresh grape juice to give the wine a touch of sweetness.

Soft: A smooth glycerol feeling of the wine on the tongue, usually associated with wines that have some residual sugar.

Structure: The shape of a wine, defined by its fruit, acidity and alcohol.

Sulphur: The burnt match-head smell in a wine. Sulphur is used to clean barrels and sulphites are employed as anti-oxidants. If too much is used and gets bound into the wine, it will be evident on the nose.

Tannin: The bitter-tasting compound in the skins, stalks and pits of grapes that gives young red wines a rasping, astringent finish. Tannins can also taste dusty in maturing wines.

Unctuous: An oiliness that coats the tongue, usually in sweet wines.

Varietal character: A wine should smell and taste of the grape from which it is made.

Volatile: The smell of acetone, balsamic vinegar or nail polish; a fault when too evident.

Young vines: A green, immature taste in the wine.

TASTE

If a wine reminds me of a well-known style, then I have described it as such; that is, Chablis-like, Mâconnais-style. I have indicated whether the wine is dry, off-dry or sweet, and when it is full-bodied I have drawn attention to the fact. The mark of a great wine is how long it lingers on the palate once you have swallowed it. This characteristic is evident in such descriptions as "good length."

Ontario Wines

Brights *White*

☆½   Brights Vidal 1992 (11% alc)

Colour: Straw   **Bouquet**: Oily, apple peel
Taste: Unctuous, heavy, acidic

Red

☆☆½   Brights Vintage Selection Baco Noir 1993 (12% alc)

Colour: Ruby   **Bouquet**: Bovril
Taste: Smoky, earthy, medicinal, fresh acidic finish

Cartier *Red*

☆   Cartier L'Ambiance Red (11% alc) screwtop litre (non-VQA)

Colour: Ruby   **Bouquet**: Sweetish
Taste: Thin, raspberry flavour, sweetish middle palate, not a lot of taste

Cave Spring Cellars *White*

☆☆☆
(>☆☆☆☆)   Cave Spring Chardonnay Reserve 1993 (13% alc) (barrel fermented and aged in Allier and Nevers oak for four months)

Colour: Bright straw   **Bouquet**: Vanilla, apple
Taste: Well balanced, dry green apple, Chablis-style. Good length. Needs time

☆☆☆
(>☆☆☆☆)   Cave Spring Chardonnay Bench 1994 (12.5% alc)

Colour: Grassy straw   **Bouquet**: Pear, grapefruit
Taste: Full-bodied, grapefruit and passionfruit flavours, good acidity, clean with a vanilla finish

☆☆☆
(>☆☆☆☆)

Cave Spring Chardonnay Reserve 1994
(barrel sample—aged in one-year-old Nevers)

Colour: Straw **Bouquet**: Grassy, grapefruit
Taste: Closed in behind the oak but sufficient fruit and acidity to mature well

☆☆☆☆

Cave Spring Riesling Dry 1993 (11.2% alc)

Colour: Pale straw **Bouquet**: Grapefruit
Taste: Ripe grapefruit, good middle fruit, well balanced

☆☆☆
(>☆☆☆☆)

Cave Spring Riesling Reserve 1994 (11.5% alc) tank sample

Colour: Pale straw, green highlights **Bouquet**: Fresh grapefruit
Taste: Very dry, lemony, grassy, grapefruit, zesty acidity, long lingering finish

☆☆☆
(>☆☆☆½)

Cave Spring Off-Dry Riesling 1994 (10% alc)

Colour: Pale straw, green highlights **Bouquet**: Yeasty, grapefruit skin **Taste**: Off-dry, grapefruit and kiwi flavours, good length. Nose will develop with some bottle age.

☆☆☆½

Cave Spring Indian Summer Riesling 1991 (12.5% alc) half bottle

Colour: Straw **Bouquet**: Apple
Taste: Off-dry, peachy-apricot. Full in the mouth. Good length.

Red

☆☆☆
(>☆☆☆☆)

Cave Spring Cabernet/Merlot 1991 (12.5% alc)

Colour: Purple **Bouquet**: Blackberry
Taste: Good extract, rich blackberry flavour, tannic finish

☆☆☆½
(>☆☆☆☆)

Cave Spring Cabernet/Merlot 1993 (12.5% alc)
(53% Cabernet Sauvignon/32% Merlot, aged eight months in Allier and Nevers oak)

Colour: Purple **Bouquet**: Vanilla, floral, blueberry
Taste: Medium-bodied, sweet fruit, blackberry and blueberry flavour with a fine spine of acidity, a tannic wrapping and an overlay of oaky vanilla

☆☆½	Cave Spring Gamay Noir 1992 (11% alc)
	Colour: Purple **Bouquet**: Cherry **Taste**: Fresh, dry, cherry. Acidic finish

☆☆☆½	Cave Spring Gamay Noir 1993 (12% alc)
	Colour: Purple-ruby **Bouquet**: Vanilla, cherry **Taste**: Light-bodied, black cherry and pepper. Hint of almond on the finish, clean with some tannin

☆☆☆	Cave Spring Gamay Noir 1994 (12% alc)
	Colour: Purple-red **Bouquet**: Cooked cherries **Taste**: Light-bodied, cherry and plum flavours, underlying acidity

Rosé

☆☆☆	Cave Spring Rosé 1994 (11% alc) (65% Gamay/19% Cabernet Sauvignon/16% Cabernet Franc)
	Colour: Pink with blue tints **Bouquet**: Redcurrant **Taste**: Fresh, lively redcurrant flavour, zingy finish, clean

Cedar Springs *White*

☆☆½	Cedar Springs Riesling 1993 (11.5% alc)
	Colour: Pale straw **Bouquet**: Apple, aromatic **Taste**: Sweet, appley taste, soft, clean fruit, off-dry character

☆☆	Cedar Springs Reserve Cuvée (11.5% alc) non-VQA
	Colour: Pale straw **Bouquet**: Lemony, hay **Taste**: Earthy, herby, not much definition

☆½	Cedar Springs Vidal 1993 (11.5% alc)
	Colour: Pale straw **Bouquet**: Chemical **Taste**: Sweetish, browning apple, oxidized fruit flavour

Red

☆☆☆½	Cedar Springs Baco Noir 1992 (11.5% alc)
	Colour: Light ruby **Bouquet**: Cassis **Taste**: Good extract, lots of acidity, lingering cassis flavour

☆☆☆ Cedar Springs Maréchal Foch 1993 (11.5% alc)

Colour: Ruby   **Bouquet:** Earthy plum
Taste: Sweetish fruit, good length, well made

Château des Charmes *White*

☆☆☆☆ Château des Charmes Auxerrois 1994 (11.5% alc)

Colour: Pale straw   **Bouquet:** Peachy nose
Taste: Crisp, fresh, peach and lemon flavours. Good length

☆☆ Château des Charmes Estate Chardonnay 1992 (12.5% alc)
Black label

Colour: Old gold   **Bouquet:** Butterscotch
Taste: Mature, maderised taste

☆☆☆½ Château des Charmes Estate Chardonnay 1993 (12.5% alc)

Colour: Straw   **Bouquet:** Spicy, vanilla and pear
Taste: Well balanced, sweetish vanilla, pear and pineapple
flavours. Soft middle palate, good length

☆☆☆☆ Château des Charmes Estate Chardonnay 1994 (12.5% alc)
(aged in Allier oak)

Colour: Straw   **Bouquet:** Creamy vanilla
Taste: Medium weight, sweet pear and apple flavours.
Good acidity, nicely balanced

☆☆☆☆ Château des Charmes Chardonnay 1993 Paul Bosc Estate
(12.5% alc) (barrel fermented, Allier oak)

Colour: Straw   **Bouquet:** Butterscotch, vanilla
Taste: Rich, soft, spicy and mouthfilling, Burgundian style.
Tangerine and caramel flavours. Elegant

☆☆☆½ Château des Charmes Estate Gewürztraminer 1992
(11.5% alc)

Colour: Straw   **Bouquet:** Developed lychee and rose petal
nose   **Taste:** Dry, spicy, aromatic. Good length and good
varietal character

☆☆☆

Château des Charmes Riesling Late Harvest 1990 (11% alc)

Colour: Straw **Bouquet:** Petrol, lime
Taste: Apricot, sweet, soft, peachy finish

☆☆☆☆

Château des Charmes Riesling Late Harvest 1992 (10.5% alc)

Colour: Straw, green highlights **Bouquet**: Petrol, grassy, sweet grapefruit
Taste: Medium-dry with tangy acidity, apricot and lemon flavours. Finishes well

Red

☆☆☆½

Château des Charmes Cabernet 1989 (12% alc)
(Estate bottled)

Colour: Ruby **Bouquet**: Cedar, blackcurrant
Taste: Medium weight, clean fruit, good length, well balanced light claret style

☆☆☆½

Château des Charmes Cabernet 1993 (12.5% alc)
(Cabernet Sauvignon, Cabernet Franc, Merlot)

Colour: Ruby **Bouquet**: Leafy blackcurrant, Cabernet Franc predominating
Taste: Medium bodied, delicate blackcurrant-blueberry flavours. Well balanced, elegant

☆☆½

Château des Charmes Gamay Noir 1993 (12% alc)

Colour: Light ruby **Bouquet**: Raspberry
Taste: Lean, green raspberry, light, acidic finish

☆☆☆½

Château des Charmes Gamay Nouveau 1993 (12% alc)

Colour: Purple **Bouquet**: Floral, plum
Taste: Black cherry, lots of extract, lively acidity, overlaid with a rose-like flavour. Acidic finish

☆☆½

Château des Charmes Pinot Noir 1990 (12.5% alc)

Colour: Aged plum **Bouquet**: Earthy
Taste: Dry, lean, austere, bitter chocolate flavour, woody. Not much extract

CHÂTEAU DES CHARMES   COLIO

☆☆☆½ **Château des Charmes Pinot Noir 1992 (12% alc)**

Colour: Tawny plum   **Bouquet:** Sweet, jammy
Taste: Light-bodied, dry raspberry, good varietal character, mature with a touch of tannin

Sparkling

☆☆☆☆ Château des Charmes Canadian Champagne Brut

Colour: Pale straw   **Bouquet:** Soft, creamy
Taste: Appley flavour, too much residual sugar to be Brut but a fine sparkling wine nonetheless

Colio   *White*

☆☆½ Colio Chardonnay 1992 (12% alc)

Colour: Straw   **Bouquet:** Flinty, apple
Taste: Soft, sweetish apple flavour, acidic

☆☆ Colio Riesling 1993 (12% alc)

Colour: Pale straw   **Bouquet:** Sweet peachy nose
Taste: Off-dry, short with a powerful acidic finish

☆☆½ Colio Riesling Traminer 1993 (12% alc)

Colour: Pale straw   **Bouquet:** Spicy, earthy nose
Taste: Dry, orange flavour, lively acidity with a tangerine-like finish

☆☆☆ Colio Vidal 1993 (12% alc)

Colour: Pale straw   **Bouquet:** Green plum
Taste: Off-dry, clean, well balanced, good acidity

Red

☆☆☆ Colio Cabernet Franc 1993 (12.5% alc)

Colour: Light ruby   **Bouquet:** Vanilla, black cherry
Taste: Fruity, cherry and raspberry flavours, light-bodied, simple and straightforward, some tannin and acidity

☆☆ Colio Maréchal Foch 1994 (12% alc)

Colour: Ruby   **Bouquet:** Sweaty
Taste: Sweetish, grapey, medium weight, acidic finish

Rosé

☆☆☆	Colio Blanc de Noir 1994 (10.5% alc) (Villard Noir grapes)
	Colour: Pale salmon **Bouquet**: Strawberry and rhubarb **Taste**: Off-dry, fruity, strawberry flavour, nicely balanced

Culotta *White*

☆☆☆	Culotta Gewürztraminer 1992 (12.2% alc)
	Colour: Pale straw **Bouquet**: Earthy, aromatic **Taste**: Rose petal, spicy, off-dry, good acidity, hot finish
☆☆½	Culotta Seyval Blanc 1994 (11.5% alc)
	Colour: Pale straw **Bouquet**: Earthy-flinty **Taste**: Herbaceous, green fruit flavours, acidic finish
☆☆	Culotta Vidal 1993 (11.5% alc)
	Colour: Pale straw **Bouquet**: Appley, slightly oxidized **Taste**: Off-dry, grassy, good acidity

D'Angelo *White*

☆☆½	D'Angelo Chardonnay 1992 (11.5% alc) Bordeaux-shaped bottle
	Colour: Palest straw **Bouquet**: Barnyard, sweet grass **Taste**: Tart, green apple flavour, acidic finish
☆☆☆	D'Angelo Chardonnay 1993 (11.5% alc) (oak fermented, aged five months on the lees in French oak)
	Colour: Straw **Bouquet**: Vanilla, caramel **Taste**: Smoky, tarry, toasty flavours. Oak predominates over the fruit
☆☆☆	D'Angelo Riesling 1993 (11.5% alc)
	Colour: Pale straw **Bouquet**: Piney **Taste**: Dry, crisp grapefruit flavour with a green apple finish

Red

☆☆ (>☆☆☆)	D'Angelo Cabernet Franc/Merlot 1993 (12% alc) (one year in American oak)
	Colour: Ruby **Bouquet**: Vanilla oak overpowering red currant fruit **Taste**: Oak flavours predominate over blackcurrant flavour. High acid finish

COLIO

CULOTTA

D'ANGELO

☆☆☆☆   D'Angelo Maréchal Foch 1993 (11.5% alc)

Colour: Ruby   **Bouquet:** Oaky, blackcurrant
Taste: Succulent sweet fruit, intense blackcurrant flavour, beautifully balanced

Domaine Vagners   *White*

☆☆½   Domaine Vagners Pinot Gris 1994 (11% alc)

Colour: Almost water white, pinkish tinge   **Bouquet:** Peach skin   **Taste:** Peachy flavour, good extract but somewhat green on the finish. Young vines. A good first effort

Red

☆☆½   Domaine Vagners Cabernet Franc 1993 (12% alc)

Colour: Deep cherry   **Bouquet:** Leafy. Blackcurrant and rhubarb   **Taste:** Spicy redcurrant. Lively acidity, green finish

☆☆☆   Domaine Vagners Cabernet Franc 1994 (barrel sample)

Colour: Purple   **Bouquet:** Vanilla, closed
Taste: Blackberry. Better extract than the 1993, but still acidic and green on the finish. Soft tannins. Young vines

☆☆½   Domaine Vagners Merlot 1994 (barrel sample)

Colour: Purple   **Bouquet:** Vanilla, blueberry
Taste: Initial fruit gives way to an acidic and tannic finish. Not enough extract, young vines

Henry of Pelham   *White*

☆☆½   Henry of Pelham Chardonnay 1992 Barrel Fermented (12.3% alc)

Colour: Straw, slightly murky   **Bouquet:** Buttery, alcoholic
Taste: light on extract, appley, heavy on the finish. Not enough fruit for the oak content. A clumsy wine

☆☆☆☆   Henry of Pelham Chardonnay 1993 Barrel Fermented (12.9% alc)

Colour: Straw   **Bouquet:** Buttery, pineapple
Taste: Elegant, spicy, pear and pineapple flavours, grows in the mouth. Great balance, beautifully made

☆☆☆☆

Henry of Pelham Chardonnay 1993 Proprietors' Reserve (12.5% alc)

Colour: Pale straw **Bouquet:** Spicy butterscotch
Taste: Medium-bodied, ripe on the palate, well balanced, apple and pineapple flavours. Rich and opulent

☆☆½
(>☆☆☆½)

Henry of Pelham Chardonnay 1994 Proprietors' Reserve (12.5% alc) (aged 3 months in Allier and Tronçais)

Colour: Pale straw **Bouquet:** Oaky, lactic nose
Taste: Spicy, lean apple flavour, still closed in

☆☆☆½
(>☆☆☆☆)

Henry of Pelham Riesling 1993 (11.5% alc)

Colour: Pale straw **Bouquet:** Grapefruit peel
Taste: Fresh, lively, grapefruit, tangerine and lime flavours. Lingering acidity

☆☆☆½

Henry of Pelham Riesling 1994 (10.5% alc)

Colour: Pale straw **Bouquet:** Grapefruit, minerally
Taste: Grapefruit and lime, crisp finish, good length

☆☆☆

Henry of Pelham Riesling 1993 Proprietors' Reserve (12.1% alc)

Colour: Pale straw, lime hints **Bouquet:** Earthy, grapefruit
Taste: Initial roundness on the palate gives way to citrus acidity. Lacks the balance of the simpler Riesling 1993.

☆☆☆½
(>☆☆☆☆)

Henry of Pelham Riesling 1994 Proprietors' Reserve (11% alc)

Colour: Pale straw **Bouquet:** Floral-lime
Taste: Well structured, grapefruit and spring flowers, fine acidic spine. A little closed.

☆☆☆

Henry of Pelham Vidal 1993 (11.5% alc)

Colour: Straw **Bouquet:** Grapefruit peel **Taste:** Good fruit, lively melon and grapefruit flavours. Good length

☆☆☆

Henry of Pelham Vidal Select Late Harvest 1994 (10.5% alc) half bottle

Colour: Deep straw **Bouquet:** Icewine style nose, apricot
Taste: Initial honeyed apricot and pear flavour thins to a lively acidic finish

Red

☆☆☆½ | Henry of Pelham Baco Noir 1992 (American oak)

Colour: Dense purple **Bouquet**: Smoky blackberry
Taste: Intense blackberry flavour with an acidic punch at
the end

☆☆☆☆ | Henry of Pelham Baco Noir 1993 (12.5% alc)

Colour: Ruby **Bouquet**: Black cherry
Taste: Smoky, tarry, lively in the mouth, clean finish

☆☆☆
(>☆☆☆☆) | Henry of Pelham Baco Noir 1994 (12.5% alc)
(aged seven months in American oak, 35% new oak)

Colour: Purple-ruby **Bouquet**: Coconut, blackberry
Taste: Smoky blackberry, lively acidity, tight fruit. Not as
intense as the 1993, but elegant

☆☆☆
(>☆☆☆☆) | Henry of Pelham Cabernet/Merlot 1993 (12.5% alc)
(46% Cabernet Sauvignon, 5% Cabernet franc, 49% Merlot;
aged fourteen months in Allier and Tronçais)

Colour: Purple-ruby **Bouquet**: Blueberry
Taste: Light bodied, nicely tuned berry character. Elegant, youthful

---

☆☆☆ | Henry of Pelham Gamay Noir 1992 (12% alc)

Colour: Purple **Bouquet**: Cherry, leather
Taste: Light, dry, lively pomegranate flavour, acidic finish

☆☆½
(>☆☆☆½) | Henry of Pelham Merlot 1991 (13.2% alc)

Colour: Purple **Bouquet**: Closed
Taste: Closed-in fruit, powerful, full-bodied, tannic

Rosé

☆☆☆ | Henry of Pelham Cabernet Franc Rosé 1994 (10.5% alc)

Colour: Pinkish with blue tints **Bouquet**: Intense varietal
nose, red currant, elderberry
Taste: Fresh, almost Sauvignon Blanc-like in character.
Surprising for a rosé but quite delicious

Hernder Estate *White*

☆½	Hernder Estate Chardonnay 1992 (11.5% alc)
	Colour: Pale straw **Bouquet**: Caramel
	Taste: Browning apple flavour, short. Oxidized fruit

☆☆	Hernder Estate Vidal 1992 (11% alc)
	Colour: Pale straw **Bouquet**: Cooked nose
	Taste: Baked apple flavour, acidic, browning apple finish

☆☆☆½	Hernder Riesling 1994 (11% alc)
	Colour: Pale straw **Bouquet**: Apricot
	Taste: Ripe fruit flavours, crisp citrus and peach. Good length and well balanced

Red

☆☆☆	Hernder Baco Noir 1994 (11% alc)
	Colour: Ruby **Bouquet**: Smoky, tarry
	Taste: Medicinal, cooked blackberry, smoky, lots of character

Hillebrand Estates *White*

☆☆☆	Hillebrand Chardonnay 1992 (12.5% alc) (French oak and 30% American)
	Colour: Straw **Bouquet**: Buttery, vanilla
	Taste: Medium-bodied, light nutty and lemony tones. Touch of toastiness on the finish. Chabliesque but a little short. Good value

☆☆☆	Hillebrand Gewürztraminer 1992 (11.5% alc)
	Colour: Pale straw **Bouquet**: Sweet apple
	Taste: Not much Gewürz character. Soft, sweetish with a spicy flavour

☆☆☆	Hillebrand Gewürztraminer 1993 (12% alc)
	Colour: Straw **Bouquet**: Barnyard, spicy
	Taste: Sweetish lychee and rose petal. A little on the heavy side

☆☆½	Hillebrand Gewürztraminer 1994 (11.5% alc)
	Colour: Pale straw **Bouquet**: Not much Gewürz character, quite neutral **Taste**: More Riesling-like, spicy, aromatic, sweetish middle palate, dry finish

☆☆☆
🍷

Hillebrand Muscat Reserve 1992 (10.5% alc) (Morio Muscat and Muscat Ottonel)

Colour: Straw **Bouquet**: Tangerine
Taste: Medium-bodied, grapey, off-dry, clean

☆☆☆½
🍷

Hillebrand Muscat Reserve 1993 (11.5% alc)

Colour: Straw **Bouquet**: Perfumed, spicy
Taste: Clean, dry Muscat flavour, light on the palate, good length

☆☆☆☆
🍷

Hillebrand Muscat Reserve 1994 (11.5% alc) (66% Morio Muscat/33% Muscat Ottonel)

Colour: Pale straw **Bouquet**: Good intensity, perfumed Muscat nose
Taste: Sweet, perfumed, exotic, tangerine flavours. Clean and true. Good length and fine dry finish

☆☆☆
🍷

Hillebrand Pinot Gris 1992 (11.5% alc)

Colour: Deep straw **Bouquet**: Peachy
Taste: Fruity, medium-bodied, clean peach and melon flavours. Good length but could do with more extract. Slightly hot finish

☆☆☆½
🍷

Hillebrand Harvest Riesling 1992 (11% alc)

Colour: Straw **Bouquet**: Lime
Taste: Fresh citrus, grapefruit, good length with a hint of residual sugar. Soft finish. Good value

☆☆☆
(>☆☆☆☆)
🍷

Hillebrand Trius Riesling Dry 1992 (12% alc)

Colour: Pale straw **Bouquet**: Lime, apricot
Taste: Very dry, lemon and lime. Acidic finish. Needs time in the bottle

☆☆½
🍷

Hillebrand Riesling 1994 (10.5% alc)

Colour: Pale straw **Bouquet**: Fresh, green plum
Taste: Rather insipid with an acidic finish

☆☆☆½
🍷

Hillebrand Sauvignon Blanc 1994 (12% alc)

Colour: Pale straw **Bouquet**: Stony, grassy
Taste: Soft, initially sweetish grassy, gooseberry, asparagus flavours give way to lemony acidity. Very true to the variety

☆☆☆

Hillebrand Seyval Blanc 1994 (12.5% alc)

Colour: Pale straw **Bouquet**: Sweaty, grassy
Taste: Sweet grapefruit and elderberry, good acidity and lingering flavour

☆☆☆½

Hillebrand Vidal 1994 (13% alc)

Colour: Pale straw **Bouquet**: Stony, green fruit
Taste: Full-bodied, very dry, green plum and citrus flavour, crisp finish

☆☆

Hillebrand Vidal Late Harvest 1991 (10% alc) half bottle

Colour: Straw **Bouquet**: Mushroom
Taste: Off-dry, bitter

Red

☆☆☆

Hillebrand Cabernet Franc 1994 (12% alc)

Colour: Light purple **Bouquet**: Woody, blueberry
Taste: Floral, blackberry, light-bodied, elegant berry flavour, acidic, light tannic finish

☆☆☆½

Hillebrand Gamay 1992 (12% alc)

Colour: Purple ruby **Bouquet**: Rose, raspberry
Taste: pomegranate, sweet rhubarb, light, soft, delicate. Good value

☆☆☆

Hillebrand Gamay Noir 1994 (12% alc)

Colour: Deep cherry **Bouquet**: Smoky, earthy, gamey
Taste: Light-bodied, sour cherry, fresh, fruity, lively acidity, slightly bitter finish

☆☆

Hillebrand Maréchal Foch 1993 (12% alc)

Colour: Light ruby **Bouquet**: Smoky, sweaty
Taste: Lean fruit, astringent with an acidic finish

☆☆☆☆

Hillebrand Trius Red 1991 (12% alc)

Colour: Dense purple **Bouquet**: Blackcurrant, vanilla
Taste: Rich blackcurrant flavour with well-integrated oak. A lovely wine; one of the best Canadian reds.

Rosé

☆☆½   Hillebrand Pinot Noir Rosé 1994 (11.5% alc)

Colour: Tawny-salmon   **Bouquet:** Roasted, earthy nose
Taste: Citric, tart, lacking Pinot Noir character, medium-bodied, hot finish

Inniskillin *White*

☆☆☆☆   Inniskillin Alliance Chardonnay 1993 (13% alc) (first joint venture wine with Burgundy shipper Jaffelin: fermented and aged for eleven months in Nevers and Allier *barriques*)

Colour: Straw   **Bouquet:** Vanilla, spicy lemon and pear
Taste: Elegant, pineapple and citrus flavour with a toasted nut nuance, giving way to a toasty butterscotch finish. Very elegant, in Pouilly-Fuissé style

☆☆☆½   Inniskillin Auxerrois 1993 (11% alc)

Colour: Pale straw   **Bouquet:** Vanilla, lemony
Taste: Fresh, well balanced pear flavour, good length

☆☆☆½   Inniskillin Beamsville Bench Chardonnay 1991 (12.5% alc) (aged eight months in French oak)

Colour: Straw   **Bouquet:** Butter, caramel
Taste: Rich, toffee-like, mature, dry honey taste. Good fruit and length, lively acidic finish

☆☆☆½   Inniskillin Chardonnay Reserve 1991 (12.5% alc) (barrel fermented and aged in French oak)

Colour: Pale straw   **Bouquet:** Lemony, vanilla
Taste: Dry, appley, well balanced, Chablis style

☆☆☆½
(>☆☆☆☆)   Inniskillin Chardonnay 1992 Butler's Grant (12% alc) (aged eight months in French *barriques*)

Colour: Light straw   **Bouquet:** Toasty vanilla, sweetish nose
Taste: Crisp apple flavour, Mâcon-style. Good length

☆☆½   Inniskillin Chardonnay 1992 Seeger Vineyard (12% alc)

Colour: Pale straw   **Bouquet:** Musty, butterscotch
Taste: lean, buttery middle palate, acidic finish

☆☆☆½
(>☆☆☆☆)

Inniskillin Chardonnay Reserve 1993 (12.8% alc)

Colour: Pale straw, green highlights **Bouquet:** Bench nose, grassy-grapefruit
Taste: Well balanced, apple and green fruit, nicely integrated oak. Showing well now and will develop in the bottle

---

☆☆☆½

Inniskillin Chardonnay 1994 (12% alc)

Colour: Pale straw **Bouquet:** Barnyard, apple and pear nose
Taste: Well balanced, well made wine, medium-bodied, apple-pear flavour, good length

---

☆☆☆½
(>☆☆☆☆)

Inniskillin Chardonnay Reserve 1994 (12.8% alc)

Colour: Straw **Bouquet:** Spicy, barnyard with vanilla
Taste: Soft initial flavours of apple, pear and toffee. Medium weight. Good length. California style

---

☆☆☆½
(>☆☆☆☆)

Inniskillin Chardonnay 1994 Klose Vineyard barrel sample

Colour: Straw **Bouquet:** Spicy, vanilla
Taste: Oaky, pineapple, strong acidity, smoky, toasty spine, great length with a nutty, lemony finish

---

☆☆☆☆

Inniskillin Chardonnay 1994 Seeger Vineyard (barrel sample)

Colour: Pale straw **Bouquet:** Apple
Taste: Leaner and more forward than Klose Vineyard Chardonnay. More Burgundian in style with a pineapple flavour, elegant with good length

---

☆☆☆½
(>☆☆☆☆)

Inniskillin Chardonnay 1994 Schuele Vineyard (barrel sample)

Colour: Pale straw **Bouquet:** Apple and pear
Taste: Chabliesque, leanest of the single vineyard Chardonnays. Pear and apple flavours, good acidity, nutty, lemony finish

---

☆☆☆

Inniskillin Melon 1992 (11% alc) (Muscadet grape)

Colour: Pale straw **Bouquet:** Lemon, herbs
Taste: Very crisp, Muscadet-style. Not as full as the '91

INNISKILLIN

INNISKILLIN

☆☆½
(>☆☆☆½)   Inniskillin Pinot Grigio 1994 (12.5% alc)

Colour: Pale straw   **Bouquet:** Yeasty nose
Taste: Dry peachy flavour, good middle taste and good length. Will lose some of its yeasty flavour with bottle age

☆☆☆   Inniskillin Riesling 1993 (11% alc) (non-VQA, some Washington fruit)

Colour: Pale straw   **Bouquet:** Spicy, aromatic
Taste: Grapefruit taste, good middle fruit, lingering acidity, crisp finish

☆☆☆½   Inniskillin Riesling 1994 (12% alc)

Colour: Palest straw   **Bouquet:** Mealy
Taste: Off-dry, grapefruit, nicely balanced, good length

☆☆½
(>☆☆☆)   Inniskillin Late Harvest Riesling 1993 (non-VQA, some Washington fruit)

Colour: Pale straw   **Bouquet:** Baked apple, petrol
Taste: Medium sweet, grapey, mango flavours

☆☆½   Inniskillin Sauvignon Blanc 1992 (11% alc)

Colour: Pale straw   **Bouquet:** Herbaceous
Taste: Light, grassy, green fig. Good acidity but lacking punch. Young vines?

☆☆☆   Inniskillin Seyval Blanc 1992 (11.5% alc)

Colour: Pale straw   **Bouquet:** Earthy, fennel
Taste: Tangerine flavour with good citric acid finish

☆☆½   Inniskillin Seyval Blanc 1993 (12% alc)

Colour: Straw   **Bouquet:** Floral, green plum
Taste: Sweetish fruit but not really together. The acid kicks in where the fruit stops

☆☆   Inniskillin Late Harvest Vidal 1993 (11% alc)

Colour: Pale straw   **Bouquet:** Sulphur, grapefruit peel
Taste: Sweet, grapey, soft

Fortified

☆☆☆☆   Fleur d'Ontario (16% alc) (aperitif wine in Pineau des Charentes style, made from Vidal and Geisenheim grapes stopped in early fermentation with grape brandy)

Colour: Pale straw   **Bouquet**: Sweet vanilla
Taste: Off-dry, tangerine flavour, rich and mouth-filling

Red

☆☆½   Inniskillin Cabernet Franc 1992 (12% alc)

Colour: Light plum   **Bouquet**: Cedar, rose, raspberry
Taste: Light-bodied, dry raspberry flavour, lacking extract

☆☆☆   Inniskillin Cabernet Franc 1993 (12.5% alc)

Colour: Medium ruby   **Bouquet**: Cherry-berry
Taste: Light, earthy, cherry flavour prolonged by acidity. Soft tannins

☆☆☆   Inniskillin Cabernet Sauvignon 1994 (barrel sample)
(>☆☆☆½)

Colour: Purple   **Bouquet**: Smoky, perfumed
Taste: Red currant and green pepper flavours

☆☆☆☆   Inniskillin Cabernet Sauvignon 1991 Klose Vineyard (12.5% alc)

Colour: Purple   **Bouquet**: Vanilla, blackberry
Taste: Rich, ripe blackcurrant, creamy texture, soft on the palate. Drinking well now

☆☆☆   Inniskillin Maréchal Foch 1993 (12% alc)

Colour: Ruby   **Bouquet**: Flinty, earthy cherry
Taste: Smoky cherry flavour, acidic finish

☆☆☆   Inniskillin Petite Syrah 1992 (barrel tasting)
(>☆☆☆½)   (Allier, Nevers and Tronçais oak)

Colour: Purple   **Bouquet**: Oaky
Taste: Blackberry and pepper, evident acidity. Reminiscent of Chinon

☆☆☆
(>☆☆☆½)

Inniskillin Alliance Pinot Noir 1993 (13% alc)
(first joint venture wine with the Burgundy shippers
Jaffelin: fermented in stainless steel, aged eleven months
in French *barriques)*

Colour: Deep cherry **Bouquet**: Flinty, cherry-raspberry
Taste: Lean and sinewy, elegant, raspberry and mulberry.
Savigny-les-Beaune-style, but lacking concentration of
middle fruit, good acidity, evident tannin

☆☆☆☆

Inniskillin Pinot Noir Reserve 1991 (12.8% alc)

Colour: Ruby-purple **Bouquet**: Vanilla, flinty, raspberry
Taste: Lively raspberry, well balanced, some tannin

☆☆½

Inniskillin Pinot Noir Reserve 1992 (12% alc)

Colour: Light ruby **Bouquet**: Rust, tomato
Taste: Earthy, lean, unripe raspberry, lively acidity, tart finish

☆☆☆
(>☆☆☆½)

Inniskillin Pinot Noir Reserve 1993

Colour: Pale ruby **Bouquet**: Earthy, flinty **Taste**: Earthy,
cherry, light extract, some tannin. Minty finish, delicate

☆☆☆
(>☆☆☆½)

Inniskillin Pinot Noir Reserve 1994 (barrel sample)

Colour: Purple **Bouquet**: Vanilla, mulberry
Taste: Firm, black cherry, lean, well-knit, good tannins

Rosé

☆☆☆☆

Inniskillin Rosé de Saignée 1994 (11.5% alc) (blend of Pinot
Noir, Cabernet Franc, Cabernet Sauvignon, Merlot; juice
bled off from tanks to intensify those varietal wines)

Colour: Pink with blue highlights **Bouquet**: Minty, wild
strawberry **Taste**: Fresh, wild strawberry flavour. Good
body and length. Refreshing

Sparkling

☆☆☆☆

Inniskillin L'Allemand (Charmat process) (Riesling and a
little Pinot Noir)

Appearance: Active mousse **Colour**: Pale straw, hint of
lime **Bouquet**: Floral, lemon-lime
Taste: Fruity Riesling taste, beautifully balanced with a
clean lemony finish. Good value.

Jackson-Triggs *White*

☆☆☆	Jackson-Triggs Chardonnay 1992 (11.5% alc) (55% Ontario, 35% Chardonnay from California and Western Europe)
	Colour: Pale straw **Bouquet**: Vanilla, spicy **Taste**: Appley, light fruit character. Good value

☆☆½	Jackson-Triggs Chardonnay 1993 (11.5% alc) (non-VQA, aged in American, Slovenian and French oak)
	Colour: Pale straw **Bouquet**: Vanilla, sweetish, toasty **Taste**: Soft on the palate, a touch of residual sugar, a little short, good acidity

☆☆☆	Jackson-Triggs Chenin Blanc 1993 (11.5% alc)
	Colour: Pale straw **Bouquet**: Pear **Taste**: Good fruit, medium-bodied, green apple and quince flavours, lively acidity and good length

☆☆	Jackson-Triggs Gewürztraminer 1992 (11% alc)
	Colour: Pale straw **Bouquet**: Sweet, aromatic **Taste**: Sweetish with tart lemony acidity. Not much varietal character, more Riesling in style

☆☆☆	Jackson-Triggs Gewürztraminer 1993 (11% alc) non-VQA
	Colour: Pale straw **Bouquet**: Spicy, vegetal **Taste**: Sweet lychee and melon flavours, well balanced

☆☆☆	Jackson-Triggs Dry Riesling 1993 (11.5% alc)
	Colour: Pale straw **Bouquet**: Hay, green fruit **Taste**: Crisp, green apple, acidic finish

☆½	Jackson-Triggs Johannisberg Riesling 1992 (11% alc)
	Colour: Straw **Bouquet**: Gummy, apple **Taste**: Baked apple and grapefruit flavours, tired finish

Red

☆☆½	Jackson-Triggs Cabernet Franc 1993 (12.5% alc)
	Colour: Light ruby **Bouquet**: Cherry pits **Taste**: Dry, lean redcurrant flavour. Not much extract, acidic finish

☆☆½ Jackson-Triggs Cabernet Sauvignon 1992 (11.5% alc) (blend of Ontario and imported wines)

Colour: Light ruby **Bouquet**: Raspberry
Taste: Light, fruity, candied raspberry, fresh acidity

☆☆½
(>☆☆☆) Jackson-Triggs Cabernet Sauvignon 1993 (11.5% alc) (non-VQA, 30% Ontario fruit)

Colour: Ruby **Bouquet**: Vanilla, cherry
Taste: Redcurrant, light-bodied, evident acidity

☆☆☆ Jackson-Triggs Cabernet Sauvignon Reserve (12.5% alc) (non-VQA, 30% Ontario fruit)

Colour: Ruby **Bouquet**: Vanilla
Taste: Black cherry, medium-bodied, acidic with a tannic finish, good length

Kittling Ridge *White*

☆½ Kittling Ridge Dry Reserve White (11.5% alc) screwtop litre (non-VQA)

Colour: Pale straw **Bouquet**: Gummy
Taste: Dry pear, not much extract, soft on the palate

☆☆½ Kittling Ridge Sauvignon Blanc 1992 (11.5% alc)

Colour: Pale straw **Bouquet**: Grassy, peapod
Taste: Crisp, citric, herbaceous and herby. Long acidic finish but short on middle fruit

Red

☆☆½ Kittling Ridge Cabernet Sauvignon 1992 (11.5% alc)

Colour: Light ruby **Bouquet**: Smoky plum
Taste: Light cherry and plum flavours, good acidity but not much Cabernet character. More Beaujolais in style. Good value

☆☆ Kittling Ridge Dry Reserve Red (11.5% alc) screwtop litre (non-VQA)

Colour: Ruby-purple **Bouquet**: Cooked cherry
Taste: Dry, cherry skin, plum, austere and slightly bitter

Konzelmann *White*

☆☆☆☆
🍷

Konzelmann Chardonnay Reserve 1993 (12.5% alc) barrel fermented

Colour: Deep straw **Bouquet**: Buttery-melon
Taste: Sweet fruit, spicy melon taste, beautifully balanced with a long crisp finish

☆☆☆
(☆☆☆>½)
🍷

Konzelmann Riesling 1993

Colour: Pale straw **Bouquet**: Apricot, floral, clean
Taste: Elegant, off-dry, good length with good acidity

☆☆☆½
🍷

Konzelmann Riesling (2) 1994 (11.4% alc) (Green label)

Colour: Straw **Bouquet**: Sweet, aromatic
Taste: Off-dry, Spätlese character. Good fruit character and good length

☆☆☆
🍷

Konzelmann Late Harvest Riesling 1991 (12% alc)

Colour: Straw **Bouquet**: Apple
Taste: Off-dry, apple flavour, well balanced

☆☆
🍷

Konzelmann Vidal 1993 (11.2% alc)

Colour: Straw **Bouquet**: Kirsch-like nose
Taste: Dry yellow cherry, acidic, tart finish

☆☆☆½
🍷

Konzelmann Late Harvest Vidal 1991 (11.5% alc) half bottle

Colour: Old gold **Bouquet**: Toffee **Taste**: Apricot and honey, burnt sugar. Good acidity. Orange and toffee finish

Red

☆☆☆
🍷

Konzelmann Cabernet Sauvignon Merlot Reserve 1991 (12% alc) (25% Merlot, part six months in old Slovonian oak, part three months in Nevers)

Colour: Purple **Bouquet**: Jammy blackcurrant
Taste: Good extract, soft, defined berry taste

☆☆½
(>☆☆☆)
🍷

Konzelmann Pinot Noir 1993

Colour: Cherry **Bouquet**: Fruity, raspberry
Taste: Lean and sinewy with a lively acidic spine and peppery finish. Needs time

KONZELMANN

Lakeview Cellars *White*

☆☆☆

Lakeview Cellars Chardonnay 1993 (12.4% alc)

Colour: Pale straw **Bouquet:** Creamy, caramel and pear
Taste: Oaky, caramel with underlying acidity, toasty finish,
a little short

☆☆

Lakeview Cellars Pinot Gris 1992 (11.4% alc)

Colour: Pale straw **Bouquet:** Shy nose
Taste: Green peach flavour, acidic. Tinny finish. Young vines?

☆☆☆

Lakeview Cellars Pinot Gris 1993 (13.7% alc)

Colour: Pale straw **Bouquet:** Alcoholic nose
Taste: Full-bodied, heavy on the palate, peachy flavour,
good extract. Tart finish

☆☆☆½

Lakeview Cellars Pinot Gris 1994 (12.5% alc)

Colour: Pale straw **Bouquet:** Vanilla, peachy
Taste: Dry, lots of extract, good acidity but a little short on
the finish

☆☆

Lakeview Cellars Riesling 1993 (11.7% alc)

Colour: Straw **Bouquet:** Lemon crystals
Taste: Lemonade, citric finish, unbalanced, hot finish

☆☆☆☆

Lakeview Cellars Vidal 1992 (10.9% alc)

Colour: Pale straw **Bouquet:** Fruity
Taste: Off-dry, good fruit, lively peachy flavour. Well balanced with a lingering fresh finish

---

☆☆½

Lakeview Cellars Vidal 1993 (11.9% alc)

Colour: Pale straw **Bouquet:** Licorice
Taste: Grapefruit and orange, some sweetness on the finish, a little heavy on the palate

---

☆☆☆½

Lakeview Cellars Vidal Late Harvest 1994 (11.1% alc) half
bottle

Colour: Straw **Bouquet:** Sweet
Taste: Sweet, soft, intense peach, rich and full in the
mouth. Good length

☆☆☆½ Lakeview Cellars Riesling 1992 (11.7% alc)

Colour: Very pale straw **Bouquet**: Earthy, greengage
Taste: Lively, lemony, good length

Red

☆☆½ Lakeview Cellars Baco Noir 1993 (11.9% alc)

Colour: Dense purple **Bouquet**: Volatile, balsamic vinegar
Taste: Rose, black cherry, tannic finish

☆☆☆ Lakeview Cellars Cabernet Sauvignon 1992 (barrel sample)
(>☆☆☆½) (seven-year-old vines; American oak, 75% new, 25% two
years old)

Colour: Purple **Bouquet**: Spicy plum
Taste: Spicy, medium-bodied, blackcurrant, lively finish

☆☆☆½ Lakeview Cellars Cabernet Sauvignon 1993 (11.9% alc)
(>☆☆☆☆)

Colour: Dense purple **Bouquet**: Floral, rose, cinnamon,
spicy blueberry
Taste: Blueberry-blackberry, concentrated fruit, good
focused fruit, tannic finish

Leblanc Estate *White*

☆☆½ LeBlanc Estate Pinot Blanc (12.2% alc) non-vintage

Colour: Palest straw **Bouquet**: Earthy
Taste: Dry, herby, Italianate, grapefruit zest. Good length.

☆☆½ LeBlanc Estate Riesling 1993 (11.5% alc)

Colour: Very pale straw **Bouquet**: Herbaceous
Taste: Dry, citrus and grapefruit flavours, browning apple
finish

☆☆½ LeBlanc Estate Vidal 1993 (11.5% alc)

Colour: Straw **Bouquet**: Browning apple
Taste: Viscous, heavy on the palate, dry appley flavour

Rosé

☆☆ LeBlanc Estate Chant d'Eté (11.5% alc) (Cabernet and Vidal)

Colour: Tawny pink-gold **Bouquet**: Dry, rather tart, green
fruit flavours

Red

☆☆☆
(>☆☆☆½)

LeBlanc Estate Cabernet 1993 (12% alc) (non-VQA)

Colour: Purple   **Bouquet**: Good blackcurrant nose
Taste: Soft blackcurrant and licorice flavour, soft tannins, easy drinking

London *White*

☆☆☆

London Late Harvest Vidal 1993 (11.7% alc) half bottle
(Late Harvest Vidal with some Icewine blended in)

Colour: Light gold   **Bouquet**: Candy apple
Taste: Starts sweet and honeyed raisin character in the mouth and then thins out with a dry apricot flavour

Magnotta *White*

☆☆½
(>☆☆☆)

Magnotta Chardonnay 1993 (12% alc)
(65% Lenko Vineyard, 35% Niagara Peninsula)

Colour: Straw   **Bouquet**: Oaky, popcorn
Taste: Perfumed, vanilla oak, lean green apple fruit, oak predominates on the finish. Australian style

☆☆☆½

Magnotta Select Late Harvest Riesling 1993 (11% alc) half bottle

Colour: Old gold   **Bouquet**: Caramel, lime
Taste: Rich, sweet, honeyed with a orangey-floral back taste

☆☆☆

Magnotta Select Late Harvest Vidal 1993 (11% alc) half bottle

Colour: Straw   **Bouquet**: Baked apple   **Taste**: Sweet, honeyed grapefruit, unctuous. Needs more acidity

Red

☆☆☆☆

Magnotta Cabernet/Merlot 1993 (12% alc)

Colour: Ruby-purple   **Bouquet**: Vanilla, blueberry, blackcurrant   **Taste**: Nicely focused fruit, good intensity, ripe blackcurrant and blueberry flavours. Well balanced, good length

☆☆☆

Magnotta Pinot Noir 1992 (12% alc)

Colour: Tawny ruby   **Bouquet**: Cooked cherry
Taste: Raspberry and cherry flavours, medium-bodied, nice balance

Maple Grove *White*

☆☆½	Maple Grove Chardonnay 1993 (11.5% alc) non-VQA
	Colour: Straw **Bouquet**: Apple
	Taste: Spicy apple, chunky, sweetish, not in harmony

Red

☆☆	Maple Grove Cabernet Sauvignon 1991 (12% alc) non-VQA
	Colour: Light purple **Bouquet**: Shy
	Taste: Sweetish plum and cherry, nicely balanced but not much excitement here. Some tannin on the finish

Marynissen Estates *White*

☆☆½	Marynissen Cabernet Sauvignon Blanc 1992 (11.5% alc) (Blanc de Noirs)
	Colour: Pale straw **Bouquet**: Shy nose
	Taste: Dry, nutty flavour, finish of white chocolate and toast. A bizarre wine, but interesting

☆☆☆½	Marynissen Barrel-Fermented Chardonnay 1993 (13% alc)
	Colour: Straw **Bouquet**: Apple, milky **Taste**: Sweet, spicy fruit, soft on the palate, caramel. Good balancing acidity

☆☆☆☆	Marynissen Barrel-Fermented Chardonnay 1992 (12% alc) (four months in one-year-old Allier, Tronçais, Nevers oak)
	Colour: Straw **Bouquet**: Vanilla, toast
	Taste: Toasty, buttery, lively acidity. Big in the mouth, a classy wine

☆☆☆☆	Marynissen Gewürztraminer 1992 (12.4% alc)
	Colour: Straw **Bouquet**: Spicy, lychee nose
	Taste: Intense lychee fruit, opulent and lingering on the palate. A fine Gewürz

☆☆☆☆	Marynissen Riesling 1993 (12% alc)
	Colour: Straw **Bouquet**: Ripe mango and grapefruit
	Taste: Rich and spicy with a touch of residual sugar, exotic flavours that linger on the palate

☆☆½	Marynissen Sauvignon Blanc 1994 (12% alc) (first harvest, fermented in French oak)
	Colour: Pale straw **Bouquet**: Flinty, earthy **Taste**: Light fruit character, fresh and pleasing, but not much varietal flavour

☆☆☆☆ Marynissen Vidal 1993 (12% alc)

Colour: Pale straw **Bouquet**: Passionfruit
Taste: Off-dry, grapefruit and mango flavour, grassy mid-taste, well balanced

---

☆☆☆½ Marynissen Winter Wine 1993 (11.5% alc) half bottle

Colour: Gold **Bouquet**: Peachy, fresh, honeyed
Taste: Honeyed and spicy with lively acidity. Not as concentrated as Icewine, but well worth the money

Red

☆☆☆½ Marynissen Cabernet Franc 1991 (12.7% alc)

Colour: Purple **Bouquet**: Leafy
Taste: Spicy plum and blackberry flavours. Almond aftertaste with some tannin

---

☆☆½ Marynissen Cabernet Sauvignon 1992 (12% alc)

Colour: Tawny ruby **Bouquet**: Lean, candied chaptalised nose
Taste: Dry, sinewy, red currant with a hint of sweetness. Chalky tannins

---

☆☆☆☆ Marynissen Cabernet Sauvignon 1991 Lot 31A (13.2% alc) (American oak)

Colour: Ruby **Bouquet**: Vanilla, blackcurrant
Taste: Lots of blackcurrant flavour, hint of coconut, some tannin in the finish. Softer and broader than Lot 31F. Forward

---

☆☆☆☆ Marynissen Cabernet Sauvignon 1991 Lot 31F (13.2% alc) (French oak)

Colour: Purple **Bouquet**: Vanilla, blackcurrant
Taste: Leaner than the 31A, but more elegant with a chocolaty, slightly roasted finish and soft tannins. Will keep better than 31A

☆☆☆½
(>☆☆☆☆) Marynissen Cabernet/Merlot 1993 (13% alc)

Colour: Purple-ruby **Bouquet**: Vanilla, perfumed
Taste: Floral, black cherry, cassis flavours, high-toned fruit flavours, nicely balanced, tannic asperity on the finish

☆☆☆☆ Marynissen Cabernet/Merlot 1991 (12.6% alc) (50% Cabernet Sauvignon, 25% Merlot, 25% Cabernet Franc; one year in French oak)

Colour: Purple **Bouquet**: Vanilla, raisiny **Taste**: Lots of extract, but closed-in and tannic. Needs three years

☆☆☆ Marynissen Gamay Noir 1993 (12% alc)

Colour: Ruby with orange tints **Bouquet**: Peppery plum **Taste**: Dry, plum with underlying acidity, medium-bodied, some tannin on the finish

☆☆☆½ Marynissen Merlot 1992 (11.9% alc)

Colour: Ruby **Bouquet**: Blackberry-blueberry nose **Taste**: Lovely sweet fruit, delicate blueberry flavour, well balanced, good length. Tannic finish. A very good wine for the vintage

☆☆½ Marynissen Pinot Noir 1991 (12% alc)

Colour: Purple **Bouquet**: Oaky, cherry **Taste**: Bitter cherry, evident acidity, lacking fruit

☆☆☆ Marynissen Pinot Noir 1992 (11.9% alc)

Colour: Ruby with a tawny hue **Bouquet**: Perfumed, candied raspberry, touch of volatility on the nose **Taste**: Racy raspberry, good length, fresh underlying acidity. Tannic finish adds structure

Pelee Island *White*

☆☆☆½ Pelee Island Chardonnay 1993 (12.1% alc) (aged in Limousin)

Colour: Straw **Bouquet**: Spicy oak, apple **Taste**: Full-bodied, spicy oak and apple. Good length. Good value

☆☆☆ (>☆☆☆½) Pelee Island Chardonnay 1994 (12.9% alc)

Colour: Pale straw **Bouquet**: Sweet, buttery nose **Taste**: Sweet apple, touch of oak, well balanced. A touch of yeast on the finish that will disappear with some bottle age

☆☆☆½ Pelee Island Chardonnay Barrique 1993 (12.5% alc)

Colour: Pale straw **Bouquet**: Citrus, vanilla, spicy **Taste**: Grapefruit, lean and crisp with nicely integrated oak, clovey finish

☆☆½

Pelee Island Pinot Gris 1992 (12.3% alc)

Colour: Pale straw **Bouquet**: Citric
Taste: Dry, fresh, lively lemony flavour, citric finish

☆☆☆½

Pelee Island Pinot Gris 1994 (12.1% alc)

Colour: Straw **Bouquet**: Earthy peach
Taste: Well balanced, clean, dry peachy flavour. Elegant

☆☆☆
(>☆☆☆½)

Pelee Island Riesling Dry 1993 (11.9 % alc)

Colour: Straw **Bouquet**: Lemon and peach
Taste: Crisp, citrus flavours, touch of sweetness in the middle palate giving way to a long lemony, green apple finish

---

☆☆☆☆

Pelee Island Riesling Dry 1992 (12.1% alc)

Colour: Pale straw **Bouquet**: Sweet tropical fruit
Taste: Off-dry. Orange and mango flavours, good length

☆☆☆½

Pelee Island Monarch Vidal 1994 (12.2% alc)

Colour: Pale straw **Bouquet**: Green plum, floral
Taste: Ripe tropical fruit, off-dry, well balanced

Red

☆☆

Pelee Island Country Red 1992 (12.1% alc)

Colour: Light cherry **Bouquet**: Raspberry candy
Taste: Sour cherry, light and fresh with a tangy, slightly hot finish

---

☆☆☆½

Pelee Island Fenian's Cuvee 1993 (12.8% alc) (Zweigelt and Gamay blend)

Colour: Purple with a blue tint **Bouquet**: Blackberry, cherry
Taste: Dry, fruity but less Beaujolais-like than previous vintages. More Zweigelt in the blend?

☆☆☆

Pelee Island Pinot Noir 1994 (12.1% alc) non-VQA

Colour: Light ruby **Bouquet**: Raspberry
Taste: Light-bodied, good raspberry flavour, well balanced with a tannic finish

Sparkling

☆☆☆ | Pelee Island Canadian Champagne (12.2% alc) (Riesling and Riesling Italico; Charmat process)

Colour: Palest straw **Bouquet**: Spicy, aromatic
Taste: Clean, green fruit flavours, good finish

Peller Estates *White*

☆☆☆ | Peller Estates Chardonnay 1994 (11.8% alc)

Colour: Straw **Bouquet**: Spicy caramel
Taste: Medium body, soft, sweetish, creamy, butterscotch flavour. Well made. Could use a little more acidity

☆☆☆½ | Peller Estates Oak-Aged Chardonnay 1994 (11.5% alc)

Colour: Straw **Bouquet**: Spicy, lemon and vanilla
Taste: Sweetish, soft, pineapple flavour, good length. A little light on balancing acidity. Nicely integrated oak

☆☆☆☆ | Peller Estates Chardonnay Sur Lie 1993 (11.5% alc)

Colour: Straw **Bouquet**: Oaky, rich, spicy
Taste: Oaky vanilla, full and fleshy on the palate, elegant balance, rich fruit flavours with a lingering nutty finish. Puligny-Montrachet style. An excellent wine

☆☆½ | Peller Estates Kerner 1994 (11.5% alc)

Colour: Very pale straw **Bouquet**: Grapey, stemmy
Taste: Medium sweet, melon flavour, clean fruit but slightly bitter on the finish

☆☆☆ | Peller Estates Muscat Ottonel 1994 (11.5% alc)

Colour: Pale gold **Bouquet**: Spicy Muscat nose **Taste**: Dry, grapey, spicy, Alsatian style. A touch bitter on the finish

☆½ | Peller Estates Dry Riesling 1993 (11.5% alc)

Colour: Pale straw **Bouquet**: Cardboard-like
Taste: Not much varietal character, acidic finish

☆☆
(>☆☆☆) | Peller Estates Vidal 1993 (12% alc)

Colour: Pale straw **Bouquet**: Candy-like
Taste: Exotic, tangerine flavour with lots of acidity giving it a lemony tartness on the finish

☆☆☆ Peller Estates Madrigal (Muscat Aperitif) (13% alc) half bottle

Colour: Tawny plum   **Bouquet**: Sweet Vermouth
Taste: Sweet, herby, minty, blackcurrant. Hot finish

Red

☆☆☆½
(>☆☆☆☆) Peller Estates Cabernet Franc 1993 (11.5% alc)

Colour: Ruby with purple tints   **Bouquet**: Floral, blueberry
Taste: Ripe fruit, blueberry-cassis flavour, medium-bodied, nicely balanced. Elegant with a touch of tannin on the finish

☆☆½ Peller Estates Cabernet Sauvignon 1993 (11.5% alc)

Colour: Ruby   **Bouquet**: Vanilla, Minty
Taste: Light, lean fruit, red currant and cranberry flavours. Green finish. Young vines?

☆☆ Peller Estates Gamay Noir 1993 (12.5% alc)

Colour: Tawny cherry   **Bouquet**: Alcoholic nose
Taste: Black licorice, austere, heavy, not much guiding fruit

☆☆ Peller Estates Gamay Noir 1994 (11.5% alc)

Colour: Cherry   **Bouquet**: Candied raspberry
Taste: Light, dry, not much fruit extract, touch of tannin

☆ Peller Estates Merlot 1993 (11.5% alc)

Colour: Ruby   **Bouquet**: Geranium nose
Taste: Dry, lean, no varietal character

☆☆
(>☆☆☆) Peller Estates Showcase Merlot 1993

Colour: Purple   **Bouquet**: Sappy, coffee bean
Taste: Oak predominates over the fruit, acidic finish

Pillitteri *White*

☆☆☆
(>☆☆☆½) Pillitteri Barrel-Aged Chardonnay 1994 (12% alc)
(50% barrel fermented in French and American oak)

Colour: Straw   **Bouquet**: Spicy, earthy
Taste: Medium-bodied, citrus and melon flavours. Lively acidity. Still closed

☆☆½ Pilliterri Oak-Aged Chardonnay 1993 (12.6% alc)

Colour: Straw **Bouquet**: Grassy, green plum
Taste: Soft, melon and green peppers, Sauvignon Blanc character

☆☆☆ Pillietteri Oak-Fermented Chardonnay 1993 (12.6% alc)

Colour: Straw **Bouquet**: Grassy **Taste**: Better balanced than the oak-aged wine. Elegant, grassy, herbaceous flavour, again Sauvignon Blanc in character

☆☆½ Pillitteri Riesling 1992 (11.5% alc)

Colour: Pale straw **Bouquet**: Lime, herbaceous
Taste: Not much varietal character, soft middle palate, red pepper character. Young vines?

☆☆☆ Pillitteri Riesling 1994 (10.5% alc)

Colour: Pale straw **Bouquet**: Flinty, lemony
Taste: Peach and lemon flavours, good acidity, earthy finish

☆☆☆ Pillitteri Riesling Medium Dry 1992 (11.5% alc)

Colour: Pale straw **Bouquet**: Green plum
Taste: Soft, light fruit character, good acidity, sweet grape-fruit flavour

☆☆☆½ Pillitteri Riesling Semi Dry 1993 (11.5% alc)

Colour: Straw **Bouquet**: Spicy-floral
Taste: Perfumed, exotic, well balanced with a lingering taste of cardamom

☆☆☆½ Pillitteri Oak-aged Seyval Blanc 1992 (11.8% alc) (two months in new American oak)

Colour: Pale straw **Bouquet**: Grapefruit, lime, vanilla
Taste: Spicy gooseberry, soft, well balanced, licorice flavour. Good length

☆☆ Pilliteri Oak-Aged Seyval Blanc 1993 (11.8% alc)

Colour: Straw **Bouquet**: Sweaty, grassy
Taste: Green fruit, sweaty taste, licorice finish

☆☆☆☆ Pillitteri Oak-Fermented Seyval Blanc 1992 (11.8% alc) (two months in new American oak)

Colour: Pale straw **Bouquet**: Leather, grapefruit
Taste: Sweet grapefruit, zesty, well balanced, hint of banana. Crisp finish

☆☆☆½ Pillitteri Vidal 1992 (11.3% alc)

Colour: Pale straw **Bouquet**: Grapefruit, floral
Taste: Soft, peachy, fruity middle taste, clean, good length

☆☆ Pillitteri Vidal 1993 (11.3% alc)

Colour: Pale straw **Bouquet**: Browning apple
Taste: Acidic orange, lacking middle fruit, acidic finish

☆☆½ Pillitteri Vidal Semi Dry 1993 (11.3% alc)

Colour: Pale straw **Bouquet**: Grassy
Taste: Fruity, crisp, sweet grassy, grapefruit taste, lively acidity

☆☆☆ Pillitteri Reserve Vidal 1993 (9.5% alc)

Colour: Pale straw **Bouquet**: Grassy, grapefruit
Taste: Sweet grapefruit, good acidity, good length

Red

☆☆☆ Pillitteri Baco Noir 1994 (11% alc)

Colour: Ruby **Bouquet**: Cherry **Taste**: Smoky, plum and cranberry flavours with a zingy acidic spine

☆☆☆ Pillitteri Cabernet Franc 1993 (12% alc)

Colour: Cherry **Bouquet**: Red fruits
Taste: Light berry flavour, colour belies depth of fruit, dry redcurrant and pomegranate flavours

☆☆½ Pillitteri Cabernet Sauvignon 1992

Colour: Light purple-ruby **Bouquet**: Vanilla, beetroot, leafy
Taste: Light, vegetal, acidic, tannic

☆☆½
(>☆☆☆) Pillitteri Cabernet Sauvignon 1993 (12% alc)

Colour: Deep cherry **Bouquet**: Herbaceous
Taste: Lean, redcurrant, medium-bodied, tannic finish

☆☆☆☆ Pillitteri Chariot 1992 (Maréchal Foch and Baco Noir)

Colour: Deep strawberry **Bouquet**: Strawberry
Taste: Delicate strawberry, clean, light. Good value

☆☆ Pillitteri Merlot 1992 (10.9% alc) (barrel sample)

Colour: Light purple-ruby **Bouquet**: Green **Taste**: Leafy, lean, unripe blackberry. Acidic finish, touch of tannin

Reif *White*

☆☆☆ Reif Estate Premium Dry White (11.5% alc) litre

Colour: Pale straw **Bouquet**: Fresh, citrus
Taste: Off-dry, melon, lemony-floral flavours, lots of character. Good final acidity. Good value

☆☆☆½ Reif Chardonnay Reserve 1992 (12.4% alc)

Colour: Pale straw **Bouquet**: Spicy oak and pineapple
Taste: Lean fruit, pear and grilled nuts. Elegant, acidic finish

☆☆☆
(>☆☆☆½) Reif Chardonnay 1993 (12.2% alc)

Colour: Very pale straw **Bouquet**: Buttery nose, hint of nuts
Taste: Caramel, good length, well balanced

☆☆☆½ Reif Premium Unfiltered Chardonnay 1991 (12.% alc)

Colour: Straw **Bouquet**: Barnyard, crème caramel
Taste: Rich, spicy green plum flavours, good acidity

☆☆☆ Reif Chardonnay 1994 (12.5% alc)(20% French oak)

Colour: Bright straw **Bouquet**: Apple, hints of barnyard
Taste: Lively, appley fruit, well balanced, fades a little on the final taste

☆☆½ Reif Gewürztraminer Dry 1993 (12.5% alc)

Colour: Pale straw **Bouquet**: Spicy baked apple
Taste: Dry lychee, rather austere, fruit doesn't carry through. Middle drop out to an appley finish

☆☆☆ Reif Gewürztraminer Medium Dry 1993 (12% alc)

Colour: Pale straw **Bouquet**: Spicy, browning apple
Taste: Medium sweet, round on the palate, lychee flavour. A little short

REIF

☆☆☆   Reif Johannisberg Riesling Dry 1993 (12.2% alc)

Colour: Pale straw **Bouquet:** Lime, grapefruit skin
Taste: Crisp, viscous, hint of honey and flowers, good length, acidic appley finish

☆☆☆½   Reif Riesling Dry 1994 (12% alc)

Colour: Pale straw **Bouquet:** Citrus nose, mineral
Taste: Clean, well balanced, lemony finish

☆☆☆   Reif Riesling Medium Dry 1994 (12% alc)

Colour: Very pale straw **Bouquet:** Grapefruit
Taste: Off-dry, well balanced, melon and grapefruit flavours, earthy finish

☆☆☆   Reif Late Harvest Riesling 1994

Colour: Very pale straw **Bouquet:** Sweet
Taste: Well balanced, melon and peach

☆☆☆½   Reif Riesling Trollinger (Kerner) 1993 (11.2% alc)

Colour: Pale straw **Bouquet:** Aromatic nose, green, grassy
Taste: Perfumed off-dry exotic flavour. Round on the palate, good length, well balanced

☆☆½   Reif Seyval Blanc 1994 (11.5% alc)

Colour: Very pale straw **Bouquet:** Green fruit
Taste: Apple and lemon flavours, medium-bodied, shy finish

☆☆☆½   Reif Vidal 1993 (11.8% alc)

Colour: Pale straw **Bouquet:** Sweet tropical fruit nose
Taste: Off-dry, clean fruit flavours, melon and mango

☆☆
(>☆☆☆)   Reif Vidal 1994 (11.5%)

Colour: Pale straw **Bouquet:** Earthy, orange peel
Taste: Earthy citrus flavour, acidic finish

☆☆½   Reif Vidal Select Late Harvest Dry 1993 (12% alc) half bottle

Colour: Yellow straw **Bouquet:** Apple juice
Taste: Sweet, rush of fruit and then it fades, hot finish

☆☆☆

Reif Vidal Select Harvest 1992 (12.2% alc) half bottle
(second pressing of Icewine)

Colour: Pale gold   **Bouquet**: Spicy baked apple
Taste: Sweet apple and dried peach, good acidity. Could do
with more acidity

☆☆☆
(>☆☆☆☆)

Reif Vidal Late Harvest 1994 (12% alc)

Colour: Pale straw   **Bouquet**: Not yet developed
Taste: Medium dry, soft, perfumed, exotic flavours, mango
and tropical fruits, nicely balanced

Red

☆☆½

Reif Estate Premium Dry Red (11.5% alc) litre
(70% Cabernet Sauvignon/20% Gamay/10% Baco Noir)

Colour: Ruby   **Bouquet**: Tobacco
Taste: Medium-bodied, red berry flavour. An attractive
blend. Good value

☆☆☆

Reif Cabernet Gamay (11.5% alc)

Colour: Purple ruby   **Bouquet**: Vanilla, plum and cherry
Taste: Dry, red berry fruit, acidic, some tannin, good length

---

☆☆☆½

Reif Cabernet Sauvignon 1991 (12.2% alc) (unfiltered, barrel-fermented, nine months in French and American oak)

Colour: Ruby   **Bouquet**: Damson, cherry
Taste: Ripe berry fruit, medium weight, good acidity. An
elegant wine

☆☆☆☆

Reif Merlot 1991 (12.5% alc) unfiltered

Colour: Ruby   **Bouquet**: Vanilla, plum and blackberry
Taste: Full-bodied, fresh acidity, plummy fruit, chocolaty
finish. Soft tannins

☆☆☆
(>☆☆☆½)

Reif Pinot Noir 1992 (12% alc)

Colour: Tawny cherry   **Bouquet**: Expressive nose—jammy
strawberry
Taste: Sweetish, good varietal character, wild strawberry,
cranberry flavours. Acidic finish

Southbrook Farms *White*

☆☆☆ | Southbrook Farms Chardonnay 1991 (12.6% alc) (oak cuvée)

Colour: Pale straw **Bouquet**: Shy
Taste: Lean, evident oak, slightly bitter, astringent finish. Oak predominates at this time of tasting

---

☆☆☆½ | Southbrook Farms Dry Riesling 1992 (12.5% alc)

Colour: Palest straw **Bouquet**: Lime, spring flowers
Taste: Green mango, kiwi, acidic, long lemony finish

☆☆☆ | Southbrook Farms Medium Dry Riesling 1992 (12.5% alc)

Colour: Pale straw **Bouquet**: Sweetish, melon, rhubarb
Taste: Off-dry, grassy grapefruit flavours, acidic finish. A little clumsy on the palate

---

☆☆½ | Southbrook Farms Gewürztraminer 1992 (12.5% alc)

Colour: Palest straw, almost water white **Bouquet**: Spicy, delicate, lychee and roses
Taste: Light Gewürz spiciness, tends to fade in the middle. Good acidity

---

☆☆☆ | Southbrook Farms White House White (12% alc)

Colour: Pale straw **Bouquet**: Grapefruit peel
Taste: Sweet grapefruit, high acid, good length

Red

☆☆☆½
(>☆☆☆☆) | Southbrook Farms Cabernet/Merlot 1991 (12.5% alc) (75% Sonoma Cabernet Sauvignon, 25% Ontario Merlot; eighteen months in oak)

Colour: Bright ruby **Bouquet**: Vanilla
Taste: Ripe red berry fruit, medium weight, good acidity, soft tannins

---

☆☆☆☆ | Southbrook Farms Framboise 1992 (15.5% alc) half bottle (fruit wine—non-VQA: raspberry juice fortified with grape spirit)

Colour: Ruby **Bouquet**: Raspberry jam
Taste: Sweet, liquid raspberry taste. Well balanced with clean fruit flavour, lingering finish. Better than the 1991

☆☆☆☆ Southbrook Farms Framboise 1993 (15% alc) half bottle
(fruit wine—non-VQA)

Colour: Ruby **Bouquet**: intense raspberry jam
Taste: Concentrated raspberry flavour, beautiful balance,
long lingering finish. Liquid raspberries

☆☆☆ Southbrook Farms Framboise 1994 (15% alc) half bottle
(fruit wine—non-VQA)

Colour: Purple-ruby **Bouquet**: Cooked raspberry, more
vinous **Taste**: Drier than 1993, more winey, not as delicate
and fresh

☆☆☆☆ Southbrook Farms Framboise d'Or 1994 (15% alc) half bottle
(fruit wine—non-VQA)

Colour: Golden bronze **Bouquet**: Eau-de-vie
Taste: Sweet raspberry, full fruit flavour, well balanced, lingering raspberry taste. Elegant

Stonechurch *White*

☆☆☆½ Stonechurch Barrel-Fermented Chardonnay 1993 (12.3% alc)

Colour: Pale straw **Bouquet**: Vanilla, lemon, apple
Taste: Sweetish, soft fruit flavours with a candy apple finish
and a touch of bitterness

☆ Stonechurch Gewürztraminer 1992 (12% alc)

Colour: Straw **Bouquet**: Heavy, muddy **Taste**: Licorice
and citrus, unbalanced, not much varietal character

☆☆☆ Stonechurch Seyval Blanc 1993 (11.5% alc)

Colour: Palest straw, almost water white **Bouquet**: Flinty,
grapefruit **Taste**: Well balanced, clean, green berry
flavours, quite delicate

☆☆☆ Stonechurch Seyval Blanc 1994 (11.8% alc)

Colour: Palest straw **Bouquet**: Fresh, citrusy
Taste: Light lemony flavour, fresh, green plum flavour, good
acidity

☆☆☆ Stonechurch Vidal 1993 (12.4% alc)

Colour: pale straw **Bouquet**: Banana
Taste: Soft on the palate, caramel with a dry finish

Red

☆☆☆☆ **Stonechurch Baco Noir 1993** (11.3% alc) (three months in new American oak)

Colour: Dense purple **Bouquet**: Smoky, tobacco, plum
Taste: Smoky, tarry fruit with a coconut and black cherry taste. Acidic spine

Stoney Ridge Cellars *White*

☆☆☆½ **Stoney Ridge Chanson 1994 Anniversary Series** (11% alc) (blend of Oraniersteiner, Ehrenfelser and Morio Muscat)

Colour: Palest straw **Bouquet**: Sweet, aromatic
Taste: Medium-dry, Gewürz-like middle taste, soft, easy drinking, good length

☆☆☆☆ **Stoney Ridge Chardonnay 1994 Anniversary Series** (12% alc)

Colour: Straw **Bouquet**: Spicy vanilla, apple
Taste: Sweet fruit, soft middle palate, toasty finish, good length

☆☆☆☆ **Stoney Ridge Chardonnay Reserve 1993 Butler's Grant Vineyard** (12% alc)

Colour: Straw **Bouquet**: Vanilla, flinty, buttery
Taste: Well balanced, sweetish melon and pear, rich fruit extract

☆☆½ **Stoney Ridge Gewürztraminer 1991** (11% alc)

Colour: Pale straw **Bouquet**: Exotic, orange
Taste: Perfumed, off-dry, soft

☆☆☆ **Stoney Ridge Gewürztraminer 1992** (11% alc) Eastman and Butler's Grant vineyards

Colour: Straw **Bouquet**: Spicy
Taste: Soft, roses and spice. A little short on the finish

☆☆☆ **Stoney Ridge Late Harvest Semillon 1991** (12% alc) half bottle (Botrytised Sonoma Semillon and Niagara Gewürztraminer)

Colour: Deep gold **Bouquet**: Botrytis, peach, apricot
Taste: Unctuous, soft, sweet, canned peaches

☆☆☆½ **Stoney Ridge Riesling 1993 Plekan Vineyard** (11% Alc)

Colour: Pale straw **Bouquet**: Sweet, white chocolate
Taste: Sweet, grapey, Auslese style, good finishing acidity

☆☆☆ Stoney Ridge Riesling Bench Reserve 1994 (11% Alc)

Colour: Pale straw, hint of lime **Bouquet:** Barnyard, sweetish
Taste: Soft apricot flavour on the initial palate and then the acidity kicks in

☆☆½ Stoney Ridge Country Selection Seyval Blanc 1993 (11.9% alc)

Colour: Straw **Bouquet:** Earthy, sweet
Taste: Sweetish fruit, good extract but rather soft and short

☆☆☆½ Stoney Ridge Country Selection Fumé 1994 (oak-aged Seyval Blanc)

Colour: Straw **Bouquet:** Toasted nuts
Taste: Sweet, toasty, nutty. well balanced, good length

Rosé

☆☆½ Stoney Ridge Cabernet Franc Rosé 1992 (10.5% alc)

Colour: Tawny pink **Bouquet:** Tobacco
Taste: Raspberry, light, tannic finish

Red

☆☆☆½ Stoney Ridge Cabernet Sauvignon 1993 Lenko Vineyard (12% alc)

Colour: Ruby-purple **Bouquet:** Vanilla, sweet blackberry-blackcurrant
Taste: Medium-bodied, sweet berry fruit, cherry and pomegranate tones. Acidic finish. Soft tannins

☆☆☆ Stoney Ridge Cabernet/Merlot 1992 (11% alc) (50% Cabernet Franc, 10% Cabernet Sauvignon, 40% Merlot from Eastman and Butler's Grant vineyards. Ten months in American oak.)

Colour: Purple ruby **Bouquet:** Cherry, leather
Taste: Fresh berries, red currant, raspberry. Light

☆☆☆ Stoney Ridge Maréchal Foch 1994 (11% alc)

Colour: Deep purple **Bouquet:** Grapey
Taste: Plummy sweet fruit, good extract and balancing acidity

STONEY RIDGE CELLARS

☆☆☆☆ Stoney Ridge Merlot Reserve 1991 (11% alc) (aged in American and French oak)

Colour: Purple   **Bouquet:** Coconut
Taste: Sweet, soft blackberry flavour, touch of tannin

☆☆☆☆ Stoney Ridge Merlot Reserve 1993 (12% alc)

Colour: Ruby   **Bouquet:** Vanilla, blackberry   **Taste:** Well balanced, cherry-blackberry fruit, good supporting tannins

☆☆½ Stoney Ridge Pinot Noir 1992 (11% alc)

Colour: Tawny strawberry   **Bouquet:** Cherry
Taste: Light, sweetish raspberry

☆☆☆½ Stoney Ridge Pinot Noir 1994 Butler's Grant Vineyard (12% alc) (aged almost eight months in American oak)

Colour: Light ruby   **Bouquet:** Vanilla, raspberry
Taste: Sweet raspberry, good extract, flavourful and a touch of sweetness

☆☆½ Stoney Ridge Cranberry Wine 1993 (11% alc) (fruit wine)

Colour: Cherry   **Bouquet:** Cooked cranberries
Taste: Syrupy, cooked sour cherries, lemony acidity, tart finish

Thirty Bench *White*

☆☆½
(>☆☆☆½) Thirty Bench Riesling Dry 1994 (11.5% alc)

Colour: Pale straw   **Bouquet:** Grapefruit and apple peel
Taste: Spicy, grapefruit and lemony, a little hollow in the middle taste with a zesty acidic finish

☆☆☆ Thirty Bench Riesling Reserve 1994 (11.5% alc)

Colour: Straw   **Bouquet:** Apple juice   **Taste:** Ripe appley and lime flavours. Fine acidic spine but a touch of oxidation of the fruit before fermentation gives it a browning apple finish

☆☆☆
(>☆☆☆½) Thirty Bench Riesling Semi-Dry 1994 (11.5%) half bottle

Colour: Straw   **Bouquet:** Floral, baked apple
Taste: Exotic, soft fruity attack, but drops out in the middle palate before a lively acidic finish

THIRTY BENCH

VINELAND ESTATES

☆☆☆☆ Thirty Bench Riesling BA 1994 (tank sample)

Colour: Old gold **Bouquet**: Nutty, apricot
Taste: Viscous, Botrytis flavours of dried peach and honey.
Great acid balance and lingering baked apple flavour

Red

☆☆☆½
(>☆☆☆☆)
Thirty Bench Red 1994 (barrel sample) (80% Cabernet Franc,
20% Cabernet Sauvignon; eight months in French
barriques)

Colour: Dense purple **Bouquet**: Smoky plum and blackcurrant **Taste**: Blackcurrant and blackberry, intense earthy
fruit flavour, well integrated oak, medium-bodied. Good
length

Vineland Estates *White*

☆☆☆ Vineland Estates Gewürztraminer 1992 (11.7% alc)

Colour: Pale straw **Bouquet**: Grassy, grapefruit
Taste: Spicy grapefruit flavour. More Riesling than Gewürz,
but a good-tasting wine

☆☆☆☆ Vineland Estates Riesling 1991

Colour: Pale straw **Bouquet**: Sweet grapefruit peel
Taste: Crisp, clean, very dry, grapefruit flavour

☆☆☆
(>☆☆☆☆)
Vineland Estates Riesling Dry 1992 (11% alc)

Colour: Pale straw, hints of lime **Bouquet**: Grapefruit
Taste: Dry, lean, lemony, fine acidic spine

☆☆☆☆ Vineland Estates Riesling Dry 1994 (10.8% alc)

Colour: Pale straw **Bouquet**: Mineral-floral
Taste: Crisp, lime and grapefruit flavours, medium-bodied,
good length, elegant

☆☆☆☆ Vineland Estates Riesling Reserve 1992 (11.2% alc)

Colour: Straw **Bouquet**: Concentrated lemon and peach
Taste: Dry, lemon-lime and kiwi flavours, rich extract, well
balanced with a lingering grapefruit finish. The acidity will
help this wine to age well

☆☆☆
(>☆☆☆☆)

Vineland Estates Riesling Reserve 1993 (11.4% alc)

Colour: Pale straw **Bouquet:** Petrol and lime
Taste: Crisp grapefruit, closed, tart with a long citric finish

Rosé

☆☆☆½

Vineland Estates Rosé 1994 (12% alc) (80% Seyval Blanc/20% Cabernet)

Colour: Deep salmon **Bouquet:** Wild strawberries
Taste: Dry, mouth-filling, strawberry flavour, good intensity with a crisp finish

Vinoteca *White*

☆☆½

Vinoteca Chardonnay 1992 (11.5% alc) Mosel-shaped bottle

Colour: Straw **Bouquet:** Apple and hay
Taste: Dry, lean, red licorice flavour. Not enough extract

☆☆☆

Vinoteca Chardonnay 1993 (11.5% alc) Mosel-shaped bottle

Colour: Straw **Bouquet:** Spicy
Taste: Crab apple and clove. Lean on the palate, hot alcoholic finish

☆☆☆

Vinoteca Riesling 1992 (11.5% alc)

Colour: Straw, lime tints **Bouquet:** Floral, honeysuckle
Taste: Exotic, melon flavours, perfumed finish. Unusual flavour for Riesling, but appealing

Red

☆☆

Vinoteca Cabernet Sauvignon 1992 (12% alc)

Colour: Cherry **Bouquet:** Tobacco leaf, red fruits
Taste: Light, minerally extract, black cherry and smoke

☆☆½

Vinoteca Cabernet Sauvignon 1993 (12% alc)

Colour: Light ruby **Bouquet:** Vanilla **Taste:** Vanilla oak and candied cherry flavour giving way to an acidic, tannic finish

☆☆

Vinoteca Pinot Noir Reserve 1991 (12% alc)

Colour: Ruby **Bouquet:** Vanilla, leather
Taste: Sweetish, bound in sulphur, earthy, blood orange flavour, some tannin on the finish

Willow Heights *White*

☆☆☆☆   Willow Heights Chardonnay 1993 (13.3% alc)

Colour: Straw **Bouquet**: Toasty vanilla
Taste: Burgundian style, apple and butterscotch flavours.
Well made with good length and lots of heft

☆☆
(>☆☆☆)   Willow Heights Riesling Dry 1993

Colour: Pale straw, hints of lime **Bouquet**: Apple peel, petrol
Taste: Austere, lean fruit flavours, acidic lemony finish

British Columbia Wines

Blue Mountain *Sparkling*

☆☆☆½ Blue Mountain Sparkling Wine Brut 1992 (12.5% alc)

Colour: Straw, light mousse **Bouquet**: Yeasty, Chardonnay nose
Taste: Dry, well balanced, full in the mouth, green apple finish. Good length

Brights *White*

☆☆☆½ Brights Proprietors' Reserve Chardonnay 1992 (12% alc)

Colour: Straw **Bouquet**: Lemon, butter
Taste: Kiwi, vanilla, medium bodied. Good fruit and nice length. Well balanced

☆☆☆ Brights Proprietors' Reserve Dry Riesling 1992 (12.7% alc)

Colour: Pale straw **Bouquet**: Aromatic, sweetish, pear
Taste: Sweet apple and pear, rich extract, good length. Soft finish. A little low on acidity and high on alcohol

Calona Vineyards *White*

☆☆☆ Calona Vineyards Pinot Blanc 1993 (12.1% alc)

Colour: Palest straw **Bouquet**: Fresh, lemony, peachy
Taste: Light, delicate, peachy, crisp lively acidity

☆☆½ Calona Semillon 1993 (11% alc)

Colour: Very pale straw **Bouquet**: Elderberry, grassy
Taste: Crisp, green bean flavour, long acidic finish

CedarCreek *White*

☆☆☆☆ CedarCreek Chardonnay 1993

Colour: Pale straw **Bouquet**: Vanilla, apple, pear
Taste: Apple and pear flavours with a fine spine of lemony acidity to carry the flavours

☆☆☆½ CedarCreek Pinot Blanc 1993 (11.8% alc)

Colour: Pale straw **Bouquet:** Vanilla, sweetish peach
Taste: Good middle fruit, medium-bodied, dry peachy
flavour, fresh finish

Domaine de Chaberton *White*

☆☆☆ Domaine de Chaberton Chardonnay 1993 (12% alc)

Colour: Pale straw **Bouquet:** Anise, pear
Taste: Dry, crisp, narrow focus of fruit, Chablis-style

Red

☆☆☆ Domaine de Chaberton Pinot Noir 1993 (12% alc)

Colour: Light ruby **Bouquet:** Sweet cherry-like and leather
nose
Taste: Cherry and cranberry flavour, light on the palate,
elegant. Evident acidity matched by dusty tannins. Good
Pinot character but more extract needed

Gehringer Brothers *White*

☆☆☆½ Gehringer Bros. Pinot Auxerrois 1993 (11% alc)

Colour: Pale straw **Bouquet:** Fresh, citrus, green plum
Taste: Clean, sweetish, hint of anise, soft middle and soft
finish

☆☆☆½ Gehringer Bros. Johannisberg Riesling 1993 Dry Select
(12% alc)

Colour: Pale straw **Bouquet:** Petrol, licorice
Taste: Off-dry, floral-citrus character, well made

☆☆☆☆ Gehringer Bros. Riesling 1994 (12% alc)

Colour: Pale straw **Bouquet:** Dry apricot
Taste: Off-dry, clean, crisp, well-balanced with a lingering
peachy flavour

Gray Monk *White*

☆☆☆½ Gray Monk Late Harvest Ehrenfelser 1992 (11.5% alc)

Colour: Pale straw **Bouquet:** Ripe, perfumed, tropical fruit
Taste: Sweet, ripe soft fruit flavours, off-dry, opulent

☆☆ Gray Monk Gewürztraminer Reserve 1989 (11.6% alc)

Colour: Straw **Bouquet**: Earthy, spicy
Taste: Mature, drying out with oxidized finish

☆☆☆ Gray Monk Pinot Blanc 1991 (11.9% alc)

Colour: Pale straw **Bouquet**: Grapefruit, grass
Taste: Sauvignon Blanc-like, grapefruity with a soft middle palate, elegant

☆☆☆½ Gray Monk Pinot Gris 1992 (11% alc)

Colour: Pale straw **Bouquet**: Aromatic, peachy
Taste: Perfumed, sweet rhubarb. Good length

Hainle Vineyards *White*

☆☆☆½ Hainle Chardonnay Estate Bottled 1992 (12.7% alc)

Colour: Pale straw **Bouquet**: Butterscotch, touch of barnyard
Taste: Full-bodied, appley, heavy in the mouth

☆☆☆ Hainle Chardonnay Estate Bottled 1993 (11.5% alc)

Colour: Pale straw **Bouquet**: Hay-like
Taste: Dry, apple, viscous, good acidity

☆☆☆ Hainle Kerner 1993 (12.1% alc)

Colour: Pale straw, lime tints **Bouquet**: Aromatic, Muscat-like **Taste**: Spicy, exotic, hints of Muscat and Riesling, full in the mouth, fresh acidity, good length

☆☆☆ Hainle Pinot Blanc 1993 (12% alc)

Colour: Pale straw **Bouquet**: Mineral, earthy, peach skin
Taste: Full-bodied, dry, appley, taste of the soil. Somewhat alcoholic on the finish

☆☆☆
(>☆☆☆☆)
Hainle Riesling 1993 Estate Bottled (12.1% alc) (organic vineyard)

Colour: Deep straw **Bouquet**: Petrol, apricot skin
Taste: Very crisp, aromatic, steely grapefruit. A cross between Alsatian power and Mosel delicacy and spice. Needs time

☆☆☆☆   Hainle Traminer 1993 (12.9% alc)

Colour: Pale straw   **Bouquet**: Lychee, red peppers
Taste: Spicy, very dry, lychee and rose petal, full-bodied
and voluptuous in the mouth. Alsatian style

Red

☆☆☆½   Hainle Merlot 1992 Elisabeth Vineyard

Colour: Purple-ruby   **Bouquet**: Grapy, leesy nose
Taste: Sweet fruit, tobacco leaf. Italianate style

☆☆☆
(>☆☆☆☆)   Hainle Merlot 1993 (12% alc)

Colour: Purple   **Bouquet**: Earthy, smoky, blackberry
Taste: Focused black cherry fruit, good extract, hefty acidic
spine

☆☆½   Hainle Vineyard Pinot Noir 1992 (12.2% alc)

Colour: Tawny cherry   **Bouquet**: Feral, rhubarb
Taste: Earthy, dry cherry and rhubarb. Not a lot of extract,
lean and nervous, overly alcoholic

☆☆½   Hainle Pinot Noir 1992 Elisabeth Vineyard (14% alc)

Colour: Pale ruby   **Bouquet**: Wild strawberry
Taste: Heavy in the mouth, rather clumsy, not much
extract. Too high alcohol, tannic finish

☆☆☆½   Hainle Pinot Noir 1993 Elisabeth Vineyard (12% alc)

Colour: Deep cherry   **Bouquet**: Raspberry
Taste: Elegant, light, Savigny-les-Beaune style. Well balanced

Jackson-Triggs *White*

☆☆½   Jackson-Triggs Chenin Blanc 1993 (12% alc)

Colour: Straw   **Bouquet**: Butterscotch
Taste: Ripe fruit flavours, Chardonnay-like. Very dry on the
finish with excessive acidity

☆☆☆   Jackson-Triggs Late Harvest Ehrenfelser 1993 (11% alc) half
bottle

Colour: Straw   **Bouquet**: Exotic, tropical fruit, vanilla
Taste: Sweet, unctuous, perfumed, cardamom. A little more
acidity would have helped

☆☆☆ Jackson-Triggs Pinot Blanc 1993 (11% alc)

Colour: Pale straw **Bouquet**: Peach yoghurt
Taste: Butterscotch, peach and orange flavours with green apple acidity

☆☆☆ Jackson-Triggs Dry Riesling 1993 (12.5% alc)

Colour: Pale straw **Bouquet**: Sweet, red licorice
Taste: Soft and creamy, spicy middle palate, off-dry. Good length

☆☆☆ Jackson-Triggs Gewürztraminer 1993 (12% alc)

Colour: Palest straw **Bouquet**: Spicy, perfumed peach
Taste: Aromatic, tropical fruit, well balanced, lingers on the palate with a hint of lychee

Red

☆☆☆½ Jackson-Triggs Merlot 1993 (11.5% alc) (aged in American and French oak)

Colour: Ruby **Bouquet**: Sweet blackberry-blueberry
Taste: Good extract, jammy redcurrant and strawberry flavours, nicely balanced, medium bodied, good length

Mission Hill *White*

☆☆☆ Mission Hill 49 North (Pinot Auxerrois, Riesling, Bacchus)

Colour: Light straw **Bouquet**: Sweetish peach, aromatic, perfumed
Taste: Forward ripe tropical fruit flavours, easy drinking. Good acidity on the finish. Good value

☆☆☆☆ Mission Hill Chardonnay Grand Reserve 1993 (12% alc) (50% American oak, 50% stainless steel)

Colour: Straw **Bouquet**: Spicy, tropical fruit
Taste: Rich amalgam of apricot, tangerine and pineapple with a buttery overlay. Great length

☆☆☆
(>☆☆☆½) Mission Hill Grand Reserve Gewürztraminer 1993 (12% alc)

Colour: Pale straw **Bouquet**: Sweet, spicy apple
Taste: More Riesling than Gewürz character, touch of rose petal, orange and honeysuckle, clean, good length, off-dry

JACKSON-TRIGGS

MISSION HILL

☆☆☆½ Mission Hill Grand Reserve Pinot Blanc 1993 (11.5% alc) (25% American barrels, 75% stainless steel)

Colour: Light straw   **Bouquet**: Vanilla peachy, spicy
Taste: Peach, tangerine and pear flavours, good length, well balanced

☆☆☆☆ Mission Hill Grand Reserve White 1993 (11.5% alc) (40% Chardonnay, 20% Semillon, 40% Chenin Blanc)

Colour: Straw   **Bouquet**: Peachy, grassy   **Taste**: Lively, fresh, elderberry, grass and peach flavours. Fresh finish

☆☆☆½ Mission Hill Private Reserve Pinot Blanc 1993 (11.5% alc)

Colour: Straw   **Bouquet**: Melon and gooseberry
Taste: Crisp, green fruits, fresh grapefruit, well balanced, good length, lemony finish

Red

☆☆☆ Mission Hill Grand Reserve Barrel Select Red 1993 (11.5% alc) (60% Pinot Noir, 25% Maréchal Foch, 15% Gamay)

Colour: Ruby-plum   **Bouquet**: Warm, cakey
Taste: Well balanced, raspberry, rust, pepper, candied flavour. Good intensity, lively acidity and a touch of tannin

Nichol Vineyard   *White*

☆☆☆☆ Nichol Vineyard Pinot Gris 1993 (13.7% alc)

Colour: Amber-copper   **Bouquet**: Caramel, peach
Taste: Rich, mouth-filling, big-boned but well balanced

Okanagan Vineyards   *White*

☆☆☆ Okanagan Vineyards Johannisberg Riesling 1993 (11.5% alc)

Colour: Pale straw   **Bouquet**: Aromatic
Taste: Thick in the mouth, sweet peach and melon flavours give way to a crisp finish

Red

☆☆½ Okanagan Vineyards Merlot 1993 (11.5% alc)

Colour: Cherry   **Bouquet**: Minty, cherry
Taste: Light cherry-berry flavour, soft, easy drinking. Not varietally correct but pleasant drinking

Peller Estates *Red*

☆☆☆
(>☆☆☆½)

Peller Estates Merlot 1994 (12.5% alc) (barrel sample)

Colour: Deep red   **Bouquet**: Classic Merlot nose with oak overtones
Taste: Blackberry, cassis, chocolate, coffee. Great depth of flavour but a little closed

Sumac Ridge *White*

☆☆☆½

Sumac Ridge Pinot Blanc 1992 Private Reserve (12% alc)

Colour: Straw   **Bouquet**: Buttery, vanilla
Taste: Peachy-apple flavour, good middle intensity and a fine lingering oaky finish

☆☆☆½

Sumac Ridge Riesling 1993 (11.9% alc)

Colour: Straw   **Bouquet**: Biscuity, lime and grapefruit
Taste: Grassy grapefruit, good intensity of flavour and length

Summerhill *White*

☆☆

Summerhill Nordique Blanc (Ehrenfelser) (12.5% alc)

Colour: Straw   **Bouquet**: Vanilla, citrus
Taste: Earthy, slightly soapy, short

Sparkling

☆☆☆☆

Summerhill Cipes Brut (12.5% alc)

Appearance: Good mousse, tiny bubbles   **Colour**: Pale straw-green   **Bouquet**: Soft, hint of residual sugar, lemony. Good length

☆☆☆☆

Summerhill Brut (12.5% alc)

Appearance: Active mousse, tiny bubbles   **Colour**: Straw
Bouquet: Chalky
Taste: Very dry, austere, green apple. Will age well

PELLER ESTATES

SUMAC RIDGE

SUMMERHILL

Quails' Gate *White*

☆☆½   Quails' Gate Dry Riesling 1993 (12% alc)

Colour: Pale straw **Bouquet**: Leafy, citrus nose
Taste: Crisp, green fruit flavour, medium-bodied

Red

☆☆☆½   Quails' Gate Baco Noir 1992 (12% alc)

Colour: Tawny ruby **Bouquet**: Vanilla, plum
Taste: Spicy, jammy plum, good extract, well made

Wild Goose Vineyards *White*

☆☆☆   Wild Goose Johannisberg Riesling Dry 1992 (12.5% alc)

Colour: Pale straw, lime **Bouquet**: Spicy apricot, anise
Taste: Off-dry, spritzig, full-bodied, tangerine flavour. Good
length but slightly alcoholic on the finish

Red

☆☆½   Wild Goose Pinot Noir 1992 (12% alc)

Colour: Light cherry **Bouquet**: Wet earth, raspberry
Taste: Unripe raspberry, sweetish (chaptalised), touch of
tannin

Quebec Wines

Domaine des Côtes d'Ardoise *Red*

☆☆

Domaine des Côtes d'Ardoise Haute Combe 1994 (Maréchal Foch/De Chaunac)

Colour: Medium cherry red **Bouquet**: Small red fruits, pretty Burgundian-style floral perfume
Taste: Light but fine, pure, raspberry flavours. Quite elegant

☆☆

Domaine des Côtes d'Ardoise Gamay 1994

Colour: Fairly deep red **Bouquet**: Bright berries: strawberry, raspberry
Taste: A richer, thicker mouthfeel than the Haut Combe, slightly chalky. Old wood finish that adds complexity

La Vitacée *Red*

☆☆☆

La Vitacée Barbe Rouge 1994 (Red Beard) (vat sample)

Colour: Intense black, vivid purple with a blue tinge; looks like you expect a Concord wine would **Bouquet**: Intense, with burnt, peppery, Rhône-style blackberry fruit, and no foxiness
Taste: Juicy black fruit flavours, decent weight, some tannins present, nice finish

Vignoble Angell *White*

☆☆

Vignoble Angell Blanc 1994

Colour: Palest yellow **Bouquet**: Bright green lime with flinty overtones
Taste: Round mouthfeel, typically Montérégie-like riper, but flatter fruit, honeyed finish

Vignoble de l'Orpailleur *White*

★★½

Vignoble de l'Orpailleur Vin Blanc 1993 (11% alc)

Colour: Almost water white with a hint of blush **Bouquet:** Papery nose
Taste: Tart, lemony, light and lively

★★★

Vignoble de l'Orpailleur 1994 (no malolactic)

Colour: Palest yellow **Bouquet:** Complex: spicy, flinty, minerally white pepper notes, Sauvignon-blanc-style, fresh pink grapefruit
Taste: Good light green apple, hay-herbaceous flavours, dry, long finish for a wine of this type. A classic Seyval

★★½
(>★★★½)

Vignoble de l'Orpailleur 1994 élevé en fût de Chêne (barrel sample)

Colour: Light yellow **Bouquet:** Lovely use of wood, harmonious with fresh fruit, coffee/toasted wood overtones
Taste: Medium-bodied, supple, caramelly finish. More restrained use of wood than in years past

Sparkling

★★★

Vignoble de l'Orpailleur Méthode Champenoise 1992 (sparkling)

Colour: Very pale, fine bubbles persist **Bouquet:** Fresh-fruited, classic toasty-yeasty nose with mineral notes
Taste: Light, dry a little austere, crisp green apple and lemon finish but satisfying in the mouth, clean finish

Fortified

★★★½

Vignoble de l'Orpailleur Apéri d'or (Pineau de Charentes style)

Colour: Mid yellow to light gold **Bouquet:** Sweet, pleasantly, lightly oxidized fruit nose
Taste: Peaches, bananas, and other flavours mingle. Sweet but balanced with good acidity

Vignoble des Pins *White*

☆☆   Vignoble des Pins Blanc '94 (blend of Seyval and Aurore)

Colour: Palest yellow   **Bouquet**: Alive, floral, melony, peppery fruit
Taste: Sauvignon-like green flavours. Medium-bodied, acidic finish with a touch of nuttiness

Sparkling

☆☆   Vignoble des Pins Mousse des Vins

Colour: Almost water white, fine bubbles   **Bouquet**: White pepper, smoky-yeasty nose
Taste: Fruit is rounded off by just enough residual sugar to make it a great crowd-pleaser as an apéritif

Vignoble Dietrich-Jooss *White*

☆☆½   Vignoble Dietrich-Jooss Vin Blanc 1994

Colour: Very pale yellow   **Bouquet**: Typical Seyval, peppery/herbaceous nose
Taste: Full fruity mouthfeel rounded off by a kiss of residual sugar

☆☆☆½   Vignoble Dietrich-Jooss Cuvée Speciale 1994

Colour: Light pale yellow   **Bouquet**: Very fruit/floral, with a light spicy/Muscat edge (Cayuga component)
Taste: Good body, lovely long elegant finish

☆☆☆½   Vignoble Dietrich-Jooss Cuvée Storikengold 1994

Colour: Light yellow   **Bouquet**: Spicy nose with American oak notes and a pungent floral edge; quite elegant
Taste: Solid fruit, long, nutmeg inflected, ever-so-slightly-sweet finish. Great acid balance

Red

☆☆☆½   Vignoble Dietrich-Jooss Vin Rouge 1994

Colour: Good dark red   **Bouquet**: One of the nicest reds produced in Quebec, not unlike a lighter Loire red but with American oak overtones on the finish
Taste: Black raspberry and dark spices

Rosé

☆☆☆   Vignoble Dietrich-Jooss Vin Rosé 1994 (11% alc)

Colour: Tawny-coral   **Bouquet**: Candied strawberry
Taste: Good extract, off-dry, orangey-strawberry flavour, well-made, lingering taste

Vignoble du Marathonien   *White*

☆☆☆ | Vignoble du Marathonien Vin Blanc 1994

Colour: Light yellow, quite pale   **Bouquet**: Spicy, peppery, lemony nose, very attractive, open
Taste: Great concentration for Quebec. Very Sauvignon-like, long and lemony with a light residual sugar which lets the winemaker de-acidify a little less and leaves more of the character in the wine. Refreshing with food

☆☆☆½ | Vignoble du Marathonien Vendange Tardive 1994 (vat sample)

Colour: Yellow/gold, quite a deep colour   **Bouquet**: Honeyed, herbal and green apple notes
Taste: Floral, decent weight of fruit, Riesling-like on long, honeyed, glycerine-laden finish. This wine is somewhere between a late-harvest and an Icewine, harvested December 1st when grapes were semi-frozen

☆☆☆ | Vignoble du Marathonien Cuvée Stephanie Vendange Tardive 1994 (vat sample)

Colour: Medium yellow   **Bouquet**: Flowers and honeyed notes compete for attention
Taste: This wine is light for a Late-Harvest, but flawlessly made with good balance, complex fruit, and a long, honeyed finish

Vignoble La Bauge   *White*

☆½ | Vignoble La Bauge Seyval Blanc 1994

Colour: Almost colourless, light yellow   **Bouquet**: Very faint floral perfume
Taste: Decent mouthfeel, slight nail polish finish

Rosé

☆ | Vignoble La Bauge Bête Rousse

Colour: Light orange/red   **Bouquet**: Light fruit and nail polish
Taste: Clean, but very light, refreshing

Vignoble Le Cep d'Argent   *White*

☆☆½   Vin Blanc 1994

Colour: Almost water white   **Bouquet**: Herbed, yeasty, white pepper, lemons
Taste: Very clean, resembles a light Sauvignon Blanc. Good acidity with a bright green apple finish

Sparkling

☆☆   Vignoble Le Cep d'Argent Sélection des Mousquetaires Méthode Champenoise Blanc des Blancs 1992 Brut Zero

Colour: Palest yellow, fine bubbles that are very persistent
Bouquet: Toasty, complex nose is almost Chardonnay-like
Taste: Lighter than expected in mouth, chalky finish, good acidity

Fortified

☆☆½   Vignoble Le Cep d'Argent l'Archer (made from dry wine *muté* with Cognac, Maple Syrup, dried and fresh fruits)

Colour: Orange-tinged red   **Bouquet**: Slightly rancio, Tawny Port nose.
Taste: Rich, long, maple flavours come through mostly on finish. A delicious, intriguing digestif

Vignoble Le Royer-St. Pierre   *White*

☆☆½   Vignoble Le Royer-St. Pierre Les Trois Sols—Cayuga 1994

Colour: Light yellow   **Bouquet**: Fruity, lemons and floral with a lovely light Muscat overtone, bit too much SO_2
Taste: Good concentration, mouthfilling fruit, good acidity

Red

☆☆   Vignoble Le Royer-St. Pierre Le Saint Cambrert (barrel sample)

Colour: Deep purple   **Bouquet**: Big blackberry fruit, lovely with hazelnut notes
Taste: Still young, prominent acidity, good concentration, pure fruit, some tannin. Nose promises more than mouth-feel delivers, typical of our cool-climate reds. This wine was late harvested and, remarkably, did not have to be chaptalized!

Vignoble Les Arpents de Neige   *White*

☆☆☆

Vignoble Les Arpents de Neige, Cuvée 1er Neige 1994

Colour: Very pale yellow   **Bouquet:** Light Muscadet-type nose, with a smoky, minerally pepper edge, yeasty
Taste: Clean lime and grapefruit, really quite a surprisingly big Sauvignon Blanc flavour for Quebec, good acid balance

Vignoble Les Blancs Coteaux   *White*

☆☆

Vignoble Les Blancs Coteaux La Taste Seyval Blanc 1994

Colour: Very light   **Bouquet:** Very citrus nose, appley
Taste: Nice concentration of floral green apple flavours with a very slight, refreshing spritz on the slightly peppery finish

Fortified

☆☆☆½

Vignoble Les Blancs Coteaux Empire Cidre Apéritif (16% Calvados and Cider blend)

Colour: Light golden   **Bouquet:** Buttery, butterscotchy wood and sweet nutmeg bouquet
Taste: Rich, not too sweet, with a caramelly-appley edge, very satisfying finish

Vignoble Les Trois Clochers   *White*

☆☆½

Vignoble Les Trois Clochers Vin Blanc 1994 (vat sample)

Colour: Almost water white   **Bouquet:** White pepper, grapefruit, lemon and herbal overtones
Taste: Medium mouthfeel with a yeasty, refreshing finish, dry, touch of spice and lemon

Vignoble Morou *White*

☆☆

Vignoble Morou Vin Blanc 1994 (Seyval, Cayuga, V20501)

Colour: Pale yellow   **Bouquet**: Herbaceous, slightly peppery fruit

Taste: Dry, adequate clean fruit, green apple finish

☆☆☆½

Vignoble Morou Clos Napierois 1994

Colour: Canary yellow   **Bouquet**: Beautiful butterscotchy, citrus and floral nose, very elegant

Taste: Made from the Geisenheim clone with a little skin pre-fermentation maceration. This wine, if not terribly full in the mouth, still exhibits lots of finesse in the pure fruit, with just a touch of Riesling "petrol" on the finish

Red

☆☆☆

Vignoble Morou Vin Rouge 1993

Colour: Medium red   **Bouquet**: Aromatic nose of small red fruit: raspberry, cherry, strawberry, Burgundian-style

Taste: Light raspberry fruit in mouth with an American oak finish. Clean

Vignoble St-Alexandre *Red*

☆☆

Vignoble St-Alexandre Domar 1994

Colour: Cherry red colour   **Bouquet**: Vinous, clean red cherry nose with hazelnut notes, like a light Italian Merlot

Taste: Mellow, smooth, no wood-style, pleasant, good balance, no hint of hybrid flavours

Vignoble Sous les Charmilles *White*

☆☆☆

Vignoble Sous les Charmilles Vin Blanc 1994

Colour: Water-white, almost colourless   **Bouquet**: Attractive lemony/floral nose with a touch of peppery yeastiness, pleasant herbal/celery overtones; a fairly complex nose

Taste: Medium-light fruit weight in mouth, very clean, refreshing finish, well-balanced

Nova Scotia Wines

Jost Vineyards *White*

☆☆☆	**Jost Avondale Blanc 1992** (12.8% alc) (322-57 Gesienheim variety) **Colour:** Straw **Bouquet:** Tropical fruit **Taste:** Kiwi fruit, driving acidity, dry, lingering flavour, full-bodied
☆☆½	**Jost Beaver Creek Geisenheim 1992** (12.9% alc) **Colour:** Pale straw, lime tints **Bouquet:** Earthy, apple **Taste:** Minerally, apple and pie crust flavour, high alcohol, appley finish
☆☆½	**Jost Eagle Tree Muscat 1993** (11% alc) **Colour:** Pink-gold **Bouquet:** Spicy, baked apple **Taste:** heavy, off-dry Muscat flavour, long finish of apple peel flavour
☆☆½	**Jost Habitant Blanc 1991** (12.8% alc) **Colour:** Straw **Bouquet:** Sweet lemon **Taste:** Sweetish plum, good acidity but the hand of the winemaker is obvious
☆☆½	**Jost Habitant Blanc 1992** (l'Acadie Blanc grape) **Colour:** Light yellow **Bouquet:** Germanic nose with floral and spice nuances complementing the fruit. Some Cayuga-like peachy *labrusca* overtones **Taste:** Soft Germanic fruit in the mouth, finishes slightly sweet with good balancing acidity
☆☆☆	**Jost Habitant Chardonnay 1991** (12.9% alc) **Colour:** Pale straw **Bouquet:** Earthy, apple **Taste:** Tobacco leaf, apple, full on the palate, good length, nice acidic finish

☆☆   Jost Riesling Vidal 1991 (12.6% alc)

Colour: Pale straw   **Bouquet**: Sweet and fruity
Taste: Sweetish, grapey, vanilla, not much structure

☆☆☆½   Jost Seyval Blanc 1992 (12.2% alc)

Colour: Pale straw   **Bouquet**: Sweet, clean
Taste: Sweet melon, good fruit flavour, well balanced, finishes well, off-dry

Red

☆☆☆   Jost Grand Cru Rouge 1992 (11.8% alc)

Colour: Medium ruby   **Bouquet**: Burgundian nose, slightly volatile
Taste: Full cherry-raspberry flavour, lots of extract, dry with some tannin on the finish

☆☆☆   Jost Maréchal Foch 1992 (12% alc)

Colour: Tawny ruby   **Bouquet**: Black cherry
Taste: Sweet fruit, plum, cherry and tobacco leaf flavours, well balanced with a tannic finish

Sainte Famille *White*

☆☆   Ste. Famille Chardonnay 1990 (12.5% alc)

Colour: Pale straw   **Bouquet**: Shy
Taste: Appley, dry Mâconnais style. Slight oxidation in the final taste

☆☆☆½   Ste. Famille Estate Seyval Blanc 1993

Colour: Pale yellow-white   **Bouquet**: Honeyed, perfumed, Sauvignon-style nose
Taste: Good round fruit, zesty, yeasty finish

☆☆☆   Ste. Famille Fleur de Blanc 1993 (95% l'Acadie Blanc/15% Vidal)

Colour: Very pale straw   **Bouquet**: Light floral nose, slight Germanic, fruity overtones
Taste: Green apple fruit in the mouth, surprisingly good body, sweet character, but finishes yeasty and dry

☆☆½   Ste. Famille Riesling 1990 (12% alc)

Colour: Pale straw   **Bouquet**: Petrol-floral
Taste: Perfumed, cardamom, lively acidity, good length

Red

☆☆☆   Ste. Famille Maréchal Foch 1990

Colour: Medium ruby   **Bouquet**: Lovely berry, almost
Burgundian-style nose with light spiciness and some
herbal nuances
Taste: Light soft, mature tobacco-tinged fruit in the mouth.
The acidity is balanced by a slight residual sugar content

P.S. The 1994 red wine, from Maréchal Foch/Michurinetz,
tasted from cask, looks to be one of Suzanne Corkum's (and
Nova Scotia's) best reds yet. It will need some ageing, but so
far appears to be, despite its deep concentration, mercifully
free of any *labrusca* taint.